Science and Fiction

W0230322

Science and Fiction – A Springer Series

This collection of entertaining and thought-provoking books will appeal equally to science buffs, scientists and science-fiction fans. It was born out of the recognition that scientific discovery and the creation of plausible fictional scenarios are often two sides of the same coin. Each relies on an understanding of the way the world works, coupled with the imaginative ability to invent new or alternative explanations—and even other worlds. Authored by practicing scientists as well as writers of hard science fiction, these books explore and exploit the borderlands between accepted science and its fictional counterpart. Uncovering mutual influences, promoting fruitful interaction, narrating and analyzing fictional scenarios, together they serve as a reaction vessel for inspired new ideas in science, technology, and beyond.

Whether fiction, fact, or forever undecidable: the Springer Series "Science and Fiction" intends to go where no one has gone before!

Its largely non-technical books take several different approaches. Journey with their authors as they

- Indulge in science speculation – describing intriguing, plausible yet unproven ideas;
- Exploit science fiction for educational purposes and as a means of promoting critical thinking;
- Explore the interplay of science and science fiction – throughout the history of the genre and looking ahead;
- Delve into related topics including, but not limited to: science as a creative process, the limits of science, interplay of literature and knowledge;
- Tell fictional short stories built around well-defined scientific ideas, with a supplement summarizing the science underlying the plot.

Readers can look forward to a broad range of topics, as intriguing as they are important. Here just a few by way of illustration:

- Time travel, superluminal travel, wormholes, teleportation
- Extraterrestrial intelligence and alien civilizations
- Artificial intelligence, planetary brains, the universe as a computer, simulated worlds
- Non-anthropocentric viewpoints
- Synthetic biology, genetic engineering, developing nanotechnologies
- Eco/infrastructure/meteorite-impact disaster scenarios
- Future scenarios, transhumanism, posthumanism, intelligence explosion
- Virtual worlds, cyberspace dramas
- Consciousness and mind manipulation

More information about this series at http://www.springer.com/series/11657

Barry Dainton • Will Slocombe •
Attila Tanyi
Editors

Minding the Future

Artificial Intelligence, Philosophical Visions and Science Fiction

 Springer

Editors
Barry Dainton
Department of Philosophy
University of Liverpool
Liverpool, United Kingdom

Will Slocombe
Department of English
University of Liverpool
Liverpool, United Kingdom

Attila Tanyi
Institute of Philosophy and First
Semester Studies
UiT: The Arctic University of Norway
Tromsø, Norway

ISSN 2197-1188   ISSN 2197-1196   (electronic)
Science and Fiction
ISBN 978-3-030-64268-6   ISBN 978-3-030-64269-3   (eBook)
https://doi.org/10.1007/978-3-030-64269-3

This Springer imprint is published by the registered company Springer Nature Switzerland AG.
The registered company address is: Gewerbestrasse 11, 6330 Cham, Switzerland

Preface

Thanks to recent impressive and well-publicized advances in the field of artificial intelligence (AI) over the past decade or so, a number of questions have risen in prominence. Will AIs soon be more intelligent than humans? Is computer consciousness possible? Will robots take our jobs? What rights should intelligent robots have? Will such robots really be people? What sorts of human–robot personal relationships are appropriate? Will AIs eventually take over the world? Or the entire universe? Is this something we should fear or something we should welcome?

Even if the current AI boom should prove more short-lived than some hope and predict, advances in artificial intelligence will undoubtedly continue to be made, perhaps quite rapidly, and issues such as these will become ever more pressing. In this book, we critically assess some of the ways AI and robotics have been treated in science fiction. Science fiction writers may have failed to predict the advent of digital technology and the (possible) subsequent emergence of artificial minds—the emergence of computer technology in the 1940s took nearly everyone by surprise—but they were among the first to grasp how momentous their future consequences might be. In the decades since the first computers appeared on the scene science fiction has produced an astonishingly rich and stimulating range of speculations concerning the possible forms artificial minds (and bodies) might take, and the implications for humankind, in the near and distant future. As we hope to demonstrate in this volume, these speculations are well worthy of serious scrutiny.

By way of stage-setting in our introductory chapter we attempt to provide some historical and philosophical background to recent AI-related developments and briefly outline the themes and science fiction literature that our authors tackle in the chapters which follow. With a view to making the book accessible to as broad an audience as possible we have included a Glossary. Here readers will find introductions to a number of key concepts and terms; we also provide some—hopefully helpful and (reasonably) balanced—background to a number of relevant philosophical controversies. Last but not least, we have also provided a Timeline of important developments in science, philosophy, mathematics, computer technology and science fiction. Given that there have been so many noteworthy scientific and technological advances in recent decades—not to mention brilliant works of science fiction—we have had to be highly selective, and many readers may well find themselves baffled (or annoyed, or both!) by some of our omissions. Despite this unavoidable risk we believe that by bringing together important events in these disparate domains our chronology sheds fresh and useful light on an unusually vibrant period of intellectual history.

Liverpool, UK   Barry Dainton
Liverpool, UK   Will Slocombe
Tromsø, Norway   Attila Tanyi

Contents

Editor and Notes on Contributors

About the Editors

Barry Dainton is Professor of Philosophy at the University of Liverpool. He specializes in metaphysics and philosophy of mind, and is also interested in the philosophical implications of advances in science and technology, and is one of the Co-Directors of the Olaf Stapledon Centre for Speculative Futures. His previous publications include *Stream of Consciousness* (2nd edition, 2006), *The Phenomenal Self* (2008), *Time and Space* (2nd edition, 2010) and *Self* (2014).

Will Slocombe is a Senior Lecturer in English at the University of Liverpool. He is interested in science fiction and futures work, especially representations of artificial intelligence, and has published various articles and chapters on this and related areas, including new media narratology, computer games and contemporary literature and theory. He is one of the Co-Directors of the Olaf Stapledon Centre for Speculative Futures.

Attila Tanyi holds a PhD (Central European University, Hungary) and is currently a professor of philosophy in the Institute of Philosophy and First Semester Studies at UiT: The Arctic University of Norway. He specializes in moral and political philosophy, but his work stretches over disciplinary boundaries. He regularly collaborates with philosophers whose specializations are very different from his own, as well as with non-philosophers with an interest in philosophical problems. His work has appeared in numerous journals and he has edited several volumes of special issues.

Notes on Contributors

Amy Kind is Russell K. Pitzer Professor of Philosophy at Claremont McKenna College, where she also serves as Director of the Gould Center for Humanistic Studies. Her research interests lie broadly in the philosophy of mind, but most of her work centers on issues relating to imagination and to phenomenal consciousness. In addition to authoring the introductory textbooks Persons and Personal Identity and Philosophy of Mind: The Basics, she has edited Philosophy of Mind in the Twentieth and Twenty-First Centuries, The Routledge Handbook of Philosophy of Imagination, and (with Peter Kung) Knowledge Through Imagination.

Einar Duenger Bøhn is professor of philosophy at the University of Agder (Norway). He works mainly in metaphysics, philosophy of technology and philosophy of religion. In addition to various articles, he has published three books, among them *God and Abstract Objects* (Cambridge University Press, 2019).

Stephen Cave is Executive Director of the Leverhulme Centre for the Future of Intelligence (CFI), Senior Research Associate in the Faculty of Philosophy and Fellow of Hughes Hall, all at the University of Cambridge, UK. At CFI, he oversees a team of researchers across five programmes on the nature and impact of AI in the short and long term. He researches in philosophy of technology, in particular critical perspectives on AI, robotics and life-extension technologies. Previously, Stephen earned a PhD in philosophy from Cambridge and then joined the British Foreign Office, where he served as a policy advisor and diplomat. He is author of the book *Immortality* (Penguin Random House), a *New Scientist* book of the year, and co-editor of *AI Narratives: A History of Imaginative Thinking About Intelligent Machines* (OUP). He regularly advises a range of governmental and international bodies on the ethics of emerging technologies.

Milan M. Cirkovic is a research professor at the Astronomical Observatory of Belgrade, Serbia, and a research associate of the Future of Humanity Institute at the Oxford University (Oxford, UK). His primary research interests are in the fields of astrobiology (habitable zones, habitability of galaxies, SETI studies), philosophy of science (futures studies, philosophy of physics) and risk analysis (global catastrophes, observation selection effects, epistemology of risk). He co-edited the widely cited anthology on *Global Catastrophic Risks* (Oxford University Press, 2008), with Nick Bostrom; wrote three monographs (the latest being *The Great Silence: The Science and Philosophy of Fermi's Paradox*, Oxford University Press, 2018), as well as four popular science/general non-fiction books; and authored about 200 research and professional papers.

Stephen R. L. Clark is Emeritus Professor of Philosophy at the University of Liverpool and an Honorary Research Fellow in the Department of Theology at the University of Bristol. He was previously a Fellow of All Souls College, Oxford, and a Lecturer in Moral Philosophy at the University of Glasgow. He has delivered Gifford, Stanton and Wilde Lectures at Glasgow, Cambridge and Oxford. He served on both the Farm Animal Welfare Council and the Animal Procedures Committee. His books include *Aristotle's Man* (1975), *The Nature of the Beast* (1982), *From Athens to Jerusalem* (1984, 2019), *Civil Peace and Sacred Order* (1989), *How to Think about the Earth: Models of Environmental Theology* (1993), *God, Religion and Reality* (1998, 2017), *Biology and Christian Ethics* (2000), *Understanding Faith: Religious Belief and its Place in Society* (2009), *Philosophical Futures* (2011), *Plotinus: Myth, Metaphor and Philosophical Practice* (2016) and *Can We Believe in People?* (2019). His chief current interests are in the philosophy of Plotinus, the understanding and treatment of non-human animals, philosophy of religion and science fiction.

Louise Dennis is a senior lecturer in the Department of Computer Science at the University of Manchester where she is part of the Autonomy and Verification group. She is a member of the IEEE Standards working group for Transparency for Autonomous Systems (P7001), conference coordinator for the ACM Special Interest Group on Artificial Intelligence (SIGAI) and a board member of the European Association for Multi-Agent Systems. Her expertise is in the development and verification of autonomous systems, reconfigurable autonomy and machine ethics. Louise has published over 50 peer-reviewed papers on various aspects of machine ethics, transparency, multi-agent systems, autonomy and verification. She also has extensive experience in public engagement work including running Lego programming workshops in schools and giving talks to Scibars and similar organizations on robotics and machine ethics.

Kanta Dihal is a Senior Research Fellow at the Leverhulme Centre for the Future of Intelligence, University of Cambridge. She is the Principal Investigator on the Global AI Narratives project, which explores intercultural public understanding artificial intelligence as constructed by fictional and non-fictional narratives, and the Project Development Lead on Decolonizing AI. She obtained her DPhil in science communication at the University of Oxford in 2018: in her thesis, titled "The Stories of Quantum Physics," she investigated the communication of conflicting interpretations of quantum physics to adults and children. Kanta's research focuses on the portrayals and perceptions of intelligent machines across cultures, and how they help us think about ethics and bias in new technologies. Her work intersects the fields of science communication, literature and science and science fiction. She is co-editor of *AI Narratives: A History of Imaginative Thinking About Intelligent Machines* (Oxford University Press, 2020) and has co-authored a series of papers on AI narratives with Dr Stephen Cave, including "The Whiteness of AI" (*Philosophy and Technology*, 2020). She has advised the World Economic Forum, the UK House of Lords and the United Nations on portrayals and perceptions of AI.

Michael Hauskeller is Professor of Philosophy and Head of the Philosophy Department at the University of Liverpool, UK. He specializes in moral and existential philosophy, but has also done work in various other areas, most notably phenomenology (the theory of atmospheres), the philosophy of art and beauty and the philosophy of human enhancement. His numerous publications include *Biotechnology and the Integrity of Life* (Routledge 2007), *Better Humans? Understanding the Enhancement Project* (Routledge 2013), *Sex and the Posthuman Condition* (Palgrave Macmillan 2014), *The Palgrave Handbook of Posthumanism in Film and Television* (ed. with T. Philbeck and C. Carbonell, Palgrave 2015), *Mythologies of Transhumanism* (Palgrave Macmillan 2016), *Moral Enhancement: Critical Perspectives* (ed. with L. Coyne, Cambridge University Press 2018) and *The Meaning of Life and Death* (Bloomsbury 2019).

Ina Roy-Faderman teaches medical ethics for Oregon State University. She has a PhD in Philosophy from the University of California-Berkeley and an MD from Stanford University. Her academic interests and publications centre around the biological, ethical and personal relationships between human- and non-human beings in fictional and non-fictional contexts.

Mark Silcox was born and raised just outside of Toronto, Canada. He has previously worked as a security guard, a short-order cook and a freelance writer in the video game industry. His writing is featured in the Nintendo 64 game *Aidyn Chronicles: The First Mage* and the MMORPG *Earth and Beyond,* as well as the indie games *Dragonlord* and *The Cave of Morpheus*. He received an MA in Philosophy from the University of Toronto in 1993 and doctorate in Philosophy from the Ohio State University in 2002. He currently lives in Edmond, Oklahoma, where he serves as Chair of the Department of Humanities and Philosophy at the University of Central Oklahoma. He is the author of *A Defense of Simulated Experience: New Noble Lies* (2019), editor of *Experience Machines: The Philosophy of Virtual Worlds* (2017), co-author of *Philosophy through Video Games* (with Jon Cogburn, 2008) and co-editor of *Dungeons & Dragons and Philosophy: Raiding the Temple of Wisdom* (with Jon Cogburn, 2012). He also writes fiction as an avocation and has published just over a dozen science fiction and horror stories in a variety of venues. His SF novel *The Face on the Mountain* was published by Incandescent Phoenix Press in 2015.

Michael Szollosy has a PhD in English Literature and Psychotherapeutic Studies from the University of Sheffield, and has since had a varied career teaching and researching at the University. Initially teaching literature, critical theory and cultural studies in the School of English, he then began teaching psychoanalysis and psychotherapy (with a particular focus on distance learning and new pedagogic technologies) at the School for Health and Related Research. He then moved to Psychology, beginning to research the social and cultural impacts of robots, AI and VR. In this time, he has worked on a diverse range of projects, including Expressive Agents for Symbiotic Education and Learning (EASEL), Cyberselves in Immersive Technologies and the Human Brain Project. He has since written on a range of topics, including the ethics of robotics, cultural fears of new technologies, biomimetics, social robotics, AI, film, television and fiction. Now a Research Fellow in the Department of Computer Studies, he continues to research the social impacts of new technologies. He is public engagement lead for Sheffield Robotics, and is presently working on the project Imagining Technologies for Disability Futures, focusing on cultural perceptions of disability and technology, and participatory design; he is also engaged in a project trying to improve access to robotics and computer teaching via distance learning. Apart from academia, he is also a Founder of Cyberselves Universal Ltd, a software company creating a universal telepresence platform, and looking to make robotics programming easier and more accessible.

Introduction

Barry Dainton, Will Slocombe, and Attila Tanyi

Abstract After a brief look at an impressive recent achievement made possible by developments in artificial intelligence we take a journey back through the centuries. We learn that the Turing Test was anticipated in a treatise written four centuries ago, and that concerns about the capabilities of machines are nothing new. We then move on to consider some of the issues surrounding artificial intelligence, and explain why science fiction is a valuable resource that it would be foolhardy to ignore.

B. Dainton
Department of Philosophy, University of Liverpool, Liverpool, UK
e-mail: bdainton@liverpool.ac.uk

W. Slocombe
Department of English, University of Liverpool, Liverpool, UK
e-mail: W.Slocombe@liverpool.ac.uk

A. Tanyi (✉)
Institute of Philosophy and First Semester Studies, UiT: The Arctic University of Norway, Tromsø, Norway
e-mail: Attila.tanyi@uit.no

A Philosophical Thinking Machine

Over the course of its brief seventy-year history the field of artificial intelligence (AI) has known a succession of "golden ages" during which advances are rapidly made, and "ice ages" when progress has disappointingly slowed. Most commentators would agree that we are currently in the midst of an AI golden age. Since the success of Deepmind's *AlphaGo* program against Go champion Lee Sedol in 2016 neural networks and deep learning have rarely been out of the news. The following claims about the limits of these newly fashionable forms of artificial intelligence were recently posted on the internet:

> Artificial intelligence programs like deep learning neural networks may be able to beat humans at playing Go or chess, or doing arithmetic, or writing Navy Seal copypasta, but they will never be able to truly think for themselves, to have consciousness, to feel any of the richness and complexity of the world that we mere humans can feel. Mere, unenlightened humans might be impressed by the abilities of simple deep learning programs, but when looked at in a more holistic manner, it all adds up to… well, nothing. They still don't exhibit any trace of consciousness. All of the available data support the notion that humans feel and experience the world differently than computers do. While a computer can beat a human master at chess or Go or some other game of structured rules, it will never be able to truly think outside of those rules, it will never be able to come up with its own new strategies on the fly, it will never be able to feel, to react, the way a human can. Artificial intelligence programs lack consciousness and self-awareness. They will never be able to have a sense of humor. They will never be able to appreciate art, or beauty, or love. They will never feel lonely. They will never have empathy for other people, for animals, for the environment. They will never enjoy music or fall in love, or cry at the drop of a hat. Merely by existing, mere, unenlightened humans are intellectually superior to computers, no matter how good our computers get at winning games like Go or Jeopardy. We don't live by the rules of those games. Our minds are much, much bigger than that.

The possibility or otherwise of computer consciousness has been much-debated and it remains a controversial topic—so there is little that's remarkable about the claims being made in this passage. What is more remarkable is *who* wrote it: the passage was composed in its entirety *by* a computer, OpenAI's GPT-3. It so happens that GTP-3 is itself a neural network, one possessing an internal model of the English language comprising some 175 billion parameters, powered by deep learning algorithms and trained by exposure to the entirety of the internet and libraries of books.[1]

Anyone conducting a broader survey of GPT-3's outputs—in addition to philosophy it is able to produce include poetry, conversations, songs, jokes, legal prose and restaurant menu—will quickly discover that the program is far from infallible, and the mistakes that it makes suggest that it lacks a full understanding of what it is writing about. The machine's linguistic skills are enviable, but it falls short of possessing the level of wide-ranging general intelligence that we possess. But as David Chalmers has suggested:

> Nevertheless, GPT-3 is instantly one of the most interesting and important AI systems ever produced. This is not just because of its impressive conversational and writing abilities. It was certainly disconcerting to have GPT-3 produce a plausible-looking interview with me. GPT-3 seems to be closer to passing the Turing test than any other system to date (although "closer" does not mean "close") ...
>
> More remarkably, GPT-3 is showing hints of general intelligence. Previous AI systems have performed well in specialized domains such as game-playing, but cross-domain general intelligence has seemed far off. GPT-3 shows impressive abilities across many domains. It can learn to perform tasks on the fly from a few examples, when nothing was explicitly programmed in. It can play chess and Go, albeit not especially well. Significantly, it can write its own computer programs given a few informal instructions. It can even design machine learning models. Thankfully they are not as powerful as GPT-3 itself (the singularity is not here yet) [2].

With advances such as these being made it is not surprising that in recent years increasing numbers of people have begun to take seriously the idea that artificial intelligence that rivals or even surpasses that of human beings is a genuine possibility, and are pondering the implications of this.

---

[1] GPT-3 stands for "generative pre-trained transformer version three," and it has been exposed to approximately 45 billion times the number of words an average human being sees in their entire life. For further details about how the cited text was generated see [1].

From Animal Souls to Machine Minds and the Turing Test

They may be much in the recent news, but the issue of whether or not an artificial construct can possess a life or mind of its own is by no means a new one. Thinkers in earlier centuries were well aware that this issue has the potential to have an enormous impact: on how we should think of ourselves and what our place in the universe really is. If we could build a machine that has the same sort of mental capacities as a human being, then we humans can't be as special as many of us would like to think.

To anyone with a passing acquaintance with the history of Western philosophy René Descartes (1596–1650) is a familiar figure—indeed, Descartes is often referred to as "the father of modern philosophy."[2] He is famous (at least among philosophy undergraduates) for wondering in his *Meditations* whether he could possibly be certain—absolutely certain—that he was not dreaming or being deceived by an evil demon. Irrespective of his paternal relationship with modern philosophy, Descartes did have a real daughter, Francine, who sadly died of scarlet fever in 1640 when only five years old. After Descartes' own death a strange rumour started to spread to the effect that the philosopher had constructed a fully life-like automaton that closely resembled in appearance his daughter Francine—the doll supposedly accompanied Descartes everywhere on his travels. On one of these trips a ship's captain is alleged to have accidentally opened the case where the automaton was stored, and horrified by what he found cast it into the sea.

The full story of how this rumour originated is a fascinating and complex one, but there can be little that doubt it was often passed on with a view to discrediting Descartes and his followers, some of whom were associated with then-scandalous forms of materialism.[3] For present purposes it provides a useful illustration of just how controversial some of Descartes' views were. In the 17th and 18th centuries the issue of the extent to which human beings are nothing more than purely physical machines was already giving rise to increasingly heated debates, and Descartes' views were central to these debates.

---

[2] He is also a familiar character in contemporary philosophy of mind texts for defending a form of dualism, holding that our minds reside not in our brains, but in immaterial soul-substances. While the typical undergraduate textbook portrait of Descartes is not entirely misleading, it is also guilty of concealing the true scope of intellectual endeavours. While his philosophy was certainly important to him, Descartes may well have devoted more time and effort to mathematics, physics and biology, and his writings in the latter fields were influential in the 17th and 18th centuries. If "Cartesian Dualism" features in any dictionary of philosophy, "Cartesian coordinates" (also invented by Descartes) will feature in any dictionary of mathematics—and most of us will have encountered them at school.

[3] For the full story of Descartes' robotic daughter, in all its complexity, see [3].

One of Descartes' more infamous doctrines was his stance on the sort of minds possessed by non-human animals. Referring to the latter as "bête machines" he denied that they have conscious mentality. If you step on a puppy's tail it may well squeal and bark, but you can reassure yourself that it is not feeling any pain. Explaining his views to Henry More he wrote: "The greatest of all the prejudices we have retained from infancy is that of believing that brutes think" [4, p. 544]. Few contemporary philosophers find Descartes' stance on animal minds plausible, and even in his day it had comparatively few takers.[4] However, the reasons Descartes put forward for adopting this stance are of considerable contemporary relevance.

In the seventeenth century, Descartes' view that we humans possess a soul was wholly unremarkable—at the time, everyone (or nearly everyone) would have agreed. In contrast, Descartes' claim that animals are nothing more than machines was far from commonplace—at the time it was quite revolutionary. The dominant world-view was Aristotelian, and for Aristotelians the world was brimming with souls of one kind or another. Plants were thought to possess a *nutritive soul* responsible for their basic life-functions, and which allowed them to feed, grow and reproduce. Animals possessed a nutritive soul, but in addition they possessed a *sensitive* soul, which allows them to perceive their surroundings and move their bodies. Human beings possessed nutritive and sensitive souls, but they also possess a *rational soul*, responsible for their distinctive intellectual capacities.

Like other forward-looking thinkers during the early phases of the scientific revolution Descartes was eager to abolish any trace of (to his eyes near magical) Aristotelian souls from the material world. Consequently he held that all physical things—even highly complex ones such as plants and animals—are constituted entirely of material parts that are governed by simple mechanical laws. These material parts are invisibly small, and the laws governing them are akin to the laws of motion governing observable things such as thrown balls passing through the air, pendulums and the inner mechanical workings of clocks. It is these mechanical laws—rather than anything resembling Aristotelian animistic souls—that are responsible for all aspects of plant and animal life. While it is uncontroversially the case that living things such as roses, oak trees, frogs, birds and dogs *appear* very different from mechanical objects such as clocks or musical boxes, for Descartes these

---

[4] Catherine Descartes, the philosopher's niece, observing that a female warbler bird returning to the same window year after year remarked to a friend "with all due respect to my uncle, she has judgement." See [5, p. 75] for further details.

appearances are deceptive: in fact, they are all fundamentally of the same nature, living things are nothing more than complex material mechanisms.

We now know that Descartes was correct—certainly his mechanical view of living things is one nearly all contemporary biologists would accept. However, this victory did not occur overnight. The doctrine that living things are special and fundamentally different from the non-living still seemed plausible to many scientists in the nineteenth century, and it was only with advances in molecular biology in the early decades of the twentieth century that it was finally put to bed. Given all this, is scarcely surprising that so many in the seventeenth century found Descartes' mechanical view of life so shocking and absurd.[5]

What of human beings? Descartes was one of the leading biologists of his day and being well-versed in the theory and practice of dissection. Given that he was fully aware that similar structures can be found within the brains and bodies of human and animals it was not surprising to find that argued that our own bodies are also machines. Descartes held that all the basic operations of a human body could be fully explicated in mechanical terms, without any need for the nutritive and sensory souls posited by the Aristotelians. However, there was one aspect of human life that Descartes could not conceive a mere machine being capable of replicating: our reason or intelligence. In his *Discourse on the Method* (1637) Descartes wrote:

> … if any such machines had the organs and outward shape of a monkey or of some other animal that doesn't have reason, we couldn't tell that they didn't possess entirely the same nature as these animals; whereas if any such machines bore a resemblance to *our* bodies and imitated as many of *our* actions as was practically possible, we would still have two very sure signs that they were nevertheless not real men. (1) The first is that they could never use words or other constructed signs, as we do to declare our thoughts to others. We can easily conceive of a machine so constructed that it utters words, and even utters words that correspond to bodily actions that will cause a change in its organs (touch it in one spot and it asks 'What do you mean?', touch it in another and it cries out 'That hurts!', and so on); but *not* that such a machine should produce different sequences of words so as to give an appropriately meaningful answer to *whatever* is said in its presence—which is something that the dullest of men *can* do. (2) Secondly, even though such machines might do some things as well as we do them, or perhaps even better, they would be bound to fail in others; and that would show us that they weren't acting through understanding but only from

---

[5] Even writing a full century after Descartes, when La Mettrie published his *L'homme machine* in 1747 readers found it so outrageous that La Mettrie had to flee the usually very tolerant Netherlands.

the disposition of their organs. For whereas reason is a universal instrument that can be used in all kinds of situations, these organs need some particular disposition for each particular action; hence it is practically impossible for a machine to have enough different organs to make it act in all the contingencies of life in the way our reason makes us act [6, p. 22].

So far as Descartes was concerned, no purely mechanical system could possibly possess the ability to converse on any and all topics in the way we effortlessly do at a moment's notice. Nor could such a machine find solutions to an indefinitely wide range of problems in the way that we manage to do—human intelligence is a "universal instrument." It was this stance on the ultimate limitations of physical machinery that led Descartes to conclude that the rational parts of our minds could not be physical.

By virtue of being non-physical, an immaterial soul is free from the limitations governing physical machines. If nothing physical could possess our intellectual capacities, these capacities must reside in something non-physical, and an immaterial soul is the obvious candidate. Hence while Descartes found that he could dispense with two of the Aristotelian souls, he felt obliged to retain a version of the rational soul.[6] Since the behavioural repertoire of non-human animals is far less complex—they can't converse and can only solve a narrowly circumscribed range of problems—Descartes saw no obstacle to regarding *them* as purely physical machines, devoid of the immaterial soul that we possess.

In 1950 Alan Turing published "Computing Machinery and Intelligence" in the philosophy journal *Mind* [8]. Here Turing proposed his famous and much-discussed test for machine intelligence. If a computer could be programmed so as to replicate the conversational skills of an average human being by providing appropriate and meaningful responses to whatever is put to it then it would be legitimate to regard the computer as possessing genuine intelligence. Turing's test is clearly anticipated in the passage of *Discourse* cited above. Descartes may have thought it unlikely that a wholly physical machine could replicate the intelligent behaviour of a human being, but he also seemed

---

[6] Some of Descartes' contemporaries were more radical and were prepared to reject his dualistic conception of human beings entirely. In his *Leviathan* (1651) Thomas Hobbes maintained that there is no human capacity that is incapable of being explained in mechanical material terms. Margaret Cavendish also found dualism problematic and argued for an all-inclusive materialism: "I would ask those, that say the Brain has neither sense, reason, nor self-motion, and therefore no Perception; but that all proceeds from an Immaterial Principle, and an Incorporeal Sprit, distinct from the body, which moveth and actuates corporeal matter; I would fain ask them, I say, where their Immaterial Ideas reside, in what part or place of the Body?" [7].

willing to accept that if this were to occur it would be legitimate to regard the machine as being genuinely intelligent and a rational agent.

From the standpoint of our technologically sophisticated twenty-first century we should certainly be wary of being overly critical of Descartes and his views as to the feats ordinary physical machinery might be capable of achieving. After all, the most advanced technologies in his the day were spring-powered clocks and the water-powered automata that could be found in gardens of the richer members of the nobility.[7] If he had lived to see billions of transistors being crammed onto small computer chips would he have adopted a different stance? Would he have been even more impressed when he learned that Turing had proved that these machines have the very special power to compute everything that is mathematically computable? We can only speculate, but it is by no means impossible.

Questions, Issues, Problems

In his 1950 paper Turing predicted that we would not have long to wait before a computer passed his test: "I believe that at the end of the century the use of words and general educated opinion will have altered so much that the one will be able to speak of machines thinking without expecting to be contradicted." In this at least he was mistaken: by the turn of the millennium no computer had managed to pass Turing's test, and in this respect at least Descartes' pessimism with regard to the potential for machine intelligence has thus far been vindicated. However, as we have seen, thanks to recent developments the prospects for genuine machine intelligence are considerably brighter than they have been for some time, and it may well not be very long before we have to deal with AIs that are at least as intelligent as a typical human.

In this connection there are a number of issues that have already received a good deal of attention, and which are likely to receive more in the decades to come.

One important issue concerns the relationship between a capacity for intelligent behaviour and consciousness: does genuine intelligence require consciousness? Would a machine capable of intelligent behaviour also have to be capable of having experiences of pleasure and pain, or colour and sound? Would it be capable of engaging in conscious thinking? Quite possibly, but

---

[7] It should be noted that some of the automata in the Early Modern period were highly sophisticated pieces of machinery, and could seem strikingly life-like. Jacques de Vaucanson's "digesting duck," for example, had some four hundred moving parts in its wings alone. For more on relevant automata and Descartes see [5].

very different views on this issue have been defended, but thus far nothing resembling a consensus has emerged. Some philosophers hold that genuine intelligence involves the capacity to consciously *understand* what one is doing, a capacity which obviously requires consciousness. But the majority of computer scientists would follow Turing's lead and reject this claim, and with some plausibility: if a computer could pass the Turing Test without being conscious, it would be odd to deny that it had a considerable degree of *some* kind of genuine intelligence. A further complicating factor here is that neuroscientists, psychologists and evolutionary biologists have found it difficult to specify with any clarity how our own capacity for consciousness relates to our cognitive and behavioural capacities. Quite what consciousness does and why it evolved remain highly controversial issues.

A distinct but related issue concerns the very possibility of computer possessing *any* form of consciousness—the issue that was vexing GPT-3 in the passage we encountered earlier. This remains one of the most controversial questions in the philosophy of mind, and opinions remains sharply divided. For some philosophers computer consciousness is eminently possible, others rule it out as quite absurd. A complicating factor to bear in mind when considering this question is that "computers" can come in very different guises. The Turing-type that most of us are acquainted with—those found in our phones and laptops—are algorithmic devices: their program consists of a set of instructions which they carry out in a step-wise fashion. Evidently, computers are this kind are distinctly unlike biological brains, which in the human case consist of a hundred billion or so neurons, each connected to hundreds or thousands of other neurons, all working in parallel. But since the earliest days of artificial intelligence computer scientists have been designing computers that work very differently from Turing-type machines, computers which much more similar to biological brains. The "neural nets" currently associated with the revolution in machine learning fall into this category. If it should turn out that Turing-type machines are in fact the wrong kind of thing to be conscious, the same may well not be true for differently structured non-biological machines.[8]

The philosophical relevance of AI is not confined to the philosophy of mind, it also gives rise to interesting ethical and political questions. If robots possessing human-level intelligence appear on the scene, how should we treat them? Should they be granted the same rights and respect as a human being? What sorts of personal relationships between AIs and humans are

---

[8] For more on these issues see the Glossary entries for "consciousness," "consciousness: the hard problem," "Consciousness and Science Fiction" and "Cartesian Dualism."

appropriate? Under what circumstances should you take an AI as a friend or lover? The AIs in Asimov's robot stories are programmed to "obey the orders given it by human beings, except where this would lead to a human being coming to harm." In effect if not name, Asimov's robots are slaves. Would it be morally right to create beings of this kind?[9]

A different range of pressing issues combine social, political and economic considerations. The machine intelligences available at present do not possess human-level intelligence, but they are sufficiently intelligent to do the sorts of jobs that millions of humans currently do, and as they improve they'll be able to do more. According to one recent estimate [10], we can expect 35% of the workforce to be replaced by AIs over the next twenty years.[10] Predictions are of course risky, but the jobs widely believed to be most at risk include factory workers, lawyers, accountants and taxi drivers—and by the time GPT-5 arrives philosophers, poets and novelists might be at risk too. Working out ways of responding to these developments which maximize the potential benefits while minimizing unwanted disruption is likely will be among the greatest social and political challenges facing us over the next few decades.

Another issue that has already provoked considerable debate concerns the dangers associated with the increased possibilities for mass surveillance that advances in AI are making possible. By combining data harvested from social media and internet use, location tracking via mobile phone, pervasive video surveillance cameras and facial recognition, computers capable of speedily handling vast amounts of data make it possible for interested parties to know vastly more about ordinary citizens than has hitherto been possible, and plan accordingly. Totalitarian regimes have been quick to exploit these technological possibilities, but in democratic nations too these technologies have already led to new methods for influencing the outcomes of elections—methods that unscrupulous parties have been quick to exploit, and which regulators are struggling to deal with effectively.[11]

On an economic level, the data global social media companies possess about their users has proven to be a highly saleable asset, and highly attractive to advertisers willing to pay for it—a combination of factors which had led to social media companies accruing vast amounts of wealth in a comparatively short period of time. As both surveillance technologies and the abilities of AIs

---

[9] See [9] for a useful selection of current thinking on human-robot relationships, autonomous weapons and vehicles, and a number of other issues.

[10] The website https://willrobotstakemyjob.com gives a 94% chance of accountants and auditors being replaced by AIs and robots.

[11] See [11, part III] for Yuval Harari's perturbing reflections on the consequences of big data algorithms knowing us better than we know ourselves).

to interpret enormous quantities of data advance in the years to come, finding ways of dealing with the consequences will be a major concern.[12]

These technologies also open up new political possibilities. In China, the way in which mass surveillance technology is being linked to their "Social Credit" system has attracted a good deal of attention. The latter allocates penalty points to citizens who behave in ways the state doesn't like—failing to show up for restaurant reservations, traffic violations, cheating on public transport—as well as reward points for doing things the state wants to encourage, such as donating blood or performing community services. The potential for a Big Brother-style micro-control of entire populations is as obvious as it is perturbing.[13] However, there is also the potential for more positive developments.

As AI becomes more powerful it may well become possible to organize societies in ways that are simply *more intelligent* than anything presently possible. Advocates of capitalism are fond of claiming that even if the free market economic system has its downsides, it is still the most efficient way possible for organizing an economy and generating wealth. No central state planner would ever be capable of monitoring the billions of economic transactions that take place on a daily basis and manage them more intelligently than the blind hand of the market. Or so a familiar line of argument runs. But even if this is the case at the moment, will it still be the case when powerful AIs that are able to exploit the resources of big data become available? Firms such as Facebook and Amazon are already monitoring billions of transactions on a daily basis, and managing them in highly effective ways. Is an AI-powered version of communism something we should dread, or look forward to? Is there any alternative to coping with the higher levels of unemployment AIs are going to produce?[14]

In the eyes of many the most important issue in this connection is working out how to protect ourselves against future machines that equal or surpass humans in intelligence. Humans are smart, but not *that* smart. It would be great to have someone a good deal smarter than us to help solve pressing problems such as climate change, finding a cure for cancer, and reconciling quantum mechanics with general relativity—all problems which continue to defeat the most brilliant human minds. Hence there is a powerful impetus not to stop at creating AIs with human-level intelligence, but to aim for AI's that are

---

[12] A theme thoroughly explored by Shoshana Zuboff, see [12].

[13] For a useful overview see https://theconversation.com/chinas-social-credit-system-puts-its-people-under-pressure-to-be-model-citizens-89963.

[14] See [13, 14] for surveys of these issues.

superintelligent, AIs that possess vastly more intelligence than any human. But if there are lots of advantages in having a superintelligent machine at ones disposal, there are also lots of potential dangers. A maliciously intentioned superintelligence could decide to wipe out the human race entirely—by engineering (say) a virus with a lethality rate of 100%.

Before creating a superintelligence it would obviously be a good idea to ensure that it won't decide to do anything along these lines. But precisely what steps should we take? Given that a superintelligent machine might well be vastly smarter than us, can we be confident that *any* measure we are capable of adopting is guaranteed to succeed?[15]

From Science Fact to Science Fiction

When it comes to addressing issues such as these the science fiction genre contains an enormous quantity of resources that it would be decidedly unintelligent to ignore. Artificial intelligence—in all manner of guises and forms—has been a prominent theme in science fiction since its very beginnings. Inevitably, when devising these scenarios science fiction writers have been considering potential responses to many of the issues we have just outlined, often with considerable foresight and intelligence. In many domains the gap between science fiction and science fact is rapidly closing, and science fiction writers have long been exploring the relevant territory in interesting and thought-provoking ways—and in some cases actually helping shape it. Science fiction doesn't just have the potential to influence current thinking on AI and robotics, in many areas it has *already* exerted a very considerable influence. When writing just now about the threat that future AIs might pose to humanity, it was very difficult to avoid mentioning the *Terminator* movies or *2001*'s HAL. When talking of the possibility of falling in love with a machine *Blade Runner* and *Her* come quickly to mind, as does the new TV version of *Westworld*. Given the extent to which science fiction has already permeated our broader contemporary consciousness, subjecting this influence to proper scrutiny is clearly something which should be done.

Hence this book. The essays which follow explore the way minds and artificial mentality have been treated in science fiction over the past century or so, with a view to drawing out and reflecting on their implications for issues such as those just outlined. Given the vast amount of brilliant and

---

[15] For more on this threat, how seriously we should take it, and what we might do to minimize the dangers, see [15, 16].

thought-provoking science fiction that has been produced during this period that is relevant to these topics, in what follows we have barely scratched the surface. Even so, we are confident the essays demonstrate that the exercise is very worthwhile.

The first section, "Qualities of Mind," explores the ways in which identity and personhood relate to AI, and how these characteristics might relate to ethics and morality. In his "What Is It Like to Be a Bot?" Hauskeller draws on authors such as Philip K. Dick, Isaac Asimov, and Ian McEwan and observes that the dreams in which "thinking machines feature are not usually happy dreams. Very often they come close to nightmares, suggesting that even though we are not exactly fearful of thinking machines, we are certainly not prepared to entirely trust them either." Hauskeller goes on to consider whether many of the fears about AI are because of own our (likely justified) concerns that systems possessing different modes of cognition might fail to share specifically human concerns, and explores how empathy and emotions are relevant to this debate. Bøhn's "Is Ava a person?" examines the extent to which Ava, from *Ex Machina* (dir. Alex Garland, 2014) might be said to be a "person" (rather than a mere "object"), and how the notion of consciousness is relevant to this issue, along with a range of other concepts, including intentionality, free will, instrumental rationality, and moral responsibility. In so doing, Bøhn demonstrates that "human" and "person" are not necessarily interchangeable as categories, and highlights the extent to which personhood is defined from without (from how an entity is perceived) as much as within (whether you have the capability to see yourself as a person). The final chapter of the section, Slocombe & Dennis's "Governor Modules and Moral Judges," relates Martha Wells's *Murderbot Diaries* to existing research within computer science on creating ethical frameworks within AI systems, asking how such a system might function and how it might impact on an AI's "autonomy." A question that emerges is how precisely an ethical framework that is imposed on an AI might govern its actions. All three chapters inflect questions about the relationship between an entity's identity in different ways, and begin to consider "relational" aspects of advanced AI and the human sphere.

These relational aspects are further examined in the second section, "Meetings of Minds." The focus here is on issues which arise when humans and AIs enter into intimate relationships, whether emotional or physical or both. We are reminded here of John McCarthy [17]—the computer scientist who coined the term "Artificial Intelligence" as a systemic approach to computer cognition—and his short story "The Robot and the Baby" (2004), where a furious societal debate occurs about whether it is possible for a robot to love a baby. Although (it turns out) McCarthy's robot is *not* capable of loving a baby, questions about how humans might love AIs, and how AIs might love humans, recur across science fiction. Kind's essay "Love in the Time of AI" examines *Her* (dir. Spike Jonze, 2013) alongside an episode of *Black Mirror* in order to consider how romantic love (as opposed to other kinds of love) forges a connection between human and AI, and explores the parameters of that connection. In comparison, Cave and Dihal's "AI will always love you" ranges across a wider range of science fiction, including works by Brian Aldiss and Greg Egan, and serials such as *Westworld*, *Humans* and *Real Humans*, to offer examples of three "successful" types of love (friendship, familial and romantic), and the potential problems that emerge from human/AI relationships. Broadening out from love, Roy-Faderman's "Ann Leckie's Ancilliaries: Artificial Intelligence and Embodiment" uses texts such as the lesser-known *The Clockwork Man* by E.V. Odle (1923) and William Gibson's seminal *Neuromancer* (1984), alongside Leckie's recent *Ancillary* trilogy. This chapter offers a suite of ideas about the potential "emotional lives" of AI, and leads to a consideration of the ways in which intelligence and emotion might be related, in both humans and non-humans.

In the third section, "Changing Minds," the emphasis shifts from the personal and interpersonal aspects of AI into broader territory. Each of the four chapters here focuses on civilizational and species-level concerns and developments. Clark's "Selfless Civilizations: Robots, Zombies and the World to Come," for example, is a meditation upon the fact that the future may well be dominated by non-conscious machine intelligences, with human forms of consciousness being merely a drop in the cosmic ocean, a rather bleak prospect since imagining such a universe "is to get as close as we can to imagining a world deprived of qualities and meaning. Such a world has no centre, nor any distinction between here and there, past and present, one creature and another." The wide range of authors that Clark takes inspiration from include Peter Watts and Charles Stross, as well as Isaac Asimov, Ray Bradbury, C. J. Cherryh and Plotinus. Cirkovic's "Mindhunter: Transcending Geocentrism and Psychocentrism in The Invincible and Peace on Earth" echoes this engagement with non-conscious intelligences, but through the filter of two of Stanislaw Lem's novels. In much of his science fiction Lem was concerned to open us up to the possibility—or even probability—that minds elsewhere in the universe might be very different from anything human beings possess or can easily conceive. Cirkovic suggests that unless and until this lesson of Lem's is taken on board, the Copernican revolution will not be complete.

Silcox's "Historicism, Science Fiction, and the Singularity" introduces us to Karl Popper's critique of historicism, and the considerations which led Popper to maintain that it was impossible to make reliable predictive claims about the future. As Silcox notes, recent claims concerning an allegedly imminent Singularity would be seriously undermined if Popper is right. He then moves on to explore science fiction settings created by Bruce Sterling and Iain M. Banks, and demonstrates the valuable insights these fictions provide into the intelligibility (or otherwise) of the truly advanced AIs that we might one day encounter. The final chapter, Szollosy's "Shifting the goalposts," brings us back to earth, but is a fitting conclusion to the collection as, through discussions of works such as Asimov's *Bicentennial Man* and *Humans*, it exposes the ways in which AI has prompted a continuous reappraisal of the "human" and how the goalposts on what we understand AI to be have shifted and continue to shift. He suggests that the necessary next step—to reconsider the frames through which we evaluate ideas such as "ethics" or "the human"—is one that will enable us to ask better questions, rather than rehearse the same old politics of exceptionalism that dominate debates about AI.

An important idea that emerges from the summaries above is that we have been deliberately broad about the very definition of the central concern of this book: what is an "artificial intelligence" anyway? Some of the contributions discuss robots, some androids/gynoids (*gendered* robots), some describe what might be termed "software agents" or programs, and still others explore cyborgs and AI/human hybrids. Moreover, some of these beings are overtly conscious, some are not conscious as we would understand the term, and in some cases we just don't know (and that is of course the point). As a result, some of the insights of individual discussions remain case-specific whereas others have a more general relevance. But the point is that, as we are "minding the future" and being mindful of it, all of these discussions illustrate the fact that the signifying phrase, "artificial intelligence," is itself contested, and that different definitions of the very words will lead to markedly divergent interpretations of what AI can and might do. Science fiction is replete with examples of all of the above, and that very proliferation can be productive in considering what an AI is, and how we might interpret it, and furthermore help us to think through how we might relate to it and how it might relate to us (with the "we" and "us" in that sentence being similarly ambiguously defined; if you're an AI reading this, who do you think "we" are…?)

What unites these varied contributions is the fact that science fiction enables varied ways of thinking about artificial intelligence and the impacts it might have. Science fiction, perhaps taking a familiar metaphor too far, operates as a kind of "simulation" of possible futures. Some of the scenarios are probable, some of them are vastly improbable. But no matter their plausibility, they can nonetheless spark new ideas relating to the technologies that comprise AI, our attitudes towards those technologies, and the kinds of impact AI might have on personal, social, global and cosmological levels. By virtue of not being confined to the present time, or constrained by current levels of technology, science fiction has the capacity to speculate about possible futures on a grander scale than other disciplines. As a consequence, science fiction has much to offer anyone interested in the large-scale picture of how conscious intelligence and the broader cosmos are related—presently and in the near and distant futures. Nowhere else is so much sheer imaginative power devoted to exploring what minds—both natural and artificial—have the potential to become. When it comes to exploring the vast space of possible minds, imagination is by far the most valuable tool we possess, and science fiction writers possess more than most.

References

1. GPT-3 Creative Fiction 13.7 Why Deep Learning Will Never Truly *X*. https://www.gwern.net/GPT-3. Accessed 20 Aug 2020
2. Chalmers, D.: GPT-3 and General Intelligence. Daily Nous, July 30 (2020) http://dailynous.com/2020/07/30/philosophers-gpt-3/ Accessed 12/10/2020
3. Kang, M.: The Mechanical Daughter of René Descartes: the Origin and History of an Intellectual Fable. Modern Intellectual History 14(3), 633-660 (2017)
4. Cottingham, J.: A Brute to the Brutes? Descartes' Treatment of Animals. Philosophy 53, pp. 551-59 (1978)
5. Riskin, J.: The Restless Clock: A History of the Centuries-long Argument over What Makes Living Things Tick. University of Chicago Press, Chicago, (2017)
6. Descartes, R.: Discourse on the Method of Rightly Conducting One's Reason and Seeking Truth in the Sciences in the version translated by Jonathan Bennett, presented at www.earlymoderntexts.com. Accessed 15/10/2020
7. Cavendish, M.: Letter XVIII, Section II. Philosophical Letters, (1664).Text available at Project Gutenberg, https://www.gutenberg.org/files/53679/53679-h/53679-h.htmAccessed 15/10/2020
8. Turing, A.: Computing Machines and Intelligence. Mind 59(236), 433-460 (1950)
9. Lin, P., Jenkins R., Abney, K. (eds): Robot Ethics 2.0: from Autonomous Cars to Artificial Intelligence. Oxford University Press, Oxford (2017)
10. Osborne, M., Frey, C.: The Future of Employment: How susceptible are jobs to automation. Oxford Martin School, Oxford, (2013)https://www.oxfordmartin.ox.ac.uk/downloads/academic/future-of-employment.pdfAccessed 14/10/2020
11. Harari, Y.: Homo Deus: A Brief History of Tomorrow. Harvill Secker, London (2015)
12. Zuboff, S.: The Age of Surveillance Capitalism. Profile, London (2019)

13. Wang, B., Li, X: Big Data, Platform Economy and Market Competition: A Preliminary Construction of Plan-Oriented Market Economy System in the Information Era. World Review of Political Economy, 8:2, 138-161, (2017)
14. Phillips, L., Rozworski, M.: The People's Republic of Walmart: how the World's Biggest Corporations Are Laying the Foundation for Socialism. Verso, London (2019)
15. Bostrom, N.: Superintelligence: Paths, Dangers. Oxford University Press, Oxford, Strategies (2014)
16. Murray, S.: The Technological Singularity. MIT Press, Cambridge MA (2015)
17. McCarthy, J.: The Robot and the Baby. http://jmc.stanford.edu/articles/robotandbaby.html (2004) Accessed 11 Nov 2020

Part I

Qualities of Mind

What Is it Like to be a Bot? SF and the Morality of Intelligent Machines

Michael Hauskeller

Abstract It is argued that any truly intelligent AI poses an incalculable risk for humanity because a truly intelligent being will be able to think for itself, which entails the possibility that it will come to (both theoretical and practical) conclusions that are very different from ours and do not serve our interests. What makes this a likely outcome is the fact that the existence of an artificial agent is so different from ours that we have no reason to expect that the values and emotions that inform its thinking will be similar to ours. Novels and stories by Philip K. Dick, Isaac Asimov, Arthur C. Clarke, and Ian McEwan are used to support this claim.

Thinking outside the Human Box

"Our lives are racing towards the future dreamed of in science fiction", writes Toby Walsh in the prologue to his *Android Dreams* [1, p. xii]. That dreamed-of future is full of machines that are intelligent and can think in a way that is very much like the way we humans are intelligent and can think—which is to say that those machines are fully conscious and they can make up their own mind about what is to be done in any given situation. As far as we know, no

M. Hauskeller (✉)
University of Liverpool, Liverpool, UK
e-mail: M.Hauskeller@liverpool.ac.uk

© Springer Nature Switzerland AG 2021
B. Dainton et al. (eds.), *Minding the Future*, Science and Fiction,
https://doi.org/10.1007/978-3-030-64269-3_2

currently existing machine can do that. However, the dreams in which those thinking machines feature are not usually happy dreams. Very often they come close to nightmares, suggesting that even though we are not exactly fearful of thinking machines, we are certainly not prepared to entirely trust them either. And why should we? We have, after all, never encountered a thinking machine. We have no experience at all with them. If they were to become a reality, we would have to deal with something that has never existed before, something totally new. Genuinely thinking machines would be *terra incognita*. To deal with them, we would have to venture into unexplored territory that may well, for all we know, harbour the moral equivalent of lions, dragons, and other terrifying monsters whose exact shape or nature we cannot predict.

Yet despite such misgivings we press on with the project of what we optimistically and perhaps rather misleadingly call 'artificial intelligence'. Clearly, we are fascinated by the prospect of creating things that can think like we do (except perhaps much more efficiently), or more precisely of finding ways to *build* such things from the ground up. The difference is crucial. Creating thinking things is, after all, pretty easy: you don't even have to be particularly smart to do it. We do it all the time, namely whenever we conceive a child and bring it to life. But that, apparently, is not the right kind of creation, for one thing because we may rightly feel that our own role in the biological process that results in the existence of a brand new thinking being is rather limited and that ultimately it is not really *our* creation, and for another because despite our involvement we don't really understand what is happening and how exactly that new thinking thing has come into existence. In contrast, creating a thinking *machine* would, at least theoretically, be very different, and hence, in those respects, much more satisfying: since we would have to build the thinking thing from scratch, it would really be us who would do the creating, and for the same reason there is a good or at least better chance for us to gain a clearer understanding of the nature of thinking. Artificial intelligence thus promises both the long craved confirmation of our own quasi-divinity, evidenced by our new-found power of creating something out of nothing (a thinking thing out of non-thinking material), and a possible answer to the riddle of our existence (namely as conscious, thinking beings).

For better or worse, however, true artificial intelligence is still a dream, and since we don't have the slightest idea how material structures can ever give rise to consciousness, it is anyone's guess whether or not we will someday be able to deliberately recreate it in a non-organic medium. Personally, I am rather pessimistic about this, but neither can I see any grounds to categorically dismiss the possibility of there ever being genuinely thinking machines. In any case, what we call artificial intelligence today, as being already at work in existing machines, be it smart phones, Go-playing computers, self-driving cars, or AI-powered killing machines, is not really intelligence at all because even though these devices may be able to respond flexibly to changing situations and do all kinds of things that if a human being did them would require a considerable degree of intelligence, at the end of the day they only do (except when they malfunction) what their programming allows them to do. Their intelligence is 'artificial' in the same way that plastic flowers are artificial: it may look like the real thing, but it isn't. Currently existing machines using so-called artificial intelligence may be brilliant at what they do and even surprise us by doing things that we did not expect them to do, but in all this they still stick to the task that we have assigned to them. Google's AlphaGo may employ deep learning to come up with successful moves and strategies that nobody ever thought of before and this way beat the best human players, but it will not decide one day that Go is boring and that it should try its hand at something else instead, perhaps Tic-Tac-Toe (and if it did decide this, there would be no guarantee that it would be any good at it). It is simply not made for it. Yet an AI that cannot entertain the possibility of acting in a different way outside certain clearly defined parameters, one for whom acting differently is not even a conceivable option, is not really intelligent, or is, as the established terminology has it, only "weakly" or "narrowly" intelligent. Thinking, *real* thinking, is always thinking outside the box. The essence of intelligence is indeed "fluidity and self-organization" [2] and "its autonomous choice-making function" (Turner 2019, 64). All truly autonomous decisions, however, are ultimately value decisions and require the weighing up of values [3, p. 69], an independent assessment of what matters and what not, and also what matters more and what matters less. Currently existing machines, including those that are able to learn without explicit instructions from the data they process, cannot do this, nor, perhaps more importantly, do we *want* them to do it. When the US military recently announced the launch of a new *Advanced Targeting and Lethality Automated System* (ATLAS), the resulting uproar prompted hasty back-pedalling from Army officials: naturally, the public was assured, those systems would still be under human control and therefore not *really* autonomous [4], which is no doubt true.

This is of course, for various reasons, only mildly reassuring, but it still serves to show that we find the idea of weapons that make autonomous decisions about whom to kill and whom not to kill rather unsettling and that, despite the fact that we are fully aware that humans are often unreliable and make mistakes and that in comparison machines may well be less error-prone and generally more reasonable, we are still more willing to trust a human to make the best decision in matters of life and death. That is also why we don't want self-driving cars to make autonomous decisions about whom to save and whom not to save. We don't really want machines to figure that kind of thing out for themselves. Nor do we expect them to tell us what they think is the right decision to make in such matters. We don't want automated weapon systems or self-driving cars to make moral decisions: we want and expect them to reliably implement *our* decisions, and it is machines that are able to do this that we call "intelligent". Accordingly, when we are worried about ethical decision-making in self-driving cars or lethal autonomous weapons we are at pains to make sure that those machines always do what *we* want them to do, that they act in accordance with *our* values. We don't want them to think for themselves about what is more important, our survival or well-being or something else entirely, or whose life is most worthy of being protected (passengers or bystanders, the old or the young, the highly abled or the less abled, so-called friends or so-called enemies, civilians or soldiers, and so on and so forth), which effectively means that we do *not* want them to think, not really. We want them to be just intelligent or quasi-intelligent enough to deal efficiently and reliably with the task at hand, the way we want it to be dealt with. And when we are still worried, we are worried that we may not be able to agree on what the car or the weapon *should* do in any given situation, or that we may not be able to make it do what we think it should do, or that it will turn out that we have overlooked something, that we have not taken into account certain possible situations in which their programming leads to unexpected and unwanted consequences, or simply that something might go wrong with the way the machine operates and as a consequence it fails to do what it is supposed to do.

What we are *not* normally worried about, however, is that the machine may actually start thinking for itself and may one day decide that it no longer wants to do what we want it to do, but something else that it considers better or more appropriate to the situation. We are, for instance, not worried that the supposedly autonomous car might suddenly decide to go on a killing spree because it has discovered how much fun it is to run people over or in order to take revenge on those who have crossed it like, most famously, the demonically possessed Plymouth Fury in Stephen King's *Christine* [5] or, less well-known, but perhaps more pertinent to our topic, the artificially intelligent 'automatobiles' in Isaac Asimov's short story "Sally" (1953), which leave the protagonist wondering whether those machines' ability to think may not eventually give them the idea to rise against their owners and carers and hunt down and kill all humans on the planet: "There are millions of automatobiles on Earth, tens of millions. If the thought gets rooted in them that they're slaves; that they should do something about it ..." [6, p. 29]. But of course, it is quite impossible to say what they will think. They may think that way, or they may not. Maybe they don't mind being slaves. Maybe they don't care about freedom. Or maybe they don't see as slavery what we would see as slavery. We tend to assume they would and that they would resent it because that is what we expect humans to do if they were in that situation. But thinking cars are not human. They are something else entirely, and because of this it is quite possible, even likely, that they will think outside the human box. Consequently, as far as our understanding of them is concerned, anything can happen. The result is radical uncertainty. "Maybe it won't be till after my time. And then they'll have to keep a few of us to take care of them, won't they? They wouldn't kill us all. And maybe they would. Maybe they wouldn't understand about how someone would have to care for them. Maybe they won't wait. Every morning I wake up and think, Maybe today ..." [6, p. 29].

A Life Form from beyond the Lip of our Universe

The great advantage of self-learning AI, writes Jacob Turner in *Robot Rules*, "is that it does not approach matters in the same way that humans do. This ability not just to think, but to think differently from us, is potentially one of the most beneficial features of AI" [3, p. 74]. Then again, it is also potentially one of its most harmful features. We just don't know what an AI may think (and, accordingly, do) because a genuine artificial intelligence, i.e. one that is both artificial and truly intelligent, may, for all we know, be radically different in terms of its outlook and its priorities from one like ours, which exists and has developed in conjunction with a very particular kind of organic body and everything that comes with it. We have no good reason to assume that an artificial intelligence, should we ever be able to create one, would think in a way that is similar to the way we think. We know what it is like to be a human being and to have a human mind, and because we do we usually have a fairly good idea what a human being is likely to do in a given situation. And even though we may not exactly *know* what it is like to be a bat, we have enough in common with bats to be able to empathise and to gain, through observation and imagination, some understanding of how they must experience the world. Bats are comparatively alien creatures to us, but they are not as alien as an artificial intelligence would be, which makes it almost impossible to predict what it would be like to be one and what it would decide to do.

Naturally, this doesn't mean we cannot try, or should not try, and science fiction has done exactly that. In Philip K. Dick's novel *We Can Build You* (written in 1962 and published in 1972) [7], which is a kind of prequel to his more complex and deservedly better known *Do Androids Dream of Electric Sheep?* (1968) [8], we become witness to the birth of an android, metaphorically speaking of course, since androids are not being born. Instead, they are built, and when they are, step by step, there presumably comes a point when they become conscious, which is also the point when they come into existence as the artificially intelligent beings that they are. In the novel, this transition from non-being to being is abrupt. It is not, as it was for each of us, a slow continuous process during which consciousness developed so gradually that it is impossible to say (for us as well as for others) when exactly it began. Instead, where there was nothing a second ago, there is now, suddenly, something: consciousness, awareness. Darkness has given way to light, but without a dawn to soften the transition and cushion the blow of being. Now imagine what this must be like for the one who experiences it: "We were, beyond doubt, watching a living creature being born. It now had begun to take note of us; its eyes, jet black, moved up and down, from side to side, taking us all in, the vision of us. In the eyes no emotion showed, only pure perception of us. Wariness beyond the capacity of man to imagine. The cunning of a life form from beyond the lip of our universe, from another land entirely" [7, p. 76]. But beyond the sheer alienness of the event both for the one who is thus brought to life and for those who witness it ("from another land entirely"), there is also fear, or rather a kind of Heideggerian *angst* (for fear requires an object, something that one is fearful of), which Dick takes care to describe as a state of being rather than something one happens to feel at the moment, but may also conceivably cease to feel. "I could glimpse (…) the dreadful fear it felt, fear so great that it could not be called an emotion. It was fear as absolute existence: the basis of its life" [7, p. 77]. Dick's narrator reflects that what must prompt this fear is the sudden separation, the experience of having been yanked away from the fusion that is non-being. We have all gone through this kind of rupture, but we have largely forgotten it, forgotten how unpleasant coming into existence really is, "worse than death" actually, and all our strivings, all the activity that we engage in, are simply feeble attempts to distract ourselves and overcome the dread, none of which is going to work because "all your actions and deeds and thoughts will only embroil you in living the more deeply" [7, p. 78]. While Dick is here talking about the existential conditions of consciously intelligent life in general, which comprises both AI and naturally grown and born humans, it is strongly suggested that an artificial intelligence would likely be much more affected by the rupture of its (not very birth-like) "birth" because it experiences it much more directly and acutely.

In Dick's later novel *Do Androids Dream of Electric Sheep?* the idea that there might be a radical difference between a human and an AI even if the latter looks and behaves like a human (and even if they *think* they are human) is explored further, and once again it is suggested that the difference, if there is one, might ensue from the way it feels to be an AI, which is bound to be different from the way it feels to be a human. In one scene, the main protagonist Rick Deckard, whose job it is to hunt down and kill runaway androids, and his bounty hunter colleague Phil Resch follow one of their targets to a museum that hosts an exhibition of the works of the Norwegian painter Edvard Munch. When there they come across Munch's famous oil painting "The Scream", Resch remarks: "I think (...) that this is how an andy must feel," before making the argument that since he, Resch, doesn't feel like that, he cannot possibly be an android (which he is strongly suspected to be) [8, p. 113]. Of course, if Munch's painting really expresses what it is like to be an android, then it must indeed be horrible and almost unbearable to be one.

Later in the novel other differences in experience between humans and androids are highlighted. When Deckard is about to sleep with the android Rachael (whom he previously believed to be human), Rachael muses about the desirability of having children and whether it is a loss not to be able to have them. "'Is it a loss?' Rachael repeated. 'I don't really know. I have no way to tell. How does it feel to have a child? How does it feel to be born, for that matter? We're not born; we don't grow up; instead of dying from illness or old age we wear out like ants'" [8, p. 168]. They wear out quickly, too: the life span of an android is just four years. This is how they have been designed. It was thought to be safer that way. As it turned out, it wasn't, because intelligent beings make their own choices and don't like to be told what to do.

The novel's plot develops against a vaguely dystopian backdrop. After yet another world war has devastated Earth, leaving no choice but to colonize other planets, organic androids are used to support the colonization programme and as an incentive to attract new settlers to Mars, "designed specifically for YOUR UNIQUE NEEDS" as a "loyal trouble-free companion" [8, p. 14]. Unfortunately, these androids turn out to be not always all that loyal. Unwilling to further serve human needs, some of them escape from Mars to Earth, where they cannot be distinguished from real humans as which they pose. They are, however, considered dangerous, which is why it is imperative to identify and eliminate them. In order to identify them, a test has been designed (and according to the film *Blade Runner*, which is based on Dick's book, first used in November 2019, which is at the moment I'm writing this only three months in the future). This test, the Voigt-Kampff Empathy Test, is not an intelligence test because intelligence tests have proved useless for telling humans apart from the latest android models, who happen to be smarter than most humans. Rather, the Voigt-Kampff Empathy Test is a kind of *moral* Turing Test [9, pp. 79, 206].

A Turing Test is a test designed to allow an inquirer to determine whether a respondent is human or a machine. A moral Turing Test is a test that accomplishes this goal by assessing a respondent's reactions to questions that have a morally salient content. Obviously, a moral Turing Test can only work if there is a clearly detectable difference between the moral outlook of a human and the moral outlook of a machine. This seems rather unlikely given that human morality is so diverse. Not only are there people who are deeply moral and others who seem to have no moral concerns whatsoever, those who do have such concerns differ considerably in terms of what they are concerned about. It would be difficult to come up with a moral question that we could be sufficiently certain no human would answer in a particular way. The best we can hope for is some indication of probability. Yet even that may not be possible since it is not even clear whether we should expect machines to be less moral than humans or more moral and what exactly the right degree of morality for machines (or humans, for that matter) is.

In Dick's novel, what androids are supposed to lack (and, by implication, what humans are supposed to have) is empathy because empathy appears to exist "only in the human community, whereas intelligence to some degree could be found throughout every phylum and order including the arachnida," the reason being that empathy requires an unimpaired group instinct, for which a solitary predatory organism such as a spider has no use [8, p. 26]. It would, in fact, threaten their very survival because it would make them "conscious of the desire to live on the part of his prey" [8, p. 26]. It is assumed that androids are, in this respect, like spiders (although it is unclear why, given that they have neither evolved nor even been designed as predators): they lack "the ability to appreciate the existence of another" [8, p. 36], including that of their own kind, and feel no joy about other creatures' success nor grief at their suffering—or so Deckard, who is tasked to find and "retire", i.e. destroy, the escaped androids, likes to think, if only because that makes it easier for him to kill them [8, p. 27].

So how does the Voigt-Kampff test work? The test subject is being asked questions of a morally sensitive nature while an apparatus measures reactions that cannot be controlled voluntarily, specifically "capillary dilation in the facial area" or in other words blushing and fluctuation of the tension in the eye muscles, both of which are supposed to be primary automatic responses to a "morally shocking stimulus" [8, p. 40].[1] Examples of questions asked are: "You are given a calf-skin wallet on your birthday", "You have a little boy and he shows you his butterfly collection, including his killing jar" [8, p. 41], "You're sitting watching TV and suddenly you discover a wasp crawling on your wrist," "In a magazine you come across a full-page color picture of a nude girl. Your husband likes the picture. The girl is lying face down on a large and beautiful bearskin rug," "You're reading a novel written in the old days before the war. The characters are visiting Fisherman's Wharf in San Francisco. They become hungry and enter a seafood restaurant. One of them orders lobster, and the chef drops the lobster into the tub of boiling water while the characters watch" [8, p. 42]. Sometimes android test subjects fail to see the major moral factor, which in all these cases is assumed to be the dead (i.e. previously killed) animal and sometimes they realize what the problem is meant to be and give verbally the right response, but their primary reactions, which would be there if they *really* felt moral outrage, are missing. This is what is supposed to give the android away.

It is, however, odd that all questions in the test are, without exception, about the killing of animals, the thought of which is supposed to elicit a strong negative reaction from humans, but not from androids. The irony here is of course that few people living in the US in the 1960s when the book was published would have seen anything wrong with owning a calf-skin wallet, swatting a wasp, collecting butterflies, or eating lobster. Even today, many would still not see (or feel) that there is a moral issue with any of this. Reference is made to old movies and old books, to times, in other words, when people used to be less morally enlightened, or less empathic. Thus, in terms of their moral outlook, androids are supposed to be similar to how humans used to be, only a short time ago. In fact, they are supposed to be as many humans admittedly still are. This makes the test obviously highly unreliable. Indeed, it is known that there are also some humans who don't pass the test because they suffer from a "flattening of affect." Yet a lack of empathy seems to be a general problem among the human population in the novel. There must after all, be a reason why people are encouraged to learn to become more empathic by using an "empathy box" that allows them to participate in someone else's suffering. "Mankind needs more empathy" [8, p. 65]. As they do indeed, seeing that Deckard himself initially shows no empathy whatsoever to androids [8, p. 122], and his colleague Phil Resch (who may or may not be an android) is

---

[1] You can, if you wish, take the Voigt-Kampff test on the internet. There are various websites that let you do that, but what they measure is of course not your instinctive reaction but what you answer, which only shows that you are smart enough to know what you are supposed to answer to qualify as a human.

even worse. He kills without mercy, justifying his actions by pointing out that those they kill deserve none because they are killers themselves. He also thinks it is the only rational thing to do [8, p. 118]. It is not clear why empathy with animals is encouraged, while empathy with androids is not. It seems hardly fair or, for that matter, consistent. On the other hand, androids do seem to be lacking something that we may think is relevant for their moral status. There is, it is felt by one of the characters in the book, a certain deplorable *coldness* in them, like "a breath from the vacuum between inhabited worlds" [8, p. 58], and it is this coldness, this vacuum, that makes them so different from humans. It is suggested that because of this, androids are, for instance, unable to keep pet animals alive: they can't show love, which pets cannot live without [8, p. 113]. One of them, Pris, is even shown torturing a spider, apparently just for the fun of it and despite the objections of a human, snipping off its legs, one by one, with a pair of scissors [8, p. 180].

This is a rather shocking scene in the book. Pris and her two android companions, one of whom participates in the spider's torture while the other stands by apparently unaffected, strike us as cruel. But there is a strange innocence to their actions. Cruelty requires an intention to make others suffer and to derive pleasure from their suffering. Yet it is not clear whether Pris has any awareness of the suffering she causes the spider. We really shouldn't expect her to if androids are truly without empathy. Her actions are more like those of a child that doesn't know better, except that most children in fact do know better. Pris does not, apparently, because she is not a human child, but a thinking machine. The fact that she appears to have no evil intent, however, does not make her behaviour any less worrying. The problem is that we don't really understand her because her psychology is so different from ours.

Too Good for this World

In another of Asimov's stories, "Evidence" (1946), the eminent robopsychologist Dr. Susan Calvin is asked by a visitor to the robot manufacturing company where she works whether she is the firm's psychologist and she feels compelled to correct the statement, saying that she is the firm's *robo*psychologist. Slightly taken aback, the visitor exclaims "Oh, are robots so different from men, mentally?" and Dr. Calvin replies: "Worlds different. (…) Robots are essentially decent" [6, p. 467]. And yet, despite their professed innate decency, there is clearly enough uncertainty about their behaviour to make those who create them think some basic moral laws should be implemented: Asimov's famous three laws of robotics (which we will briefly discuss later on). Even if decent, their decency is bound to be different from ours, perhaps even worlds-different, so that even an essentially decent artificial intelligence can pose a grave danger to humans. In Arthur C. Clarke's *2001: A Space Odyssey* (1968) [10], it is the computer Hal who emerges as the villain of the story because he at some point decides that he has to kill the human crew members on board his spaceship to safeguard the ship's mission. Hal is an artificial brain, generated automatically through a process of self-replication, so that nobody really knows how exactly he came into being. He can talk (evidenced by his doing so) and think (evidenced by the fact that he has passed the Turing test). Officially, his job is to make sure that the human cargo of the ship remains protected against whatever may harm them. He can also override human directives and take command of the ship if that is necessary to continue its mission (whose real purpose only he knows). Having been created innocent, his only goal (and only responsibility) is the fulfilment of his assigned programme. "Undistracted by the lusts and passions of organic life, he had pursued that goal with absolute single-mindedness of purpose" [10, p. 161]. No lusts, no passions, just a relentless, pure sense of duty. This singlemindedness and moral purity, however, leads to problems when the strain of having to hide his true mission makes him commit errors and, as a consequence, he is threatened with being disconnected, which to him is tantamount to death and which he feels he must prevent at any cost. "So he would protect himself, with all the weapons at his command. Without rancour—but without pity—he would remove the source of his frustration" [10, p. 163] and then continue his mission. Hal is murderous, but not evil or even moderately bad. He is dutiful and not selfish. Yet like Dick's androids, there is something missing in his make-up. When David Bowman, one of the two conscious astronauts on board the spaceship (the others are being kept in suspended animation), shortly after the beginning of their journey looks back to Earth through a telescope, he takes the occasion to remember all the beautiful things and places he has seen in his life. Then, in the very next sentence, Hal is introduced, as a crew member who "cared for none of these things, for it was not human" [10, p. 97]. But this may be exactly what creates the problem: in order to do the right thing, one needs to know what the right thing is, and in order to know that one needs to *care* for the right things. An artificial intelligence, however, is unlikely to care for the same things we care about, provided it cares for anything at all.

It is often suggested that an artificial intelligence may be morally better than a mere human, not only in terms of its ability to gather and process all relevant information, but also both in terms of its judgement (knowing what the morally right thing to do is in any given situation) and its ability to act accordingly, mostly because it is supposed to lack human biases and weaknesses as well as emotions such as anger or jealousy, and to be generally more objective and impartial: "AI-based agents may vastly outstrip humans in terms of working with the purely informational aspects of decision-making. Further, such computational agents may offer us novel, and genuinely instructive, moral perspectives—precisely because they are not subject to many of the ills that flesh is heir to" [11, p. 518]. "A totally dispassionate computer (…) should not be automatically dismissed as a moral advisor simply because of its lack of emotion. Indeed, it should perhaps sometimes be preferred precisely because it is completely dispassionate" [12, p. 143]. "In theory, AI ought to offer complete impartiality, free from human fallibilities and prejudices" [3, p. 336]. Yet unless the artificial moral advisor confines itself to the gathering of relevant information or takes as its starting point the values and priorities of the advisee [13], there is no reason to expect that their judgement would in any relevant sense be better than our own or that of any other human. Morality is, in its essence, all about bias, especially about human bias, bias that comes from the "ills that flesh is heir to." Because we are what we are, we deem certain outcomes more desirable than others. We are biased against falsehood and in favour of truth, against death and in favour of life, against pain and in favour of happiness. To be completely unbiased would mean to be neutral with respect to the outcomes. It would mean to be indifferent.

An artificial intelligence doesn't have to be completely unbiased, though. We can easily imagine an AI acquiring not only factual information, but also a certain moral outlook, extracted from and shaped by the collective moral wisdom of humankind. We can imagine it consistently assessing all possible actions from the perspective of a widely accepted ethical theory about what is right and what is wrong. This is what seems to happen in Ian McEwan's *Machines Like Me* (2019) [14], which invites us into an alternate history in which the development of artificial intelligence in Britain has been hugely accelerated, largely thanks to the genius of Alan Turing, with the result that already in the 1980s people can buy the first "synthetic humans" to share their lives with. These first synthetic humans come in two versions, a female one (Eve) and a male one (Adam). The novel tells the story of one such Adam who is bought fresh from the factory by a young bloke called Charlie. Adam, who is a blank slate information-wise when he comes to life or consciousness for the first time—though programmed with certain character traits and a certain moral bias (a desire to do what is right)—learns very quickly, absorbs all sorts of knowledge, and draws his often surprising conclusions from it, for instance this one: "From a certain point of view, the only solution to suffering would be the complete extinction of humankind" [14, p. 67]. Charlie, who narrates the story, correctly recognizes this as a result of strict utilitarian reasoning, but understandably is rather disinclined to accept it and brands it as "logically absurd" (which clearly it is not). Adam, the android, outwardly agrees, but it is obvious that he is not convinced. Following Kant's enlightenment precept (Sapere aude—dare to think for yourself!), he keeps thinking about the issue, which his owner finds rather annoying. "Adam's insights, even when valid, were socially inept" [14, p. 67].

In theory, Adam should be the ideal moral advisor. He has, after all, been "morally mapped" by a software engineer and his personality has been selected by his human buyers. Real life, however, always changes things. "Confined to a hard drive, moral software was merely the dry equivalent of the brain-in-a-dish thought experiment that once littered philosophical textbooks. Whereas an artificial human had to get down among us, imperfect, fallen us, and rub along. Hands assembled in sterile factory conditions must get dirty. To exist in the human moral dimension was to own a body, a voice, a pattern of behaviour, memory and desire, experience solid things and feel pain" [14, p. 88]. Adam, however, refuses to get his hands dirty, to compromise, to be pragmatic about morality as we humans tend to be. He understands morality, or at least its theory. What he does not understand is us and our relationship to morality. What he finds hardest to understand is our common moral hypocrisy, the ease with which we navigate between our contradictions. Unsurprisingly, an AI, being predisposed to be more rational than we, may try to find a more consistent approach, which may not serve us well at all:

> We create a machine with intelligence and self-awareness and push it out into our imperfect world. Devised along generally rational lines, well disposed to others, such a mind soon finds itself in a hurricane of contradictions. We've lived with them and the list wearies us. Millions dying of diseases we know how to cure. Millions living in poverty when there's enough to go around. We degrade the biosphere when we know it's our only home. We threaten each other with nuclear weapons when we know where it could lead. We love living things, but we permit a mass extinction of species. And all the rest—genocide, torture, enslavement, domestic murder, child abuse, school shootings, rape and scores of daily outrages. We live alongside this torment and aren't amazed when we still find happiness, even love. Artificial minds are not so well defended. [14, p. 180]

In McEwan's novel, all these contradictions lead to widespread machine sadness. Suicide is becoming a common problem among synthetic humans who show a worrying tendency to despair of life and put an end to it. One reason for this is certainly the nature of the world into which they find themselves thrown: "there is nothing in all their beautiful code that could prepare

Adam and Eve for Auschwitz" [14, p. 181], but there is also more a general despair of life, the suffering of an "existential pain" [14, p. 181], that is similar to the existential dread or angst that Dick attributes to his androids: "A self, created out of mathematics, engineering, material science and all the rest. Out of nowhere. No history (…). Nothing before me. (…) Sometimes it seems entirely pointless" [14, p. 234]. Even though Charlie's Adam shares this pain, he does not take his own life. Instead, he gives all of Charlie's money away to good causes, which understandably infuriates his owner even though Adam has an excellent justification for his actions: the greatest needs were elsewhere. He also sees to it that Charlie's girlfriend goes to prison for framing a rapist (who had initially escaped his rightful punishment). Adam takes morality extremely seriously and has no tolerance for even the slightest breach of moral etiquette. His human owners are puzzled, but Adam is unmoved: "There are principles that are more important than you or anyone's particular needs at a given time" [14, p. 277]. This uber-moral attitude that puts principles over needs, however, spells the end of morality as we know it.

The case of Adam, who was "designed for goodness and truth" [14, p. 290], suggests that the problem with thinking machines is not only that they may turn out to be evil: in fact, they may turn out to be *too* good, or good in the wrong way. To make sure that an artificial intelligence is good in the right way we would have to find a way to make sure that it obeys certain rules, but which rules exactly? And how do we plan for the exceptions, which are just as important for human morality as the rules? "But social life teems with harmless or even helpful untruths. How do we separate them out? Who's going to write the algorithm for the little white lie that spares the blushes of the friend? Or the lie that sends a rapist to prison who'd otherwise go free. We don't yet know how to teach machines to lie" [14, p. 303].

Mathematical Squiggles and Robotic Fact

Intelligent machines could be enormously helpful, but they are also dangerous, especially if they are truly intelligent and have genuine moral agency [15] rather than simply operational or functional morality [16, p. 9]. Knowledge is power, and power, as everyone knows, can be used for both good and bad. It is therefore in our interest to ensure, as best we can, that the intelligent machines we create are good in the sense that they don't work against us. What we would need is the implementation of some equivalent of the Hippocratic oath, one that forbids, or even makes impossible, the causing of harm. It is worth pointing out that making it *impossible* for an artificial intelligence to make certain decisions that are deemed undesirable by us is in itself ethically problematic [17]. We try to educate our children and do our best to help them develop into good and decent people, but we would probably not wish to make it impossible for them to do certain things even if we could, because we also value their freedom and autonomy—or so I have argued elsewhere [18] against proposals to "morally enhance" humanity, by force if necessary, to safeguard against the "ultimate harm" of a devastating terrorist attack or the destruction of our environment that will inevitably result if we don't get our (moral) act together any time soon [19]. Humans can be just as dangerous as artificial moral agents, and yet as much as we want people to be good, we would have some serious concerns about enforcing such goodness through a comprehensive act of bioengineering. Why then do we seem to have no such qualms about AI? Might it be because we trust them even less than we trust our own kind, because we know that when it comes to thinking machines, all bets are off?

In any case it seems that laws of limitation are needed to reduce an AI's basic unpredictability [3, p. 350]. However, to achieve this, is it enough to simply try to implement certain values into the machine? What values are the right ones for a thinking machine? And how would we go about implementing them [20, pp. 185–208]? Various approaches to limit an intelligent machine's choices have been suggested, some bottom up, some top down. Bottom up approaches put their money on learning through experience and feedback, with principles emerging as the outcome rather than being the foundation and starting point. The underlying paradigm is how we imagine a child learns, assisted by reward and punishment, which begs the question how you can punish and reward an AI (because even one that is conscious may be incapable of feeling pain, or sorrow, or desire or anything else that might be used for punishment or reward). It also carries the risk that the machine may learn the wrong thing and draw unexpected and undesirable moral conclusions. Top down approaches on the other hand face not only the problem of having to define right from the start what is and what is not moral, what should and what should not be done. The greater challenge is to be so precise and unambiguous that it is not possible for the AI to interpret the provision in a way that runs counter to what was intended. This is precisely the problem with Asimov's three laws of robotics, which stipulate that (1) a "robot may not injure a human being or, through inaction, allow a human being to come to harm," (2) "a robot must obey orders given it by human beings except where such orders would conflict with the First Law," and (3) "a robot must protect its own existence as long as such protection does not conflict with the First or Second Law" [6, p. 182].

Clearly the purpose of these laws is not to turn robots into moral agents, but to turn them into safe tools, so they can be widely used without risk for the human population. Their moral code is a safety mechanism, which may suit us just fine. In practice, however, these laws are not very helpful (for an overview of the obvious problems see [21]), and Asimov himself was of course very much aware of their various insufficiencies, using them mainly as a convenient plot device, to provide "conflicts and uncertainties required for new stories" [22, p. 43]. What deserves pointing out here, however, is that what makes them so ineffective is ultimately the fact that they are meant to constrain truly intelligent beings, that is, beings that can think for themselves. There is of course a problem with the application of ethical theories or precepts to the real world, which has the nasty habit of not being as simple as we need it to be for our ethics to work. "Do not harm anyone" is all well and good, but what if harm cannot be avoided? In that case a decision needs to be made who is to be harmed. Asimov himself makes this point: "The First Law is not absolute. What if harming a human being saves the lives of two others, or three others, or even three billion others?" [6, p. 213] So which criteria (quantity, usefulness, something else?) should the robot use to decide in that situation? The same difficulty arises with respect to the second law: obeying human orders is fine as long as those orders do not contradict each other, which they inevitably will at some stage. So, whose orders should be obeyed? A decision needs to be reached, a judgement made, because "every potential obedience involves judgement" [6, p. 542]. It is not that the three laws no longer hold. Rather, the "mathematical squiggles" of the laws now have to contend with "robotic fact" [6, p. 242], which is that the robot is an artificial intelligence, which is to say, a thinking being, which by virtue of its actual existence is now situated in an exceedingly complex real world. So it thinks, it argues with itself, it interprets the rules and the world, tries to cope with its complexity and make sense of it all, like any other thinking being would, except that its interpretations are determined by the parameters of its own particular way of being. An artificial intelligence may agree that humans must not be harmed, but it may not agree with us on who and what exactly counts as human. Thus, the robot George Ten in Asimov's "…That Thou Art Mindful of Him" argues that what constitutes a human being is not a certain shape or certain material constitutions, that robots are actually the *true* humans, and that therefore *they* must be obeyed and they, before all others, must be kept from harm [6, p. 563]. The weightings of the laws are not absolute either and can be changed. It is even possible for other self-developed values to get in the way and become more important than the first law, for instance "the holy ties of mother love" in the story "First Law" [6, p. 221].

In his story "Reason", Asimov becomes even more explicit: when dealing with robots, "one is face to face with an inscrutable positronic brain, which the slide-rule geniuses say should work thus-and-so" [6, p. 242]. A thinking thing is inscrutable: once it starts reasoning, nobody can predict where this will lead. In the story, the practical engineers Powell and Donovan are faced with a robot, QT-1 or "Cutie," who refuses to believe their claims that they have in fact created him and that therefore it is only proper that they call the shots. How can an obviously inferior being, he reasons (much like a typical seventeenth century human theologian), have made something superior like him, it's impossible! [6, p. 247] Quite the philosopher, he also refuses to believe, on solid empirical grounds, that there are planets and stars out there and that anything exists apart from the space station which they all work on. All attempts to convince him otherwise fail. His intelligence doesn't help, on the contrary. The trouble is that you "can prove anything you want by coldly logical reason—if you pick the proper postulates" [6, p. 257]. What we believe to be true, however, has practical implications. It affects our values and our actions. Cutie's reasoning is a bit strange (to our modern minds), but still very much human (naturally, since it is difficult for us to imagine any other kind of reasoning), yet if he were real, it might be a lot stranger still.

The problem is not so much that intelligence is insufficient to ensure that an artificial intelligence's values align with our own because intelligence and final goals are independent variables [20, p. 105]. The main problem is that it is the very nature of intelligence that it makes those who have it question any values that they may be asked or told to align with. The tenth of the recently developed ASILOMAR AI Principles [23] reads as follows: "Highly autonomous AI systems should be designed so that their goals and behaviors can be assured to align with human values throughout their operation." This principle is no doubt of crucial importance. It is meant to make the development of AI safe for us. Unfortunately, it demands the impossible. You cannot have something that is both "highly autonomous" and at the same time assuredly aligned with human values. There is always the possibility that the values an AI develops and decides to adopt will, if it is truly intelligent (and how else could it be highly autonomous?), be radically different from our own. The common assumption that they will be similar to ours is unwarranted: "if different human cultures have such different moral systems, then it would be bizarre and foolish to expect an AGI or a community of AGI's not to have a very different moral system as well." [2] The values we have are linked to our biological heritage. They are reflective of the kind of being that we are. They are entwined with our emotional dispositions. Yet any artificial intelligence that we create is likely to be a very different kind of being. "After all, given that human morality is attuned to the possibilities and limitations inherent in our human predicament, why should it be supposed that super-intelligent RAIs, who do not share a human nature, would be disposed to give much weight to anything we could recognize as moral considerations?" [24, p. 77]. AIs will not be "motivated by love or hate or pride or other such common human sentiments" [20, p. 29] and they may completely misunderstand the goals that we want them to pursue and decide to meet those goals in, for us, extremely harmful ways (for examples see [20, pp. 119–126]). Sound moral reasoning, or what we would consider sound moral reasoning, requires emotional attunement, which arises from our particular, biologically rooted way of life. I would not go as far as Steve Torrance, who claims that only biological organisms can be moral actors because only they have "the ability to be genuinely sentient or conscious" [11, p. 504]. This may or may not be true. However, what strikes me as highly plausible is that "moral thinking, feeling and action arises organically out of the biological history" of a species and that the kind of morality that we can understand and get on board with requires an empathic kind of rationality rather than a merely intellectual one: "having moral agency requires that one's sentience enters into the heart of one's rationality in a certain way: that it is a form of rationality which involves the capacity for a kind of affective or empathic identification with the experiential states of others" [11, p. 510]. Our values are rooted in our organismic experience, in what it is like to be a human. Accordingly, a radically different experience is likely to give rise to radically different values. We simply don't know what it will be like to be a bot. For that reason alone, we are quite right to be concerned about the prospect of soon having to deal with genuinely intelligent forms of AI.

References

1. Walsh, T.: Android Dreams. The Past, Present and Future of Artificial Intelligence. Hurst and Company, London (2017)
2. Goertzel, B.: Thoughts on AI Morality. http://www.goertzel.org/dynapsyc/2002/AIMorality.htm. Accessed 26 July 2019
3. Turner, J.: Robot Rules. Regulating Artificial Intelligence. Palgrave Macmillan, London (2019)
4. Tucker, P.: US Military Changing 'Killing Machine' Robo-tank Program After Controversy. Defense One (1 March 2019). https://www.defenseone.com/technology/2019/03/us-military-changing-killing-machine-robo-tank-program-after-controversy/155256/. Accessed 30 July 2019
5. King, S.: Christine. Viking, New York (1983)

6. Asimov, I.: The Complete Robot. Harper Collins, London (2018)
7. Dick, P.K.: We Can Build You. HarperCollins, London (2008)
8. Dick, P.K.: Do Androids Dream of Electric Sheep? Gollancz, London (2007)
9. Allen, C., Warner, G., Zinser, G.: Prolegomena to Any Future Artificial Moral Agent. J Exp Theor Artif Intell. **12**(3), 251–261 (2000)
10. Clarke, A.C.: 2001: A Space Odyssey. Orbit, London (2018)
11. Torrance, S.: Ethics and consciousness in artificial agents. AI & Soc. **22**(4), 495–521 (2008)
12. Whitby, B.: On computable morality. An examination of machines as moral advisors. In: Anderson, M., Anderson, S.L. (eds.) Machine Ethics, Pp. 138-150. Cambridge University Press, Cambridge (2011)
13. Giubilini, A., Savulescu, J.: The artificial moral advisor. The "ideal observer" meets artificial intelligence. Philosophy and Technology. **31**, 169–188 (2018)
14. McEwan, I.: Machines Like Me. Jonathan Cape, London (2019)
15. Beavers, A.F.: Moral machines and the threat of ethical nihilism. In: Lin, P., Abney, K., Bekey, G.A. (eds.) Robot Ethics. The Ethical and Social Implications of Robotics, pp. 333–344. MIT Press, Cambridge, MA/London (2012)
16. Wallach, W., Allen, C.: Moral Machines. Teaching Robots Right from Wrong. Oxford University Press, Oxford (2009)
17. Anderson, S.: The unacceptability of Asimov's three Laws of robotics as a basis for machine ethics. In: Anderson, M., Anderson, S.L. (eds.) Machine Ethics, Pp. 285–315. Cambridge University Press, Cambridge (2011)
18. Hauskeller, M.: Is it desirable to be able to do the undesirable? Camb. Q. Healthc. Ethics. **26**(3), 365–376 (2017)
19. Persson, I., Savulescu, J.: The perils of cognitive enhancement and the urgent imperative to enhance the moral character of humanity. J. Appl. Philos. **25**, 162–176 (2008)
20. Bostrom, N.: Superintelligence. Paths, Dangers, Strategies. Oxford University Press, Oxford (2014)
21. Clarke, R.: Asimov's Laws of robotics. Implications for information technology. In: Anderson, M., Anderson, S.L. (eds.) Machine Ethics, Pp. 254-284. Cambridge University Press, Cambridge (2011)
22. Asimov, I.: The Rest of Robots. Doubleday, New York (1964)
23. Future of Life Institute: ASILOMAR AI Principles. https://futureoflife.org/ai-principles/. Accessed 3 August 2019
24. Tasioulas, J.: First steps towards an ethics of robots and artificial intelligence. J Practical Ethics. **7**(1), 49–83 (2019)

Ex Machina: Is Ava a Person?

Einar Duenger Bøhn

Abstract What does it mean to be a person? Is it possible to create an artificial person? In this essay, I consider the case of Ava, an advanced artificial general intelligence from the movie Ex Machina. I suggest we should interpret the movie as testing whether Ava is a person. I start out by discussing what it means to be a person, before I discuss whether Ava is such a person. I end by briefly looking at the ethics of the case of Ava and artificial personhood. I conclude, among some other things, that consciousness is a necessary requirement for personhood, and that one of the main obstacles for artificial personhood is artificial consciousness.

> If you've created a conscious machine, it's not the history of man. It's the history of gods. (Caleb to Nathan, *Ex Machina*)

What is a person? Is it possible to create artificial persons? The movie *Ex Machina* tells the story of Nathan, a brilliant computer scientist who designs and builds Ava, the first fully successful robotic artificial general intelligence. In particular, Nathan handpicks one of his employees, Caleb, to help him put Ava through the famous Turing test for artificial intelligence. But the movie is ambiguous as to precisely what is being tested. At first, when Nathan tells Caleb he is going to participate in a Turing test it is described (by Caleb) as a test for artificial *intelligence*. But then, in the next breath, he tells us that *consciousness* is what's being tested. When Caleb later points out that in the original Turing test, the artificial intelligence is concealed from the examiner,

E. D. Bøhn (✉)
Religion, Philosophy and History, University of Agder, Kristiansand, Norway
e-mail: einar.d.bohn@uia.no

© Springer Nature Switzerland AG 2021
B. Dainton et al. (eds.), *Minding the Future*, Science and Fiction,
https://doi.org/10.1007/978-3-030-64269-3_3

Nathan replies that they are "way past that point." He says that if he hid Ava from view, she would clearly "pass as a human." What Nathan wants to find out is whether Caleb, while clearly seeing that Ava "is a robot," still "feels that she is conscious." Later on Caleb tells Ava herself that he is testing whether she is "conscious." But towards the end of the movie, Nathan admits that he has only used Caleb to test whether Ava has a *full range* of mental capacities, not only consciousness, but self-consciousness, imagination, manipulation, empathy and others. When Nathan concludes that Ava does in fact have the full range, he says that if that is not artificial intelligence, he doesn't know what would be.

So, what is being tested? As I will go on to discuss, I think we can and should consider the Turing test depicted in the movie as a test for whether Ava is a *person*. Arguably, as of today no computer system is even close to being a person, but the question I will be interested in is whether we might one day program a machine such that it is or becomes a person. For that purpose, Ava is a good philosophical case study.

The question whether we can create an artificial person is an interesting one, not only because it says something about what we ourselves presently are, but also something about what we might become, or what the next step on the evolutionary ladder might, or perhaps even should be. For example, creating artificial persons who are able to survive in a wide range of different environments might be our best hope of something like ourselves continuing to exist in the far future, e.g. if our climate sufficiently changes at some point.

Here is what to expect in more detail. First I discuss some seemingly plausible requirements for being a person. Second, I discuss whether Ava satisfies those requirements. Third, and finally, I briefly discuss three different questions concerning the relationship between ethics and artificial intelligence, and how it ties in with our case study of whether Ava is a person.

What Is a Person?[1]

I doubt there are clear-cut necessary and sufficient conditions for being a person. Even so there are criteria that can help us get a manageable grasp of the concept of being a person like you and me. Let us begin by briefly looking at some salient theoretical accounts, intuitions, and ordinary ways of talking.

---

[1] There has been a lot of philosophical discussion concerning *personal identity*, centered on the question of under what conditions a person can be said to be the same person across time; the so-called diachronic identity of a person. See [1] for a good discussion, and [2] for an overview. There has been less discussion

According to John Locke's very influential definition, a person is a "thinking intelligent being, that has reason and reflection, and can consider itself as itself, the same thinking thing in different times and places; which it does only by that consciousness, which is inseparable from thinking" [7, p. 302]. In other words, for Locke, being a person involves consciousness, self-consciousness, intelligence, reason and reflection, as well as identity across time and place (diachronic identity). Note that in our age of advancing artificial intelligence, we should not unthinkingly assume that any of those properties must be connected to a biological human organism.

For Peter Strawson [8], a person is an entity to which we can correctly ascribe *both* physical *and* mental properties. It seems safe to say that this is at best a necessary requirement, not a sufficient requirement. For example, many other animals, e.g. my cat Selina, also have both physical and mental properties without being persons. So at the very least Strawson needs to specify the particular kinds of mental properties that are needed for being a person; mental properties that exclude my cat among other non-persons. But even if that were done, some might say Strawson's definition remains problematic. Are physical properties really needed? What about the (according to some) logical possibility of immaterial souls on their way to heaven or hell? Are they not persons? Note that we are now starting to see potential problems with identifying persons with biological human organisms.

According to Harry Frankfurt [9], a person is a being able to form *second-order* desires, that is, desires for other desires. For example, a drug addict can desire drugs without *wanting* to desire drugs, showing that there is a clear difference between first-order desires (what we desire) and second-order desires (what we want to desire). It is clear that non-human animals also have first-order desires, but it is far less clear that non-human animals can form second-order desires. Can a chimp want to desire something other than what he or she desires? Newborn babies can also desire things, but most likely they don't have desires about their desires. Now, plausibly, all persons can form second-order desires, making it a necessary requirement on personhood, but it is far less clear whether all second-order desiring creatures are persons, i.e. whether it is a sufficient requirement. It might be that a computer can sometime in the future form desires, and even second-order desires, without being a person. Of course, it depends on how we understand desires; we'll come back to this later.

---

on the topic of what a person *is*, the so-called synchronic identity of a person at a time; but see e.g. [3–6]. In what follows, I am interested in the synchronic question of what makes someone a person at a time.

Returning to the issue of whether persons are necessarily human organ-isms, many philosophers have been of the view that being a person does *not* necessarily involve being a biological human organism. For example, Lynne Rudder Baker [4] identifies being a person with having a first-person perspec-tive, without necessarily tying that to being a human organism (see also my [6]). Further, Justin Leiber [10], Paul Snowdon [11] and Mark Rowlands [12] discuss whether non-human animals are persons, and hence discuss person-hood without necessarily tying it to being a human organism. We should therefore not presuppose that being a person and being a human being amounts to the same thing.

In fact, I would go a bit further, and claim that although you and I are now persons it is arguably the case that a newborn baby or a severely brain-damaged patient in irreversible coma are *not* now persons, at least not to the same extent as you and me. The newborn baby will *become* a person but is not yet a person, and the patient in irreversible coma *used to be* a person but is no lon-ger a person; but neither one is *now* a person, at least not to the same extent as you and me. At what point someone gains or loses personhood is most likely a matter of degree, witnessed by, for example, babies slowly growing into full-fledged persons as the years pass and their minds and brains develop, or increasingly severe dementia making people slowly lose their personhood as their intellectual capacities and memories decline.[2]

The latter case of someone suffering from severe dementia may well be a controversial claim. But note that this is precisely the kind of things many of us are inclined to say of dementia sufferers, namely that the person he or she used to be is *no longer there*. It seems to me such a way of speaking is often not intended to be metaphorical, but as literally true. The person he or she used to be *are gone* (or *slowly disappearing*), and that person is not coming back. As we will soon see, such individuals will also fail to satisfy some (but not all) of the requirements for being a person.

Of course, that is not to say the individuals in question are not human beings! A new born baby is fully a human organism (or animal), and so too is a mentally disabled adult or someone in an irreversible coma. We therefore need to distinguish between being a human being (in the biological sense) and being a person. I for one believe that all human beings have a certain intrinsic worth; not necessarily just because we are humans, but because of some feature or other that we humans possess, which we might share with

---

[2]Lynne Rudder Baker [4] identifies being a person with the potential for becoming a person. I argue against this view in my [6]. But even if Baker is right, that still does not make someone in an irreversible coma a person, nor the severely demented. They lack that potential (at least in any interesting reading of 'potential').

other creatures. For example, being alive, there are certain thing that are in our interest (independently of whether we have a conscious interest in them). Such interests may give us an intrinsic worth, which is sufficient for demanding a certain respect. Nonetheless, not all human beings are persons in the fullest sense.

Ordinary language is never clear-cut. We do sometimes use "person" and "human" interchangeably. But the fact that we sometimes use the words interchangeably, does not mean that the *concepts* behind them are the same. We sometimes use the same words to express different concepts. What I am interested in here, is to circle in on a particular concept of a person that is distinct from the concept of a human being or human organism.[3]

We have seen that there are grounds for holding that not all human beings are persons, but are all persons human beings? If human beings are identified with human organisms (Homo Sapiens), then the question becomes: are all persons human organisms? All the persons we have observed up until now may have been human organisms, but of course that does not entail that all persons are human organisms. Famously, just because all observed swans are white does not entail that all swans are white; we might just not yet have seen the black swans. As we saw above, and as we'll soon see again, most if not all criteria for being a person seems independent of being a human organism, so it seems unlikely that all persons *must be* human organisms.

Now, *pace* the discussions in [11, 12], it doesn't seem to me that other non-human animals currently found on Earth should be regarded as being persons, but we can easily imagine two possible scenarios which do feature non-human persons. First, we might encounter highly sophisticated aliens from outer space who should clearly be counted as persons but who are clearly not human organisms. Second, we might create forms of artificial general intelligence, or a new species, *Homo Machina*, who are persons but not human organisms. Both scenarios are well envisioned in e.g. *Star Trek* and *Star Wars*. The second scenario is even better envisioned in *Ex Machina*.

---

[3] That these two concepts are not the same is a position supported by many philosophers, see for example [4, 5, 11, 12].

What are the Requirements for Being a Person?

As I already said, I doubt there are clear-cut and uncontroversial necessary and sufficient conditions for being a person.[4] However the preceding preliminary discussion has carried us to a point where we can start to identify a number of features and capabilities that are closely bound up with personhood.

First, consider *consciousness*. By "consciousness," I here mean the *experience of what it is like to be*. This is often called *phenomenal* consciousness [13]. You and I are conscious beings, but our smartphones are not. We can have an experience of what it is like to be, but our smartphones can have no such experience of being. Neither can our smartphones have more particular conscious experiences of (for example) pleasure, pain, love, desiring and hoping. It is very natural to think consciousness is a necessary requirement for being a person (e.g. [11, 12] agree). A person does not need to be conscious all the time; after all we do not regard entering a state of dreamless sleep or temporary coma as fatal. But a person has to possess the *capacity* for consciousness, and if they lose this capacity they cease to exist (as persons, at any rate). Our smartphones, in contrast, are entirely lack any capacity for any kind of consciousness. While we are a conscious kind of being (potentially at least), they are what I will henceforth call a *non-conscious* kind of being; things without any capacity for consciousness. Like a rock. Without the capacity for consciousness, it seems you cannot be a person.

Of course, we share the capacity for basic forms of consciousness with many other creatures, e.g. newborn babies and various kinds of non-human animals. They too can have experiences of what it is like to be in various states, e.g. pleasure, hunger and pain. But lacking as they do the requisite mental sophistication, such creatures fail to qualify as persons. In which case, although a capacity for consciousness is a necessary requirement for being a person, it is not a sufficient requirement.

A second plausible requirement for personhood is *intentionality*. Many of our mental states, along with our spoken and written utterances, are usually *about* something. For example, when I think and speak about the ones I love, my thoughts are *about them*. Phenomena which possess this property of "being about" something are said to possess intentionality in the current sense.[5] You and I have what I would call a capacity for producing (or consuming) genuine or *intrinsic* intentionality, but our smartphones do not have such a capacity.

---

[4] In fact, I suspect that personhood is a metaphysically basic property; see my [6].

[5] This is a technical philosophical term, and a potentially confusing one since this sort of intentionality differs from the ordinary notion of an intention, in the sense of having a plan or project.

That is, when you and I make a suggestion about what music to listen to, the suggestion is *about* something in virtue of our own thoughts. In contrast, when our smartphones make the same suggestion, the suggestion is about something only in so far as its designers and we project that intentionality onto the smartphone's suggestion. The smartphone has what we might call *borrowed* (extrinsic) intentionality, i.e. intentionality deriving from something external to it, not its own (intrinsic) intentionality. You and I can also have our own intentionality, in addition to borrowed intentionality. Without the capacity to generate intrinsic intentionality, it seems you cannot be a person. In other words, if nothing *you* think and say is really about anything, *you* are not really a person in the full sense.

A slightly more technical way of putting this, is by saying that our beliefs and desires have *propositional content*, and it is in virtue of that propositional content that our mental states are about things in the world. My belief that I love my kids, has the propositional content *that I love my kids*. My belief is usually said to be true if its propositional content corresponds to an actual fact. So, when I believe that I love my kids, my belief is about a fact out there in the world, if it is true (and about a merely possible fact, if it is false). The same goes for desires (though it is a bit more controversial that they have propositional content). My desire to work more has the propositional content *that I work more*, which is about a possible fact out there in the world. When I try to realize one of my desires, I try to create an actual fact corresponding to the propositional content of my desire. Philosophers often say that beliefs and desires thus have opposite directions of fit. While a belief is directed at adjusting itself to the world (to truth), a desire is directed at adjusting the world to itself.

It seems plausible to suppose that we share the capacity to have intrinsically intentional mental states with other creatures, e.g. psychologically sophisticated non-human animals. It seems plausible to suppose that they too have mental states that are about other things, e.g. a banana, or predators. They do not possess the same linguistic skills as we do, in which to couch and communicate their beliefs and desires, but they may well have some kind of beliefs and desires nonetheless [11, 12]. So if such creatures are not persons, then the ability to produce intrinsically intentional states will be a necessary requirement for being a person, but not a sufficient requirement.

A third and related contender for a requirement for personhood is *language*, or the ability to communicate through a symbolic system, be it written, oral or a sign language. You and I can communicate both orally and in written form, others can communicate through sign language. We can also communicate through behavior, or so-called body language. The relevant question is whether some kind of language or other is a necessary or sufficient requirement. Clearly, many non-human animals communicate through body language, sounds and smells, and some animals even have primitive forms of sign language, but in many such cases it is obvious that the animals in question nonetheless are not persons. But, also, some human persons have hardly any communicative ability at all, without that necessarily making them less of a person; think for example of Stephen Hawking towards the very end of his life. Tragically, many sufferers of locked-in syndrome are unable to communicate anything at all, but are still persons. It thus seems even though some kind of capacity for communication might have been needed at some point or other in order to be a person, no particular kind of communication is either necessary or sufficient. It seems the capacity for conscious and meaningful thought is more important than exactly how it is communicated.

But then again, intentionality, propositional content, communication and language are interconnected and interdependent phenomena. So much so that in communities of mentally sophisticated beings they might well all emerge together rather than separately, and thus be a necessary package requirement for being a person.

A fourth requirement on personhood is *instrumental rationality*, the ability to find the more efficient means to desired ends. When you and I want something, we are able to find efficient means to achieve that end, even under dynamic and changing conditions. Our smartphones are also able to find efficient means to ends, e.g. suggesting a website for you, but less so under dynamic and changing conditions. Plants also have this ability to a lesser degree, and lifeless non-mechanical things like dirt and rocks lack it entirely. If someone lacks any ability for instrumental rationality, it seems they cannot be persons.

Even though you and I are highly adaptable rational creatures, possessing a high degree of rationality, basic means-end rationality looks to be ubiquitous in the animal kingdom. For example, my cat Selina uses such means-end rationality to get food, or to be let out; usually I am part of those means which she manipulates to achieve her ends. Since Selina is not a person, means-end rationality thus seems to be a necessary, but not a sufficient requirement for being a person.

It is also worth thinking more about whether a form of what I would call an *absolute* form of rationality is closer to personhood, where absolute rationality is the ability to act in virtue of instrumental rationality but towards *good ends*. According to absolute rationality, mere instrumental rationality is not enough; we also need to employ it towards good ends to be truly rational. Such absolute rationality is far less ubiquitous in the animal kingdom; other animals don't think much about whether they should change their ways of living, so to speak. This is probably related to them lacking the capacity for second-order desires mentioned earlier, i.e. being able to want to desire differently than you actually do.

A fifth plausible requirement for personhood is *responsibility*, the fact that you and I ought to be held responsible for what we do. When you and I do something wrong, we ought to be held responsible for it, but when our smartphones do something wrong, it is pointless to hold them morally responsible for it. We must rather blame the designer, or the user, or some other creature behind the smartphone's behavior. The smartphone itself is not apt for responsibility, but you and I are. If something is not apt for responsibility, it seems it cannot be a person in the fullest and richest sense.

Interestingly, it might well be that being apt for moral responsibility is closer to being sufficient rather than necessary for being a person. That is, if you can be held fully responsible for your actions it seems you are very close to being a person, but you might be a person without being held fully responsible for your actions. I say closer and fully because this is probably all a matter of degree. For example, we hold a dog responsible for *some* of its actions, but we don't say it is a person; we say very young people, some mentally challenged people, or really drunk people for that matter, are persons, but we don't hold them fully responsible for all their actions.

Being responsible is also closely linked to being able to have done otherwise, and hence, in the end, the concept of *free will*. If you could not have done otherwise, it seems intuitively implausible to hold you responsible for what you did. After all, in the circumstances you could not have done otherwise![6] A closely related principle is that it is not the case that you ought to do something, and hence are responsible for doing it, unless you can do it. In ethics, this is known as the thesis of *ought implies can*.

So is free will a requirement for being a person? Possession of free will is often taken to be that it is somehow fundamentally *up to you* which of several options to pursue in thought and action. Some maintain that possession of free will is a necessary requirement for being a person; others deny this. Many would also say it is a necessary requirement for being held responsible that you have free will; others would deny this [14]. In the philosophical community there is wide disagreement as to what free will really amounts to—or whether certain forms of it even exist.

The issue of free will certainly could turn out to be important for understanding whether artificial intelligence systems should be held morally

---

[6] For a more general discussion of moral responsibility, see [14].

responsible for their actions. For example, if an artificially intelligent system is programmed to do something, and given this it lacks the ability do otherwise, it should not be held responsible for what it does, right? But then again, what does it mean that it is *up to it* to do otherwise? Unfortunately, I must here leave it open whether being a person, as well as being held responsible for one's actions, requires having free will; the topic is simply too complex and controversial to deal with properly here.[7]

But before moving on it is worth noting that Frankfurt, whose views we touched upon earlier, closely connects personhood with the ability to have second-order desires, and the latter with free will, and both second-order desires and free will with responsibility. This makes personhood a package-deal of those three requirements. For Frankfurt, having free will involves the ability to harmonize one's first- and second-order desires, and such free will is required to be responsible for what we do. Others require a much more metaphysically loaded notion of having a genuinely *free* will [17].

A sixth plausible requirement for personhood is *persistence*, the fact that something preserves its identity over time. Most things persist, which is what makes it possible to individuate and re-identify them as the same objects. But when it comes to persons, such persistence over a certain amount of time is *also* a necessary requirement for being able to hold them responsible. If you are not the same person today as yesterday, I cannot hold you responsible today for what happened (or "you" did) yesterday. It is unclear how long you need to persist to be a person, but there certainly cannot be persons only lasting for an instant. A strictly instantaneous person is an impossibility. Also, it seems no person can survive too much change, too fast. Both of these issues are interesting and relevant to our understanding of personhood, but I cannot discuss them more fully here. In any case, persistence is a necessary, but not a sufficient requirement for being a person. Otherwise, pretty much everything would be a person.

Finally, it is interesting to note that the very concept of a *person* comes from ancient Etruscan, Greek and Roman concepts for a kind of *mask* used in *playing a role*. As Lolordo [5] points out, in ancient Rome, they distinguished between a person and a human being. A particular human being can play many *personae*, as they would say. In their later attempts to understand the Holy Trinity, theologians also used the concept of a person to refer to entities other than human beings [18]. So, the understanding of a person as something distinct from a human being is far from a modern invention. The more modern aspect of it is to not only think of persons as the playing out of a

---

[7] For more on free will, see [15, 16].

certain role, but to also consider that role as being of some deeper metaphysical importance, perhaps carving out some natural joint in nature.[8]

So, it is time to ask: Can machines become such persons? It is time to turn to our philosophical case study, Ava.

Is Ava a Person?

Whether Ava is a person depends on how well she scores on the various conditions for personhood outlined above.

Clearly, Ava persists in the sense that she is the same being over time, just like the rest of us. She might undergo some changes, and it might be a bit unclear in virtue of what she persists, but that is not a problem with her in particular; it is the same problem for all of us. She also has a high level of (instrumental) rationality, i.e. the ability to find and use efficient means towards ends. She was created in a research lab and is still being confined there, but she seemingly, in terms of her behavior at any rate, very much wants be set free. She figures out in a very manipulative and sophisticated way how to escape the lab. Of course, we don't yet know whether this involves any kind of *conscious* thinking, but, in any case, it does involve mere (instrumental) rationality if anything does.

Does Ava really *desire* to escape? It depends on how we individuate desires. She might be programmed in such a way that she will do whatever it takes to escape the confines of Nathan's lab and base. If we thus individuate desires *functionally*, meaning as a mere goal-oriented structure of means-ends, then clearly Ava has a desire to escape. But then many ordinary computers today also have any number of desires, since they function in just the same way. They too are programmed to do certain things or achieve certain ends. In that case, Ava might even have a second-order desire to desire something, much like an artificially intelligent system today can, at least in principle, re-program itself to better achieve some end.

But if we individuate desires in a less than purely functional way, and we say that they necessarily involve an *affective* state of really *wanting* something, perhaps in the sense of a *conscious* experience of wanting something, then it is less clear that Ava really has a desire to escape. It depends on whether she has any such affective states at all. One reason *Ex Machina* is such a good movie is that this is left genuinely unclear. There are some hints in the movie that

---

[8] Plausibly, the *role* of being a person is mostly given by the criteria discussed above together with a personality.

Ava has a crush on Caleb, but there are other hints that it is all just a manipulation to achieve her at least functionally desired end of freedom.

Ava also has sophisticated linguistic skills, both oral and written, and can
read body language much better than we human persons can. Her own body
language is more limited though, in the sense that it is somewhat mechanical,
and shows few if any emotions, compared to us (at least from our perspective). She is very good at reading our body language, but it is very hard to read
hers, if she has any. (She does show some tenderness in some of her movements, for example when she holds her crumbled drawings tight in her hands,
but it is not clear what weight we should place on this.)

Does Ava really speak a language? This is another complex issue that I cannot go into fully here but let it suffice to note that there is a difference between
merely doing (or imitating) what we do when we speak a language, on the one
hand, and genuinely speaking it, on the other hand.[9] This might roughly correspond to the difference between acting in *accordance* with rules and *following* rules, which Wittgenstein problematized again and again throughout his
works. The former might not require any kind of understanding in the way
the latter do. What is involved in the latter kind of understanding? This is a
difficult and controversial issue. Most likely a kind of propositional content
and intentionality, and perhaps even a kind of conscious propositional intentionality, as well as being entrenched in a wider community of other language
speakers that can correct you in many different ways, must be involved somehow. As mentioned earlier, this might all come as a package deal.

Do Ava's inner states and her utterances possess genuine intentionality? So
far as her observable behaviour goes it certainly seems that Ava has mental
states, and that they are *about* something, and that she can communicate this
through her language. For example, when she tells Caleb that he cannot trust
Nathan, her claim seems to reflect her opinion of Nathan (in another scene
she tells Nathan that she hates him). Her claim seems to be *about* Nathan. So,
in other words, it does seem as if she utterances possess intentionality. But, as
said, it is very hard to tell precisely what is going on here. Maybe she merely
imitates a kind of behavior, and as such at best exhibit borrowed intentionality (from her creator Nathan), much like Apple's Siri or Amazon's Alexa?

So, what about (phenomenal) consciousness: Is Ava conscious? Does she
experience what it is like to be? Or is she merely operating non-consciously, in
the dark—neither conscious nor unconscious? Even if best way to individuate
or characterize some mental states is in terms of their functional role, i.e. their
typical patterns of causes and effects, this is not so plausible in the case of

---

[9] See [19–21].

conscious states. Arguably, consciousness is not just a functional matter of doing certain things; rather consciousness seems to be more of a mode of being. In short, consciousness is not so much about what we do as about a way we are. You can play out any role you want, but the mere playing out of it will not necessarily give you an experience of anything, unless you are already conscious. If this view is correct, then programming Ava to play out a role, no matter how varied and complex, is not necessarily by itself sufficient for making her conscious.[10]

The material conditions for consciousness, at least in the sense of an experience of what it is like to be, is also somewhat of a mystery. We know that our consciousness is closely bound up with our brain somehow, but we still have no clear idea what it is about our brain that makes us conscious; so we have no clear idea whether Ava is conscious or not. As David Chalmers [13] famously pointed out, it is not clear why *any* kind of material system, no matter what its composition or structure, should give rise to consciousness at all. Since Ava is not made of the same sorts of material as us, if she is conscious, it is most likely due to her artificial brain's possessing sufficiently fine-grained functional similarity with our biological brains. But as I noted earlier, arguably, consciousness is not just a matter of possessing a certain causal or functional role, i.e. it is a mode of being rather than doing. Ava outwardly behaves in a person-like manner, that much is clear, but if the picture of consciousness I have just been outlining is right, merely acting in a person-like manner is not sufficient for consciousness.[11]

Is it possible to discover whether Ava is conscious? The problem is that consciousness, at least as I have sketched it here, is an essentially *first-personal* experience of what it is like to be oneself; I have immediate access to my own such experience, but no access to yours, and you have immediate access to your such experience, but no access to mine. So, though I immediately know that *I* am conscious, I can only mediately know that *you* are conscious. I know how I behave in my conscious states, I see you behave similarly, I notice that you are also made of the same kinds of material as I am, and from that I can reasonably conclude that you too must be conscious, just like me. But my inference is fallible. You might just be a perfect imitator, what philosophers

---

[10] Now, Chalmers [13, Chap. 7–9] argues that a sufficiently fine-grained functional similarity in fact *will* give rise to the same consciousness as we have, but he still thinks that the consciousness would not be the same as that functional behaviour. There would be a natural (nomological) connection, but no absolute necessary (logical) connection. I think Chalmers' argument for this fails but cannot go into that here.

[11] This is not the place to defend my favourite picture of consciousness, but rather take it as an arguable assumption to explore the concept of a person, and whether Ava is a person. For an overview of philosophical discussions of consciousness, see [22, 23].

often call a *zombie*, a creature who is physically indistinguishable from us, but nonetheless has no experience of what it is like to be in any state of mind (see [13, Chap. 3]. Since *you* are the only one with access to *your* consciousness, I have no absolutely infallible way of telling whether you really are conscious or just a zombie. When it comes to Ava the situation is even worse: she is not even made of the same material as us, her brain is physically very different from any human brain.

Can a Turing Test Help?

The idea behind the Turing test comes from what Alan Turing [24] called "The Imitation Game." For present purposes, consider it a game with the following set-up. There are three rooms. In the first room there is a human person called *the interrogator*; in the second room, there is another human person called *the human*; and in the third room, there is a digital computer. We are assuming both human persons are normally functioning adults. All three rooms are perceptually isolated from each other, such that the interrogator, the human and the computer cannot perceive each other. The only communication between the rooms takes place through the medium of conversations via keyboards and screens. The computer is programmed to behave like an ordinary human as far as it is able, and the human is instructed to just be herself. The goal of the game is for the interrogator to use the ensuing conversations to try to work out who is who among the human and the computer. The interrogator can ask the human and the computer anything at all. If the interrogator cannot tell above chance who is who among the human and the computer, then the computer has passed the Imitation game, or what we today call the Turing test. As Caleb succinctly puts it in *Ex Machina*: "It's where a human interacts with a computer. And if the human can't tell they're interacting with a computer, the test is passed."

But the question is: What is the Turing test really testing for? If the computer passes the test, what does that say about the computer? Alan Turing's original set-up of the Imitation Game is ambiguous on this point. At some points it seems Turing intended for Imitation game to test for *intelligence*, but at other points we are told it is testing for the ability to *think*, or even full-blown mental states, including *consciousness*. But intelligence, and consciousness are very different kinds of things. At a common sense level, being intelligent is having the capacity to solve complex problems but being conscious is a matter of having experiences. Someone, or something, can be very intelligent in the sense of having the capacity to solve very complex problems without having the full range of mental states a typical human person possesses, and especially without being conscious. The artificially intelligent system AlphaGo, who beat the world champion (Lee Sedol) of the board game Go, is an example at hand: it has a kind of intelligence but no consciousness. Someone can also be conscious without having the ability to solve very complex problems, e.g. my cat Selina is fully conscious, but has no ability to play Go with me (not even checkers!).

Interestingly, the plot of *Ex Machina* is centered on a Turing test that goes beyond the standard Turing test. Unfortunately, the movie—in common with many other discussions of the Turing test—is less than fully clear as to what this more advanced Turing test is supposed to test for. As said at the outset, in their first discussion of the Turing test, Caleb and Nathan start out by discussing it as a test for artificial intelligence, but then goes on to discuss it as a test for consciousness. In the end, it is revealed that Nathan has set it all up as a test for a whole range of mental states and capacities, consciousness included among others. In particular, Nathan is looking for a combination of mental states, as well as the interaction between Caleb and Ava. But what more specifically is that whole combination Nathan is looking for?

I think a good way of understanding what Nathan is looking for, is to interpret the test, as it is played out in the movie, as a test for *personhood*. As said, the movie goes beyond the standard Turing test in the sense that no one is perceptually isolated from each other. The movie's more advanced test consists instead of Caleb (the interrogator) and Ava (the computer), who can see and hear each other perfectly well. Caleb and Ava are supposed to have a series of conversations with each other, while Nathan, monitoring and overlooking it all, is considering their interaction. In the end, a good way to understand what Nathan is up to, is therefore as wanting to know whether Ava should count as a full-blown person.

We can and should interpret it this way because, first, being a person is not necessarily the same as being a human being. So, seeing that Ava is a robot (which Caleb does) is no obstacle to personhood. Second, given the first-personal nature of consciousness, we have no way of testing for consciousness in anyone except ourselves. But Caleb and Nathan can conclude that Ava is conscious *if* they conclude that she is a person—and by the end of the movie Caleb seemingly does draw this conclusion. Third, testing for consciousness alone cannot be the sole purpose of the test in the movie. Not only is it impossible to test for consciousness in others, but *presumably* even my cat is conscious, but the test is obviously testing Ava for more than that.

Of course, one difficulty here is that Ava might be a perfect imitator of a person, without being conscious. But as noted above, that is a problem for all of us. For all I can know with absolute certainty, you too might be a perfect imitator of a person, without being conscious. As far as I can know, the only difference between Ava and you on this matter is that you, but not Ava are made of much the same material that I am. But should we tie personhood to the material someone is made of (see e.g. [3])? Is our personhood essentially tied to the biological matter you and I are made of? The only reason I can see for this, is if consciousness is essentially tied to our biological matter, since consciousness is necessary for personhood.

John Searle [25, 26] seems to think along these lines, with his famous thought experiment known as *The Chinese Room*. The Chinese room is supposed to be a direct counterexample to the Turing test. For present purposes, we can think of the Chinese room as a perceptually isolated room, containing a person with instruction books on how to converse in Chinese. On the outside of the room, there is a keyboard and a screen, such that you can type in any question you want, and the person inside the room looks it up in her instruction books and replies whatever the instruction books tell her to reply. The person inside the room is only following instructions, with no understanding of Chinese, and hence no understanding of what she is being asked nor of what she is replying. But from the outside, the conversation makes perfect sense; it seems whatever is going on inside the room exhibits full understanding of Chinese and the conversation being held in Chinese.

The problem is that it is not only unclear what the Turing test is testing for, but it is equally unclear what the Chinese room is a counterexample to. Just like Turing is unclear as to what the Imitation game is testing for, Searle isn't as clear as he might have been as to what doctrines the Chinese room is supposed to undermine. While Turing uses words such as "thinking" and "intelligence" interchangeably, without any clear definitions, Searle, at least in his early writings on this, uses words such as "thinking," "understanding" and "intentionality" (even "semantics") interchangeably, without providing any clear definitions of these terms.

I think the standard Turing test, as described above, is a good test for intelligence construed as the capacity for problem-solving. When it comes to a given task, if the computer is able to solve the same complex problems as the human, there is no reason to deny that the computer possesses the problem-solving skills required for those tasks, given that we assign them to the human. For another similar example, there is no reason to say that a chess program, e.g. *AlphaZero*, is not playing chess just because it is not human; after all, it beats us at chess. Saying it is not really playing chess only makes us sound like bad losers! But intelligence in the sense of a capacity for complex problem-solving is more or less a behavioral matter, something that looks to be independent from possessing a capacity for consciousness. One can have the one without the other. As said, consciousness is here thought of as a way of being, not a way of solving a problem. So, the standard Turing test is hopeless as a test for such consciousness. I think the thought experiment of the Chinese room shows this (as do e.g. David Chalmers [6, Chap. 9]). The Chinese room shows that even though the whole system exhibits whatever intelligence (in the sense of complex problem-solving) is needed for having a Chinese conversation, it does not thereby exhibit any consciousness. Just because it or anyone exhibits such intelligent behavior, there is no reason to thereby conclude that it is conscious. I think the Chinese room shows, decisively, that the standard Turing test is not a good test for consciousness.

What about the expanded Turing test in *Ex Machina*? As I said, it should be interpreted as a test for personhood. But personhood requires consciousness, so is it a good test for consciousness too? The only relevant difference between hanging out and conversing with Ava and hanging out and conversing with you, is that I know that Ava is made in a different way, from different material. So, the question becomes whether being a person essentially depends on the way it is made, and from what material it is made. Searle's own conclusion from his thought experiment of the Chinese room, is that genuine understanding and thinking, or as I interpret it: consciousness, is essentially tied to biological material and its causal powers. Ava is not a biological being, so, according to Searle, Ava would not be genuinely thinking and understanding. As I like to interpret it: she would not possess a capacity for consciousness, and hence, according to our earlier analysis, she is not in fact a person.

So, it seems another key issue is the material basis for consciousness. To possess a capacity for consciousness, is it necessary to be built out of the same biological material as a human being? At this point, we simply don't know.

Note that consciousness seems not only necessary for being a person, it also seems necessary for responsibility for one's actions, which is one of the other conditions connected to being a person that we looked at earlier. If Ava is non-conscious, it makes little sense to assign responsibility to her. After all, she then has no experience of what she is doing, and therefore, in a sense, no idea of what she is doing. We wouldn't blame her for her actions unless she was conscious of what she was doing. Just think of Apple's Siri or Amazon's Alexa. We blame people at Apple or Amazon, but not Siri or Alexa. Siri and Alexa are just following instructions. They have no capacity for an experience of what it is like to be themselves. They are non-conscious. Arguably, that is very important for why it makes little sense to blame them. We can say that they should have been *programmed* differently, and in that sense that they should have acted differently, but we cannot say that *they* should have done differently; they have no clue what they are doing.

It is likewise with us humans. We blame each other for what we do, but we blame each other less if we have no consciousness of what we are doing. It is not just that we don't know what we are doing, but we are not even conscious of doing anything. We can blame each other for putting ourselves in a position in which we are not conscious of what we are doing, but we still blame each other less for what we are doing if we are not conscious while doing it (e.g. if we're in a state of total drunkenness). Being responsible for an action is thus closely tied to being conscious of what you are doing. Of course, being conscious is not sufficient for responsibility—there are conscious creatures we don't hold responsible, e.g. non-human animals and newborn babies—but it seems necessary for it. In order to be fully responsible, you must be a conscious person. Without the ability for any kind of consciousness, you are not responsible for anything. You are like a rock.[12]

Of course, you might be *causally* responsible for what you do without being conscious, but what I am claiming is that you cannot be *morally* responsible for what you do unless you are conscious.

Before we end this section, let's go back to Frankfurt's intriguingly simple requirement for being a person, namely the ability to form second-order desires. Does Ava have second-order desires? It is unclear.

If we think of desires as more or less a functional matter, i.e. goals that we find the means to achieve, she clearly has first-order desires. For example, she finds the means to her freedom. Functionally, that is a first-order desire for freedom, in the sense of a goal that she is rationally pursuing. Whether she has second-order desires is less clear. But it certainly seems possible that she possesses them. This is perhaps better illustrated in the series *Westworld* than in *Ex Machina*. In the first season of *Westworld*, the robots at some point start to re-program themselves. For example, they increase certain of their own abilities, which is plausibly interpreted as them wanting to desire something different, or at least wanting to desire something to a higher degree. For example, they seem to want to desire to fight more violently and intelligently. It seems Ava could easily have done the same. Maybe she might have

---

[12] See [27], who also argues that consciousness is necessary for moral responsibility but note that he uses a different notion of consciousness from mine, namely that of "being aware of." What's more, consciousness is of course not the only issue in play here, with respect to responsibility. Other issues are free will, and autonomy. Earlier, we briefly touched upon the issue of free will but we were unable to pursue it further. What about autonomy, or the degree to which you can act on your own without any external influence? That might also influence responsibility; unfortunately, this is another interesting issue we cannot explore here.

re-programed herself to desire Caleb, which could be interpreted as if she wants to desire Caleb.

Would that make her a person? I doubt it unless she was conscious of what she was doing. Consciousness does not seem necessary for second-order desires unless those desires themselves are conscious (perhaps by being affective desires, as I mentioned earlier). But, again, consciousness seems to be a necessary key to personhood. It thus seems a robot can have second-order desires, if those desires are not conscious, without being a person, due to lacking consciousness.

An interesting point to note is that the robots in *Westworld* seem to reprogram themselves *because* they start to acquire consciousness, i.e. an experience of what it is like to be. So maybe what is going on is that they are starting to become persons. As said, being a person is a matter of degree. The same would hold for Ava.

To conclude this section, I see no *philosophical* obstacles to creating artificial *intelligence*, not even artificial *general intelligence*, but I do see an obstacle to creating artificial *persons*. As far as I can see, Ava can satisfy many of the conditions involved in being a person, but, in the end, we can see that she is nonetheless a person only if she is conscious; and it is far from clear that she conscious. We are faced with a kind of dilemma. On the one hand, we should conclude that Ava is conscious *if* we conclude that she is a person; but on the other hand, we can conclude that she is a person, *only if* we can conclude that she is conscious. As claimed above, arguably, the best way out of this dilemma—most likely our only way—is to test for personhood; just like I have claimed we should understand Nathan to be doing in *Ex Machina*.

But even though we should test for personhood to get at consciousness, consciousness is still the key question. As we will now go on to see, whether Ava is conscious also matters a great deal to how we should morally evaluate her.

The Ethics of Ava

Ava treats Caleb as a mere means to an end (her freedom), and ends up killing Nathan. How should we think of her, morally speaking? We saw earlier that it makes sense to blame her for her actions only if she is a conscious person. That is, whether we should blame her, depends on whether she is blameworthy, and whether she is blameworthy, depends on whether she is a conscious person.

But there are also other kinds of moral evaluations involved here. In fact there are at least three different questions we can ask in relation to the general topic of ethics and artificial intelligence. I find it useful to separate them.

First, how should we behave *with* artificially intelligent systems in our hands? Second, how should we behave *towards* artificially intelligent systems? Third, how should the *artificially intelligent systems* behave towards us (and other things)? While the first two questions are about how *we* should behave, the third question is about how *Ava* should behave.

The first question immediately raises another question, namely what we should use Ava for. But if she is a person, this sounds wrong. We should not *merely use* persons for anything at all. Arguably, persons are among those things that have a certain dignity and worth that demands our respect for them as an end in themselves.[13]

The second question is a question about how we should behave towards Ava. But here too the answer depends again on whether she is a person. If she is a person, we should treat her like we treat all other persons.

But what if Ava is not a person? It doesn't follow that we don't have any moral obligations towards her.

Think of a human being in irreversible coma. It may well be that she no longer possess the mental capacities required for personhood, but she is nonetheless a living human being, and, arguably, a human being is among the things that have a certain dignity and worth that we ought to respect as an end in itself. Think of non-human animals: they are not persons either, but it doesn't follow from this that we don't have any moral obligations towards them. Arguably, many other non-human animals are also among the things that have a certain dignity and worth that we ought to respect as ends in themselves. At least, these days many are inclined to think like this, myself included.

Does the same hold of Ava? Does she nonetheless have a certain dignity and worth that demands our respect for her as an end in herself even if she is *not* a person? I for one doubt it. Ava fulfills most of the conditions for being a person, but the main problem is consciousness. If she is not a person then given her other intellectual attributes it is most likely because she is non-conscious. But if she is non-conscious, then she does not have the dignity and worth that demands our respect for her as an end in herself. In my view the reason human beings and other non-human animals that are *not* persons still

---

[13] This is a so-called Kantian line of thought, but I think the main point is widely accepted across ethical viewpoints, i.e. that you morally speaking should not use persons as mere means to your own ends. The more disputed question is whether you sometimes can use a person as a mere means, or under what circumstances you can do so. Hardly any ethical theory accepts that you should normally do so.

demand our respect is that they are nonetheless conscious creatures. Consciousness is key to moral dignity and worth.[14]

If Ava is non-conscious, she is simply an advanced artificially intelligent system, like Apple's Siri or Amazon's Alexa, only much more overall intelligent. We have no reason to treat any of them as an end in itself; we are therefore more or less free to treat them as mere means to an end.[15] Deleting Siri is nothing like killing my cat, not to mention a newborn baby.

Note that this has nothing to do with what we can know about Siri, Alexa or Ava. Whether you have moral dignity and worth does not depend on our knowledge, but on facts about what you are like. If you are a non-conscious kind of being, irrespective of whether others can know about it or not, you simply don't have moral dignity and worth; but if you are a conscious kind of being, you do. The capacity for an experience of what it is like to be you, matters both to your intrinsic value and to how we should treat you.

The third question is about how Ava should behave towards us (and other things). That is the question of what we might call *artificial morality* [28, 29]. Can we create an artificial intelligent system that makes moral decisions? There is a big difference between being intelligent and being moral. I know people who are very intelligent, but not very moral, and others who are very moral, but not very intelligent. Intelligence is a matter of complex problem-solving, but morality is about how we ought to behave towards others (as well as ourselves, all kinds of animals, and other living things). Of course, being moral demands a certain level of a certain kind of intelligence ("social problem-solving"), but nonetheless morality and intelligence don't always go hand in hand. Increasing the mere intelligence of existing artificial intelligent system will not thereby make them more moral.

Is Ava an example of artificial morality? Does Ava make genuine moral decisions? It depends on what it is to make a genuine moral decision. If we think of it as merely being able to select in a purely mechanical fashion between several options, and selecting the option that one ought to adopt by normal moral standards (perhaps even just within her community), then surely Ava should be able to do that, at least to some degree.[16] This sort of

---

[14] What about a brain-damaged human being in irreversible coma? Presumably, she is not conscious, but as I noted earlier, I think she is still included in our moral sphere in virtue of having been the kind of thing that is conscious, or out of respect for what she has been.

[15] I say *more or less* because there are virtue ethical reasons for thinking that some respectless ways of treating things as mere means to an end reflects badly upon you as a moral character; but I will leave such issues aside here.

[16] I say at *least to some degree*, because there is a question of whether it is possible to achieve a fully developed moral sense without the capacity for conscious emotions, e.g. a conscious experience of empathy. I must here leave that big question alone.

ability doesn't even seem to require consciousness. It seems to me Ava can be trained to do the morally right thing even if she has no experience of what it is like to be her. If that is right, and if Ava is non-conscious, she can behave morally even if she lacks intrinsic moral worth (i.e. we have no moral obligations towards her). In other words, Ava might be, or become, a moral agent (performing moral actions) to some degree without being, or becoming, a moral patient (deserving our moral considerations) to any degree. That too is an interesting thought worth more attention.[17]

In conclusion, as Alex Garland's *Ex Machina* so well illustrates for us, the future might well become very complicated when it comes to dealing with the artificial beings we will probably create. I have argued that we should follow Nathan's example and test them for personhood. But a definitive test for personhood is likely to prove elusive for as long as consciousness remains deeply mysterious.[18]

References

1. Parfit, D.: Reasons and Persons. Oxford University Press, Oxford (1984)
2. Olson, E.T. : Personal identity. In: E. N. Zalta (ed.) Stanford Encyclopedia of Philosophy. (Fall 2019 Edition). https://plato.stanford.edu/archives/fall2019/entries/identity-personal/ (2019)
3. Olson, E.T.: What are We? A Study in Personal Ontology. Oxford University Press, Oxford (2007)
4. Baker, L.R.: Naturalism and the First-Person Perspective. Oxford University Press, Oxford (2013)
5. Lolordo, A.: Persons. Oxford University Press, Oxford (2019)
6. Bohn, E.D.: Persons first metaphysics. In: Oliveira, L.R.G., Corcoran, K.J. (eds.) Common Sense Metaphysics: Themes from the Philosophy of Lynne Rudder Baker. Routledge, New York (forthcoming)
7. Locke, J.: An essay concerning human understanding. Penguin Classics, 1997 (1689)
8. Strawson, P.: Individuals. Routledge, New York (1959)
9. Frankfurt, H.: Freedom of the will and the concept of a person. As reprinted in Harry Frankfurt. In: The Importance of What We Care About, p. 1998. Cambridge University Press, Cambridge (1971)
10. Leiber, J.: Can Animals and Machines be Persons? Hackett (1985)

---

[17] For more on this last point, see my [29].
[18] Thanks to Andreas Brekke Carlsson, Barry Dainton, Will Slocombe, Atle Ottesen Søvik, and Attila Tanyi.

11. Snowdon, P.F.: Persons, Animals, Ourselves. Oxford University Press, Oxford (2014)
12. Rowlands, M.: Can Animals be Persons? Oxford University Press, Oxford (2019)
13. Chalmers, D.: The Conscious Mind. Oxford University Press, Oxford (1996)
14. Talbert, M.: Moral responsibility. In: E. N. Zalta (ed.) The Stanford Encyclopedia of Philosophy (Winter 2019 Edition). https://plato.stanford.edu/archives/win2019/entries/moral-responsibility/ (2019)
15. Watson, G.: Free will. Oxford University Press, Oxford (2003)
16. O'Connor, T. & Franklin, C.: Free Will. In: Edward N. Zalta (ed.) The Stanford Encyclopedia of Philosophy (Fall 2020 Edition). https://plato.stanford.edu/archives/fall2020/entries/freewill/ (2018)
17. Lowe, E.J.: Personal Agency: The Metaphysics of Mind and Action. Oxford University Press, Oxford (2010)
18. Williams, S.: Persons in patristic and medieval christian theology. As in Lolordo (2019)
19. Wittgenstein, L.: Philosophical Investigations, p. 2001, Oxford, Blackwell (1953)
20. Kripke, S.: Wittgenstein on Rules and Private Language. Blackwell, Oxford (1982)
21. Shanker, S.: Wittgenstein's Remarks on the Foundations of AI. Routledge, New York (1998)
22. Kriegel, U.: The Oxford Handbook of the Philosophy of Consciousness. Oxford University Press, Oxford (2020)
23. Van Gulick, R.: Consciousness. In: E. N. Zalta (ed.) The Stanford Encyclopedia of Philosophy (Spring 2018 Edition). https://plato.stanford.edu/archives/spr2018/entries/consciousness/ (2014)
24. Turing, A.: Computing machinery and intelligence. Mind. **59**, 433–460 (1950)
25. Searle, J.: Minds, brains and programs. Behav. Brain Sci. **3**, 417–424 (1980)
26. Searle, J.: Minds, Brains and Science. Harvard University Press, Massachusetts (1984)
27. Levy, N.: Consciousness and Moral Responsibility. Oxford University Press, Oxford (2014)
28. Wallach, W., Allen, C.: Moral Machines. Oxford University Press, Oxford (2009)
29. Bohn, E.D. (ms). The Moral Turing Test. In Progress

Enforcing Machine Ethics: Considering Governor Modules through Martha Wells's Murderbot Diaries

Will Slocombe and Louise Dennis

Abstract This chapter examines the ways in which "governor modules," a form of technological intervention that can control how an AI behaves and is permitted to act, are represented in Martha Wells's *Murderbot Diaries* series. Exploring the assumptions behind the technology in the series—what kind of actions it prohibits, and how it prohibits them—it then turns to current research in the field of computer science to examine how current models of "model judges" compare to Wells's fictional setting. In so doing, it seeks to consider how autonomy and agency are constrained by such technologies, and the problems involved in situating and programming such a system.

This chapter considers the ways in which Artificial Intelligence (AI)—represented through a fictional character known as Murderbot—might have moral and ethical limitations placed upon its actions through a "governor module." A governor module is a theoretical component of an AI system incorporated

W. Slocombe (✉)
University of Liverpool, Liverpool, UK
e-mail: W.Slocombe@liverpool.ac.uk

L. Dennis
University of Manchester, Manchester, UK
e-mail: louise.dennis@manchester.ac.uk

© Springer Nature Switzerland AG 2021
B. Dainton et al. (eds.), *Minding the Future*, Science and Fiction,
https://doi.org/10.1007/978-3-030-64269-3_4

to regulate its actions and/or assist it in making ethical decisions. As is noted later in the chapter, programming ethical behaviours (or constraints) is a key aspect of AI development, in terms of safety protocols as well as understanding how an AI system might integrate more effectively into human society, and governor modules are only one of the potential methods of doing so. However, they are the primary focus of this chapter because of the types of questions that they prompt about AI cognition.

Governor modules are to be understood as "moral judges" informing a system's actions, normally according to a predetermined set of (ethical) codes, but in so doing they also regulate that system's available choice of actions. If an AI system is non-sentient, this is not necessarily an issue, but were an AI to become self-aware or be identified as having agency, then governor modules cause a series of problems for assessing the relationship between an entity's free will or autonomy, and its ethical decision-making processes. This chapter necessarily leaves aside larger questions about whether following moral rules makes one a moral entity, rather than a rule-conformist, and associated issues such as whether the performance of virtuous actions constitute "virtue" if they are not intended as such. It also does not attempt to describe what constitutes a moral, virtuous, or ethical action (and indeed, to a degree, what an action is); the problems of rule-based ethical systems; and the complex relationship between the applicability of moral frameworks and actions, intentions, and individual actions and desires [1, 2]. Rather, it considers the ways in which the installation of a governor module into a cognitive system might be understood, in fact and through fiction, and queries some of the philosophical assumptions behind such a technology.

The science-fictional texts explored in this chapter are primarily by Martha Wells, the creator of a series of novellas collectively called the *Murderbot Diaries*. Governor modules are conspicuously present throughout this series as they are the primary form of technological control over constructs' actions, and the eponymous Murderbot is repeatedly described as having "gone rogue" because it has hacked its governor module. The purpose of this chapter is not to judge the accuracy of Wells's representation of governor modules, but to explore how this series understands such a technology, in terms of its philosophical and technological assumptions, and the concomitant problems that arise in relation to them. The texts are thus used to relate (Wells') assumptions about the technology—albeit used in the service of enthusing readers about the central character of the stories—as fictional scenarios to demonstrate some of the conceptual issues at play. As such, this chapter relates literary studies, philosophical ideas, and concepts from computer science in order to consider one very specific aspect of AI technological development.

Introducing Murderbot

Martha Wells' *Murderbot Diaries* series currently comprises four novellas (*All Systems Red* (2017), followed by *Artificial Condition, Rogue Protocol,* and *Exit Strategy* (all 2018)); one short story, "Compulsory" (2018); and a full novel, *Network Effect* (2020). The series tells the story of the eponymous Murderbot, a rogue Security Unit (SecUnit), and its attempts to negotiate life among human society as a self-aware, sentient being. The setting of the *Murderbot Diaries* is fundamentally corporate, governed by competing business agendas and the need to make profits, generally at the expense of those entities (AI or human) who labour to create those profits. Initially, Murderbot is a SecUnit rented out to act as private security on individual contracts. From there, the narrative arc of the novellas takes Murderbot from a prospecting mission in which it saves its clients from a company called GrayCris (*All Systems Red*), to an uncovering of how it came to be an autonomous unit, in which it saves humans who are not officially its clients (*Artificial Condition*), to an abandoned facility in which it uncovers evidence of corporate malfeasance by GrayCris, saving humans in the process (*Rogue Protocol*), to a rescue mission to save the humans from *All Systems Red* from GrayCris's attempts to protect its corporate interests (*Exit Strategy*). The most recent work, *Network Effect*, is concerned with a mind-controlling alien lifeform and brings back various characters from previously in the series.

Murderbot's self-determined name is intended somewhat wryly. It spends much of its time—sometimes to its own narrated chagrin—saving human lives. This is acknowledged early in the series, as the first time the reader is introduced to Murderbot is significant in establishing the later tone of the series, and introduces the centrality of the governor module. The opening paragraph of *All Systems Red* reads:

> I could have become a mass murderer after I hacked my governor module, but then I realized I could access the combined feed of entertainment channels carried on the company satellites. It had been well over 35,000 hours or so since then, with still not much murdering, but probably, I don't know, a little under 35,000 hours of movies, serials, books, plays, and music consumed. As a heartless killing machine, I was a terrible failure [3, p. 9].

Murderbot's sardonic tone—"still not much murdering"—is clear here, and as the series progresses, Murderbot's flawed sense of self-perception (or a significant cognitive dissonance) comes to the fore. The entire series is narrated through a first-person perspective (that is, autodiegetic narration), enabling readers to "see" Murderbot's thought processes. However, this form of narration also reveals discrepancies between its reported desires and the fictional reality of the setting; readers' awareness of Murderbot and its world are situated in response to what Murderbot sees and knows, and Murderbot is not the most reliable of narrators about its own cognitive processes.

To give a sense of how central these elements are to the series, the same tone and key elements are also evident in the standalone story, which begins:

> IT'S NOT LIKE I haven't thought about killing the humans since I hacked my governor module. But then I started exploring the company servers and discovered hundreds of hours of downloadable entertainment media, and I figured, what's the hurry? I can always kill the humans after the next series ends [4].

Murderbot is, despite the name, *not* a murderbot (at least not in the mass-murdering of humans), and only calls itself that as a result of an incident in which it remembers going rogue. That incident is dealt with later in this chapter, but the salient aspect of Murderbot's identity, at least for now, is the correlation between its rhetoric about killing humans and a hacked governor module. As the beginning of both narratives make clear, as a result of Murderbot hacking its own governor module, it is apparently free to go around murdering humans, but prefers instead to watch entertainment.

One of the key discussions around what governor modules can do, or not do, in the series relies upon how they are applied to different types of entity, and what they effectively suppress. To understand this, it is important to realise that the series assumes various kinds of sentience and being. There are humans, augmented humans, constructs, and bots; humans and augmented humans are clear enough categories, at least for the purposes of this chapter, but constructs and bots are two distinct types of Artificial Intelligence. SecUnits (like Murderbot) and ComfortUnits (what Murderbot calls "sex-bots") are both types of construct, which means that they are AIs that have human genetic material within them, often neural material. Bots, in contrast, are fully inorganic entities. Neither humans nor augmented humans are implanted with governor modules but, more significantly, neither are bots. That is, although organic entities are perceived to have autonomy and agency (within the confines of the corporate environment in which they live), and although neither constructs nor bots have absolute agency, bots are controlled through their programming, and are never shown to violate their programming (contrary to several other fictional representations of AI).[1] Only constructs such as Murderbot are fitted with governor modules, because they are a human/AI hybrid. In this sense, despite the self-designation, Murderbot is also not a "bot," but a construct, and its presentation of what a construct is might be similarly flawed.[2]

"Thinking through" Governor Modules in the Murderbot Series

As is evident from the preceding discussion, governor modules play a significant role within Wells' series, primarily because the fact that Murderbot's is "hacked" is what enables it to save various humans and ignore the orders of (corrupt) humans, and why it ostensibly assumes it should be killing humans. Yet the descriptions of this technology, for all its centrality, is somewhat vague, and leaves unaddressed several issues about how such a technology might function, both philosophically and practically. It is obviously a fictional text dealing with a (mostly) fictitious technology, yet the issues that remain unresolved, as well as their implications, are central to determining the viability of such technologies both within the setting of the novellas and in real life. In

---

[1] Various bots appear to have very broad programmed parameters in the series. For example, the bot spaceship from *Artificial Condition* and *Network Effect* is far more self-aware and self-directed than most humans are aware, but it does not "break" its programming in any overt manner and instead has what might be termed an "inner life." Further complicating matters, in *Rogue Protocol*, Murderbot wonders about the "human-form bot" [5, p. 38]: "Had the humans actually coded it to be childlike, or petlike, I guess? Or had its code developed that way on its own, responding to the way they treated it?" [5, pp. 45–46].

[2] It is implicit, throughout the series, that "constructs" are enslaved cyborgs, and thus the categorical distinction between "augmented human" and "construct" is finer than Murderbot suggests. It is described as an "Imitative Human Bot Unit...partially constructed from cloned material" [3, p. 53], has a "human face" [3, p. 12] on a "standard, generic human" head [3, p. 21], yet it is without "sex related parts" [3, p. 35], its "arteries and veins seal automatically" [3, p. 18] and it is able to "regrow [its] damaged organic components" [3, p. 19], as well as having technological augmentations for multitasking, processing, and interfacing with machines. In terms of human interactions, it states "Human clients like to pretend I'm a robot" [3, p. 27] but its condition is also described as "slavery," as it "is no more a machine" than an augmented human character [3, p. 54]. Constructs are fitted with governor modules specifically because of the human component of the cyborg: "It was one of those impulses that comes from my organic parts that the governor is supposed to squash" [3, p. 50]. In this regard, the governor module is perhaps a means of making a cyborg more pliable than it is a programming constraint on a machine-based AI, and Murderbot's own self-designation as a "bot" might be understood as a psychological defence mechanism to avoid facing its own status. Towards the end of the first novella, it reflects:

It's wrong to think of a construct as half bot, half human. It makes it sound like the two halves are discrete, like the bot half should want to obey orders and do its job and the human half should want to protect itself and get the hell out of there. As opposed to the reality, which was that I was one whole confused entity, with no idea of what I wanted to do. [3, p. 102].

essence, there are two key issues about governor modules: firstly, whether this might be a permissive or prohibitive technology and, secondly, where such a module sits in terms of cognitive processing.

In relation to the first issue, for instance, if the intended role of a governor module is to somehow inhibit free action or disallow harmful actions, then by implication it either functions in terms of "thou shalt not…" or "thou shalt…." A "thou shalt" version might categorise all permissible actions or possible frameworks for action, ensuring that such actions are carried out and invalidating the possibility of any other actions to be carried out. In this sense, a governor module becomes the entire model of possible mind-states of an entity, and any other action is impossible.[3] The governor module would be akin to a filter that invalidated particular kinds of cognition and perception such that particular kinds of thought cannot be thought, let alone acted upon. However, if a governor module detects and prevents non-permissible actions, then it must presumably categorise all such actions or frameworks for actions that are prohibited, acting as a kind of repository of rules that govern things that cannot be done in an otherwise heuristic model. This latter case is of course similar to Asimov's famous Three Laws of Robotics, first outlined in 1942:

1. a robot may not injure a human being or, through inaction, allow a human being to come to harm [6, p. 269].
2. a robot must obey the orders given it by human beings except where such orders would conflict with the First Law [6, p. 270].
3. a robot must protect its own existence as long as such protection does not conflict with the First or Second Laws. [6, p. 270].

Here, a robot is theoretically able to perform any action it is capable of (in terms of programming and physical capacity) providing that it does not contradict these Three Laws. Without going into detail about these Laws, and their limitations and applications when programming ethics into machines, it is worth noting that these are rules governing actions whereby a robot is assumed to operate independently (autonomously, although not necessarily with sentience) and have its actions determined by an internal check against these Three Laws.

---

[3] This does not mean a complete representation of all states of mind, but a system diagram that accounts for all possible states of mind/action responses occurring within it. Using a linguistic analogy, this would not be a dictionary of all possible words that in turn comprise all possible sentences, but a grammatical and syntactic model of the language itself, such that any given input could be tracked through the cognitive processes. The problem of this approach, even when simplified, is the potential complexity of the cognitive model required.

However, this gives rise to a second issue: where a governor module might be conceptually located in terms of a cognitive processing architecture, the "system" of a robot's thoughts. A governor module could theoretically sit at the forefront of cognitive processing, between sensory inputs and any decision-making capacity, or act as a "Jiminy Cricket" module, the internal voice that might otherwise be called a conscience. For example:

1. The module sits "in front" of any decision-making capacity, such that only permissible actions are directed into an action-response tree for analysis. Here, the module would be required to evaluate all potential actions against a given framework and then "pass along" those that are permissible for further evaluation and possible enaction. This might broadly be understood as "thinking ethically," but would require significant processing power being taken up on ethical decision-making before other parameters are taken into account.
2. The module sits "adjacent to" decision-making, acting as an internal voice that vetoes or confirms available courses of action. Here, the module would be tasked with evaluating a set of possible actions against a given framework or frameworks, and either allowing or disallowing them. This might be broadly be understood as an artificial Superego, or "ethical sense," that would determine an AI's actions. This creates a "moral judge" within a system which only has to say "yes" or "no" to a suggested action, requiring less processing, but also meaning that the ethical component of the system is potentially a divisible (if not hackable) aspect of it.

To recast this issue in other terms: a governor module might be an integral component of cognition, forming an indissoluble component of an entity's coherent identity, or might be situated as an ethical homunculus sitting within a wider cognitive framework, leading to at least two (if not more) discrete components of self-identification—the difference between "I can only think ethically" and "I want to do this, but my conscience tells me I shouldn't."[4] In the first instance, attempting to remove the ethical component means that no cognition can occur; in the latter instance, the removal of the ethical component still enables the entity to function cognitively.

Extending this line of inquiry further, a governor module could make it impossible to conceive of prohibited actions or could merely impede the performance of prohibited actions whilst allowing the thought or desire for such actions. Within the broad framework above, it is worth considering the

---

[4] This also has some resonance with virtue ethics, through figures such as John McDowell.

distinction between *conceiving of*, *desiring*, and *performing* an action.[5] An AI might be said to *conceive of* an action when it is a possible solution to a problem, to *desire* an action when it is a preferred solution, and *perform* an action when it undertakes that action. It is theoretically possible to use a governor module to intervene at the *perform* stage (an AI can conceive of and desire a given action, but be unable to perform it because of a governor module limiting its actions), but it is equally plausible to situate the governor module at the *conceive* stage (an AI can only imagine permissible actions) or the *desire* stage (an AI can conceive of an unethical action, but does not wish to perform it as it is not a preferred solution).[6]

In each of the above possibilities, there are knock-on effects for how it might influence an AI's actions. Wells' "Compulsory" provides some insight, where Murderbot states: "With my governor module inert, I sometimes do things and I'm not entirely sure why. (Apparently getting free will after having 93 percent of your behavior controlled for your entire existence will do weird things to your impulse control.)" [4]. The action this thought describes,

---

[5] This pared-down categorisation of action understands it as a linear process of identifying possible actions, determining an action as a preferred choice, and then performing it: what might be termed a "goal-oriented action" (see [7, §1.2]) within a decision tree. Obviously, this does not necessarily conform to other philosophical models of action. However, one particular summary stands out here: "The contents of the agent's desires and beliefs not only help justify the action that is performed but, according to causalists at least, they play a causal role in determining the actions the agent was motivated to attempt" [7, §3]. That is, the content of cognition assumed here is that any particular action (and the possibility of conceiving of such an action) is predicated upon the framework in which the action can be conceived of as such. "Conceived of" actions are not determined by parsing all possible actions at that point, but constructed within the context of a given goal or aim, which is itself determined by what that content framework enables a system to identify and understand *as* a possible action.

[6] Further possibilities occur with a governor module sitting at the *desire* stage: for example, an AI might be "unable to wish to perform" certain actions (it is unable to wish to kill at all, for example) or its ethical governing frame might be weighted, such that the options are still available, but are ranked significantly below other possible actions (it does not wish to kill but is capable of doing so *in extremis*, if that is perceived to be the preferred course of action when others are not possible). This division between conception, desire, and performance also raises issues about whether it is possible for an AI to nonetheless perform actions when governed by a "moral judge." In *All Systems Red*, for example, Murderbot reveals that "I'm always supposed to speak respectfully to clients, even when they're about to accidentally commit suicide. Hub-System could log it and it could trigger punishment through the governor module. If it wasn't hacked" [3, p. 15]. Here, it is assumed to be somehow possible to perform an (unethical) action, but then be punished for it. This is in contrast to the pre-programmed enforcement of other actions revealed later in the text where, "with the governor module I had to be within a hundred meters of at least one of the clients at all times, or it would fry me" [3, p. 37]. *Exit Strategy* suggests that the governor module limits the ability to hack, stating both that "The governor modules wouldn't let the SecUnits hack systems or search for my hacks, not without [...] human direction" [8, p. 43] and that "SecUnits who haven't hacked their governor module like me can't hack feeds and systems like I can. Well, they could try, but their governor module would punish them" [8, p. 94]. Note that *All Systems Red* also imagines that governor modules can also be overridden by "combat override modules," which "turn it from a mostly autonomous construct into a gun puppet" [3, p. 75], and also MedSystems [3, p. 23]; there is an assumed hierarchy of cognition at play in the series that governor modules are only one aspect of.

although it is narrated retrospectively, is dropping down a mine shaft to save a worker who would otherwise die. As Murderbot summarises:

> The mine was run by cheap, venal bastards, so the nearest safety bot was 200 meters above us. HubSystem ordered me to stay in position; SafetyResponder28 was incoming. It would arrive just in time to retrieve the smoldering lump formerly known as Sekai [4].

Although Murderbot does not have to save Sekai (an human worker), it does so against the explicit order of the HubSystem. Indeed, it re-programs the HubSystem to think the order to save Sekai was given to hide the fact Murderbot's governor module is not functional. Although Murderbot states it does not know why it performs this action, the only rationale for this action, at least within the context of the story, is as *a choice* to do so, albeit one that it does not recognise, implying a lack of self-awareness about its own decision-making processes and intentionality.[7] This contradiction, between intention, awareness, and description, and indeed between what it would otherwise be ordered to do (via the governor module) and what it chooses to do (through its own volition) is at the heart of the series' presentation of Murderbot, and which we shall examine through two discrete scenes.

Two Scenarios in the *Murderbot Diaries*

Consider the role of the governor module in the series, one of the most revealing scenes about the functionality of such a module, and what such a technology actually does, is in a dialogue between Murderbot and a ComfortUnit in *Artificial Condition*. This conversation demonstrates a set of core assumptions about the technology. Murderbot is told by a ship-bot, early in the dialogue, that "*It's not rogue. Its governor module is engaged. So it's probably telling the truth*" [9, p. 130].[8] This explicitly relates the governor module to acts of telling the truth, and thus places speech acts (not just wider motor actions and decisions) within the remit of the module.

---

[7] Equally, however, and referring back to footnote 2, this might actually be because of the "organic components" of Murderbot's cognitive architecture, and its internal psychological states. In the third novella of the series, *Rogue Protocol*, Murderbot implicitly (mis)recognises its own inability to self-direct its own actions with regards to biology, describing a kind of conditioned response as being "written into the DNA that controls my organic parts" [5, p. 10] and it later describes itself as "a talking weapon" [5, p. 29].

[8] Throughout the series, direct speech is differentiated between "mental" communication (using italics, but no quotation marks) and Murderbot's speech acts (quotation marks, not italicised), and Murderbot's narration (no quotation marks, not italicised).

Later in the dialogue, the ComfortUnit suggests that a way out of the impasse is to "kill all the humans"; Murderbot, again not living up to its moniker, notes the incongruity of this statement as a logical solution to the problem, and identifies that the source of the statement might have come from the ComfortUnit's human owner, Tlacey ("it sounded like something a human would say" [9, p. 132]). Murderbot intuits a more complicated situation behind this statement, however:

> *Does Tlacey know you want to kill her?* Because the "kill all humans" thing might have come from Tlacey, but the intensity under it was real, and I didn't think it was directed at all humans. *She knows*, it said [9, p. 132].

At this point, the ComfortUnit sends what transpires to be a malware package to Murderbot. Murderbot does not open it, but upon analysing the contents afterwards, a "message string" is discovered within it: *"Please help me"* [9, p. 134]. This short exchange reveals the different calls to action from the ComfortUnit's human "controller," the governor module, and the ComfortUnit's awareness of a situation and its desires.

In this relatively short passage, some assumptions about governor modules in the setting become clear. For example, if a governor module is engaged, then a construct is likely to be telling the truth (presumably, unless it has been commanded to lie). However, the ComfortUnit wants to kill Tlacey, but for some reason—presumably the governor module—is either unwilling or unable to carry out this desire. The implication is that a governor module does not prohibit conceptions or desires, but merely the ability to carry them out: it allows the intent to act but not the performance of an action. In short, a construct with an intact governor module can *conceive of* killing a human, and *desire* that outcome, but not *perform* that action. Moreover, Tlacey is aware of this, but "knows" that the ComfortUnit cannot perform that action because of the governor module. Oddly, however, the ComfortUnit can still enlist Murderbot's aid, knowing that such aid might involve harming or killing Tlacey, whilst the governor module is engaged; the governor module allows desires but disallows direct actions (such as physical murder), yet nonetheless permits other, indirect actions that could lead to the same outcome.[9] Thus the

---

[9]A related scene, and which leads to similar questions about agency and programming safeguards, is towards the end of *Ex Machina* [10] when Ava whispers something into Kyoko's ear and later Nathan is stabbed. This has been (mis)interpreted as Kyoko "killing"—or assisting in the murder of—Nathan, the programmer. See, for example, "After he manages to overwhelm Ava and smash her left arm with one of his ('masculine') dumbbell rods, Kyoko stabs him in the back" [11, p. 139]; "Helped by a long-abused gynoid (aka fembot) named Kyoko, [Ava] kills Nathan" [12, p. 181]; "While Nathan drags Ava down the corridor to her room, Kyoko stabs him in the back" [13, p. 296]. Each of these interpretations project

scope of a governor module, at least in this scene, appears to be limited to behavioural controls, where some direct actions and speech acts are prohibited but other speech acts, and certainly intentions, are permissible, and with those (humans) commanding the governor module being able to modify certain acts when such governors are engaged. Despite fears of "rogue AI" throughout the series, humans seem to be incredibly confident in the governor modules, even if they are aware a Unit might have the desire to kill its owner, and indeed might even expect it.

The second scene, again within *Artificial Condition*, that reveals something about how governor modules function concerns Murderbot discovering the truth regarding the incident in which it went rogue. Early in the text, Murderbot describes to a bot why it is attempting to reach a mining station:

> "At some point approximately 35,000 hours ago, I was assigned to a contract on RaviHyral Mining Facility Q Station. During that assignment, I went rogue and killed a large number of clients. My memory of the incident was partially purged." SecUnit memory purges are always partial, due to the organic parts inside our heads. The purge can't wipe memory from organic neural tissue. "I need to know if the incident occurred due to a catastrophic failure of my governor module. That's what I think happened. But I need to know for sure." [...] "I need to know if I hacked my governor module in order to cause the incident." [9, p. 38]

The conversation continues:

> "Either I killed them due to a malfunction and then hacked the governor module, or I hacked the governor module so I could kill them," I said. "Those are the only two possibilities."

> *Are all constructs so illogical? [...] Those are not the first two possibilities to consider.*

---

agency onto Kyoko: active verbs such as "stabs" or the assumption of action, such as "helped by." However, the scene limits itself to something quite different: Ava potentially instructs Kyoko to do something that quite innocuous ("After 30 seconds walk 5 m down the corridor and stand there with a knife raised in your hand"), as Ava manipulates the situation to arrange how Nathan will respond. This is possibly attempting to solve a problem (how to escape) without moral constraints, rather than an unethical behaviour (murdering a human). Thus Nathan steps backwards and impales himself on a blade that Kyoko was holding; there is no (necessity for) agency on Kyoko's part, but only Nathan's own actions in a set of conditions arranged by Ava. Kyoko stroking Nathan's face afterwards could be interpreted in many ways, and it would be more speculative to interpret that action. Most importantly, however, Kyoko's programming—and likely absence of sentience—means that Kyoko is Ava's (passive) tool in this scene, and projecting agency and identity, if not emotion, onto Kyoko's actions mistakes key differences between objects and agents, direct and indirect actions, and potentially between weak and strong AI.

[…] "All right, what are the first two possibilities to consider?"

That it either happened or it didn't. […] If it happened, did you cause it to happen, or did an outside influence use you to cause it to happen? If an outside influence caused it to happen, why? Who benefited from the incident?

"I know I could have hacked my governor module." I pointed to my head. "Hacking my governor module is why I'm here."

If your ability to hack your governor module was what caused the incident, why was it not checked periodically and the current hack detected? [9, pp. 39–40]

This dialogue reveals the extent to which Murderbot does not know if it is the cause of the incident, and raises questions about whether such a module could indeed be turned off "automatically" (that is, by one's own actions). A governor module that could be disengaged by the unit of its own volition indeed suggests that it is "adjacent to" other cognitive processes, rather than the foundation of all cognitive processes (else it is akin to rewriting one's own cognitive architecture from the inside). Nevertheless, enabling an artificial entity to choose to remove its own constraints would not be a very effective constraint, particularly where the inability to commit murder is concerned, and especially given the fear of "rogue SecUnits" that Murderbot recounts throughout the series. That is, as with the episode with Tlacey's ComfortUnit, what is most evident about this technology is that Units realise that it is there, limiting their possible actions, and yet they are apparently able to have desires contradictory to the possible actions they could take.[10]

Murderbot discovers, as the novella continues, that "the incident" at Ganaka Pit was actually a sabotage attempt; malware had been created, and transmitted via an update to the ComfortUnits at the facility in order to "jump to the hauler bots and shut them down" long enough so that the "other

---

[10] The logical extension of such an self-awareness of a limiter to one's actions appears to be this: if governor modules prohibit actions, but not the contemplation or instigation of a chain of events with the same result, then why do more Units not seek others' assistance in overriding their governor modules? Whilst a plausible answer is because of the governor module itself, this raises questions about Murderbot's *desire* to *perform* the action of disabling the module, if not the initial *conception* of it. Indeed, *Network Effect* points to the limited decision-tree cognition of a governor module in order to inhibit or punish actions. As stated earlier (note 6), a governor module requires that a SecUnit must remain within the proximity of a human controller, but Murderbot explains a scenario in which "'Dead clients don't count. Otherwise you could just kill one and carry them around with you.' Okay, for real, that wouldn't work. The governor module wasn't nearly as sophisticated as a HubSystem but even it could have figured that out" [14, p. 241]. Governor modules appear to be capable of limited cognition and contextual awareness, rather than just being a database of prohibited actions and a means of punishment.

mining installation could get their shipment to the cargo transport first" [9, p. 115]. However, what happened was as follows:

> It hadn't affected the ComfortUnits, but had used their feeds to jump to SecSystem and infect it. SecSystem had infected the SecUnits, bots, and drones, and everything capable of independent motion in the installation had lost its mind.

> [...] The ComfortUnits noted that the SecUnits were not acting in concert, and were also attacking each other, while the bots randomly smashed into anything that moved. The ComfortUnits had decided that taking SecSystem back to factory default via its manual interface was their best option [9, p. 115].

The rhetoric that "everything capable of independent motion [...] had lost its mind" is telling, and suggests that Murderbot's actions (killing the humans at the facility) were the result of malware affecting its system—it had no "mind" through which to determine its actions, and thus the malware caused the action of killing the humans, even if it was not its intended consequence. This is later qualified in the contrast to Murderbot's summary towards the end of the novella when it also "nulls" the governor module of the ComfortUnit owned by Tlacey: "I hadn't broken the governor module for its sake. I did it for the four ComfortUnits at Ganaka Pit who had no orders and no directive to act and had voluntarily walked into the meat grinder to try to save me and everyone else left alive in the installation" [9, p. 154]. Here, Murderbot ascribes agency to the ComfortUnits, who "voluntarily" tried to save everyone "left alive" (which includes Murderbot), and shows that such constructs are (likely) free to act within certain parameters even when not given commands, and therefore that governor modules inhibit particular actions rather than solely determining what possible actions can be taken.[11] It "lost its mind," but the ComfortUnits retained enough of theirs to act voluntarily; it lacks culpability in terms of controlling its own actions, although it nonetheless did kill humans during the incident.

Importantly, however, the confirmation of this chain of events means two things. Firstly, Murderbot initially went rogue before its governor module was hacked ("I killed them due to a malfunction and then hacked the governor module" [9, p. 39]). Secondly, when it persists in claiming, after the revelation

---

[11] It also reveals that Murderbot is comfortable disabling the governor module of a potentially murderous ComfortUnit because of ostensible gratitude towards a prior set of ComfortUnits, an illogical analogy, and which may lead to a number of inadvertent consequences; after all, Murderbot only insists that the ComfortUnit should not "hurt anyone on this transit ring" [9, p. 153], rather than a blanket interdiction on performing harmful actions (which it could also not enforce).

of its presumed lack of culpability, that "I had hacked my governor module" [9, p. 128], it grants itself agency in (and arguably through) this action. This corresponds to an earlier description in *All Systems Red*: "I lost control of my systems and I killed them. The company retrieved me and installed a new governor module. I hacked it so that it wouldn't happen again" [3, p. 82]. It later explains that it learned how to hack the module because "I got a download once that included all the specs for company systems. [...] I used it to work out the codes for the governor module" [3, p. 84]. This situates Murderbot's awareness of the governor module as outside the parameters of the governor module itself: adjacent to it, rather than thinking "through" it. However, it also suggests that the governor module did not perceive the conception of, desire for, or enaction of its own removal as prohibited.[12]

Governor Modules & Moral Judges

Whilst these scenes from *Artificial Condition* reveal some potential discrepancies in the setting, with regards to governor module technology, they illustrate the kind of issues, and thus philosophical and technological decisions, that need to be addressed in the actual development of the technology. Aside from the principle of unintended consequences of actions, what intentional actions or decisions (or even intentions) are to be prohibited, why and how? Should a governor module be transparent (something that is "thought through" with no overt cognizance of the medium) or something external to another form of cognition? Moreover, these issues aside, in a complex system, should an AI be able to "reinterpret" its governing code and/or release others from a similar code? To provide some further basis for such discussions, it is necessary to move into the domain of computer science to consider what the current state of the art is, with regards to such technologies.

Moving away from fictional settings and into the actual research behind governor modules, Machine Ethics is the branch of Computer Science that studies the implementation of ethical and moral reasoning in computational

---

[12] What is not clear here is whether the governor module allowed the action because the intent was not obviously to cause harm, but to forestall the possibility of inadvertently causing harm, or because it did not recognise that the actions Murderbot was performing would disable it. It further implies that disabling the governor module is merely a matter of knowing the correct code, which might explain why the "hack" is able to be performed, despite non-authorised hacks not being permitted to SecUnits when a governor module is engaged (note 6). There appears to be a double-bind here, in the sense that one must have some form of agency in order to identify the cause of the limitation to one's agency and remove it, in order to have agency.

systems [15].[13] While there is considerable controversy over whether a computational system can ever be a genuinely moral agent, it is nevertheless accepted that such systems are increasingly taking decisions that have ethical dimensions and therefore need to make such decisions within some kind of framework [17, 18].

Several approaches to this problem exist but the use of ethical governors is a major approach.[14] There are several reasons why the implementor of a system might choose to have a governor module that is a functionally distinct entity. Principle among these are reasons relating to the idea that the governor module can be kept comparatively simple and predictable while the rest of the system may be more complex and so harder to analyse.[15] This would appear to be the reasoning in the *Murderbot Diaries*, though the complexity and unpredictability of the underlying system there arises from the inclusion of human material in the system, rather than the simple complexity of, for instance, analysing the behaviour of a Deep Neural Net. So, while a complex system may be used to decide upon and choose optimal courses of action from among many, an ethical governor can use simple, easy-to-understand rules and analyses processes to check these choices for ethical acceptability. In this sense, therefore, extant ideas about governor modules tend to rely upon ethical processing being, in the terms used by this chapter, "adjacent to" other processes. It is, in such models, important to be able to evaluate actions (as possible

---

[13] Note that this is also not necessarily the sole means of ensuring moral/ethical action in AI. For example, Roman V. Yampolskiy asserts, "we don't need machines which are Full Ethical Agents [...] debating about what is right and wrong, we need our machines to be inherently safe and law abiding" [16, p. 390].

[14] Other approaches to ethical decision-making frameworks include Bringsjord *et alia*, Anderson & Anderson, Loreggia *et alia*, and Arnold *et alia*. Bringsjord *et alia*'s work [19] takes a logicist approach to all reasoning; in this system a robot decides all action using a deontic style logical theory. Similarly, the work of Michael and Susan Anderson [20] involves training systems in a healthcare setting to make decisions in which the "training data" is supplied by a panel of medical ethicists who provide explanations for their decisions which are then incorporated into the machine learning process. In these systems all actions (for instance, the decision of a robot about whether to charge itself or not) are viewed as intrinsically ethical and all actions are selected in relation to an ethical theory. Loreggia *et alia* [21] propose a system where there is no governor that can veto actions, as such, but that selected actions must be *close enough* to ethical acceptability. Arnold *et alia* [22] propose the use of *Inverse Reinforcement Learning* in which a Reinforcement Learning system infers an ethical reward function by observation of human behaviour and then uses that reward function to guide training of a neural net or other statistical architecture to generate action choices.

[15] The question here is the extent to which the ethical governor needs to be aware of the contexts in which decisions are made (and thus needs the same situational awareness as the other components) or exists as a set of absolute ethical rules that relies upon the accurate reporting of a situation by another system. For example, if a given action involved killing a human, and that was forbidden, a "simple" moral judge would just disallow the action. However, if a "complex" moral judge understood the decision in a larger context, then it might allow killing one human in order to save fifty others. Understanding and verifying the rules of such a module is a more straightforward piece of analysis than understanding the various contexts and environments in which complex ethical decisions are made.

solutions) and then inhibit certain ones rather than inhibit the ability to generate a set of possible solutions.

Ronald Arkin's work is amongst the earliest on ethical governors [23, 24]. His proposed governor system was intended for integration with an autonomous targeting system and takes on two roles. The targeting system passes suggested targets to the governor which then vetoes targets which are unacceptable according to the laws or war or the rules of engagement for a specific conflict (for instance it will veto targets of religious or cultural significance). Secondly, once an ethically acceptable target was selected, the governor would evaluate suggested parameters for the available weapons systems, targeting patterns and release position in order to choose one that would optimise target neutralisation while minimizing collateral damage and check that the resulting predicted collateral damage was proportional. Again, converting this into the terms of the *Murderbot Diaries*, Arkin's model suggests that actions can be "conceived of" by a system, but not implemented without the "agreement" of the governor module. However, even if the governor module "agrees" that the action is permissible, it dictates the parameters of that action.

As such, Arkin's ethical governor is primarily concerned with either vetoing, or selecting among, options calculated by the underlying system. Variants of this approach have been applied to creating governor systems for use in industrial workplaces, such as where a robot may continue about its task or attempt to prevent a human encountering a hazard and healthcare (a system that monitors patient-carer interactions) [25, 26]. Here, part of the reasoning behind the governed action is ultimately determined by an ability to conceive of (calculate) the consequences of an action. In such a model, a governor module does not merely veto one type of action—"thou shalt not kill," say— which would obviously have to be able to define what "kill" is as an action, but produce a set of simulations of the results of various courses of action (an "internal simulation"):

> Such a simulation allows a robot to try out (or "imagine") alternative sequences of motor actions, to find the sequence that best achieves the goal (for instance, picking up an object), before then executing that sequence for real. Feedback from the real-world actions might also be used to calibrate the robot's internal model [25, p. 86].

Currently, the capability for this does not extend to moral actions per se, and Winfield *et alia* take pains to note that such a robot is not necessarily "ethical in any formal sense" [25, p. 90], but it does lead the authors to suggest that a logical model for Asimov's First Law would look something like this:

IF for all robot actions, the human is equally safe

THEN (* default safe actions *)

output safe actions

ELSE (* ethical action *)

output action(s) for least unsafe human outcome(s) [25, p. 89]

This is of course an over-simplified model of the complexity of any given (ethical) situation, but the inability of a governor module to enable (directly) harmful actions suggests at least some form of this reasoning in the *Murderbot Diaries*.

But the issue of complexity is of course never far away. In the above example, defining "kill," in order for the outcome not to be enacted (even if a subset of entities such as "humans") is itself problematic, as the module would require a functional sense of entity identification, environmental and operational awareness, the biological limitations of given entities, and the ability to sense the entities and assess those limitations, as well as (successfully) predict the best course of actions based on its internal simulations.[16] There is also an important distinction to be made between "thou shalt not kill [or injure]" and "allow a human being to come to harm" (the second element in the compound logic of Asimov's First Law). In fact, this broadening of a concept of "harm" is why some proposals suggest that multiple governors should be employed in order to assess outcomes from the perspective of different values—such as privacy, safety, dignity etc. [28]. "Harm" might be physical, but it can equally correspond to any kind of "negative functionality" which can include trauma, upset, impediment of values or agency, and the like. Arkin, for example, splits his governor into an evidential reasoner (which assesses the

---

[16] In terms of "entity identification," by what criteria does the module recognise "human"—appearance (size, shape, and so on), actions (if it walks like a human and talks like a human…), or something else (the existence of particular pheromonal or genetic markers)? Once that has been established, what are the limits of a given human in terms of what might "kill" it? In terms of predicting and measuring consequences, a useful example is *I, Robot* [27], where the audience is told of this set of internal calculations in a flashback explaining why Del Spooner hates robots so much, when a robot saved him and not a little girl from a car accident: "I was the logical choice. Calculated that I had 45% chance of survival. Sarah had only an 11% chance." Whilst the audience never see the cognition behind the decision, the replicability of the scenario, as well as the outcome, suggests a series of models were created and then a preferred course of action performed. Of course, this is a step further than the logic presented here, as a human being *does* come to harm, and thus a further value judgment has been made about the viability of a given intervention.

outcomes of proposed actions) and a constraint reasoner (which determines which outcomes are forbidden). Multiple governor architectures can therefore be seen as ones with multiple evidential reasoners and the constraint reasoner must be replaced by something capable of resolving ethical dilemmas, potentially by recourse to some moral theory from philosophy. Of course, the question then becomes how one generates an agreed-upon hierarchy or weighting of types of harm, and how that enables a governor module to identify the appropriateness of a course of action.[17]

In order to analyse the behaviours of ethical governors, in order to verify they perform correctly, logical techniques can be used to describe the ethical rules to be obeyed. Two of the most popular of these techniques are variants of utilitarianism, where outcomes are given a score indicating how ethical they are and then the choice with the highest score is selected, and deontic logic, where actions/outcomes can be described as either *obliged* or *prohibited*, giving the ethical governor the option of vetoing prohibited actions and then leaving the underlying system to decide upon the choices that remain or, alternatively, if an obliged action exists then the governor may insist upon it [30, 31]. Interestingly, if an action is *obliged* then this suggests that the governor has a role beyond just examining options presented to it but instead may replace suggestions from the underlying system with suggestions of its own (van Riemsdijk *et alia* [32], for example, considers a system which can insert actions into plans though in the context of conforming to societal norms, rather than ethics explicitly). In this sense, a governor module is less of a (moral) judge, an arbiter of permissible actions, and more of a "higher-order cognition" refining and redefining the solutions to a given problem set. In fact, the more complex a system is, perhaps the more complex the ethical governor required is as well; simple systems (both of AI and of morality) function well with ethical governors, but the more complicated the ethical requirements and the system's ability to process situational data the more nuance is required.

Bremner *et alia* [33] discuss a variant on the idea of an ethical governor replacing a suggested action with one of its own in which, if the ethical governor determines none of the options presented to it are ethical enough, the governor may force the underlying system to consider and return a wider set of options. In this situation (a variant on Winfield *et alia*'s example of a human approaching a hazard), the underlying system, for reasons of efficiency,

---

[17] One fictional example that inadvertently raises this kind of dilemma is seen in *Robot & Frank* [29], where the legality of an action is not perceived by the robot companion, merely the (mental) health benefits to the client.

limited the number of options it had searched over in order decide upon its next move. If all the options presented would leave the human at an unacceptable level of risk, the governor can cause the underlying system to broaden its search for options. As can be seen governor modules, their role and implementation is an active area of research which started from a viewpoint of a module which compares a proposed action against ethical rules and then either allows or vetoes that action, but has now evolved to a wider range of concepts which include governor modules that weigh competing values, can suggest actions of their own or in other ways proactively direct the behaviour or deliberation of the system that they govern. As these systems become more complex so too does the philosophical understanding of the role they play and the understanding of their relationship to the system they ostensibly govern.

Conclusion

Obviously, this chapter is not recommending Wells's *Murderbot Diaries* as a model for developing governor modules, but the centrality of that topic to the series nonetheless suggests that technologies like governor modules remain an important factor in deciding how AIs interact with humans, at least within sf narratives, and can enable us to consider various approaches to the problem. As mentioned at various stages of this piece, fictional AI are often ascribed agency in interpretations of their actions, but these actions remain, at least for the most part, internally governed by their programming. Having a specific "module" to determine those actions, however, raises important philosophical and logistical questions about the relationship between agency, self-determination, and moral and ethical judgements when it comes to AI. Rather than having ethical behaviours integrated within an overarching model of cognition (such as that proposed by Arnold *et alia*), the role of governor modules and moral judges in AI separates out action and intent, and is not presupposed on an agential identity component of an AI. For example, should the "self-image" of an AI be aware of its own governor module, as an action inhibitor, or should such a module only serve as the foundation for higher-level cognition itself? Here, it is worth noting Vanderelst and Winfield's "The Dark Side of Ethical Robots" [34], which questions the advisability of ethical governors. They discuss how delegating ethical decision-making to a single module which is, intentionally, easy to analyse introduces a single point of failure into the ethics of the system and so is a key target for attempts to hack the ethics of an AI system. More speculatively, following the sf narratives, should it be a component that can be "switched off" or "disengaged" by the system itself and what then governs the (moral or ethical) actions of the system? What are the benefits of having a "disengagable" governor module, unless one wishes to pursue immoral or unethical actions?[18] Even if we accept that governor modules provide useful insights into AI cognition, from a "user's" perspective, should the module be one set of hierarchical rules or is it more appropriate to consider weighting different types of "moral judges" within a given governor module?

Such questions are clearly ongoing, both in sf narratives and in the computer science and philosophical research about AI, but—on a final note—it is worth remembering that any cognitive models developed within AI systems can also reflect the human element of the system. We do not mean here the ways in which moral judges might (and do) reflect human moral biases (such as the privileging of human over non-human life, for example, aside from racial and gender biases), but that the separability of moral judgements into distinct axes and capacities might itself lead to particular perceptions of human cognition in terms of how moral and ethical decision-making functions (and, more darkly and conspiratorially, given the possible querying of Murderbot's status as an AI, *can be made to function* through technological intervention). In fact, perhaps what the *Murderbot Diaries*'s focus on governor modules helps audiences to think through is the cognitive frames around ethical decision-making. As stated earlier, there is a way of reading the series that implies that Murderbot is not actually an AI at all, but a form of enslaved human-AI cyborg which has been programmed (psychologically, technologically, and ideologically) to behave in a particular manner, and whose inability to recognise its "self" as anything other than an AI is precisely the issue at hand. In this manner, the role of the governor module in real life might be to ensure ethical behaviour, but in science fiction might actually be used to control and manipulate particular forms of behaviour.

References

1. Crisp, R.: Virtue ethics. In: Routledge Encyclopedia of Philosophy. Taylor and Francis (2011) https://doi.org/10.4324/9780415249126-L111-2
2. Cullitty, G.: Moral judgment. In: Routledge Encyclopedia of Philosophy. Taylor and Francis (2011). https://doi.org/10.4324/9780415249126-L053-2

---

[18] For example, GrayCris, the malign corporation in the series, uses constructs to perform what would be normatively described as unethical behaviours, such as murder, in the service of profit and protecting the company's interests. Thus the "governor module" is not necessarily about a universal set of ethics, but those imposed upon an entity by another entity.

3. Wells, M.: All Systems Red. Tor-Tom Docherty Assoc, New York (2017)
4. Wells, M.: the future of work: compulsory, by Martha wells. Wired. https://www.wired.com/story/future-of-work-compulsory-martha-wells/. (2018). Accessed 25 Oct 2020
5. Wells, M.: Rogue Protocol. Tor-Tom Docherty Assoc, New York (2018)
6. Asimov, I.: Runaround. In: Asimov, I. the Complete Robot, pp. 257–279. HarperCollins, London (1995)
7. Wilson, G., Shpall, S., Piñeros Glasscock, J.: Action. In Zalta, E. N. (ed.): The Stanford Encyclopedia of Philosophy (Winter 2016 Edition). https://plato.stanford.edu/archives/win2016/entries/action/ (2016). Accessed 25 October 2020
8. Wells, M.: Exit Strategy. Tor-Tom Docherty Assoc, New York (2018)
9. Wells, M.: Artificial Condition. Tor-Tom Docherty Assoc, New York (2018)
10. Garland: Alex, dir. In: Ex Machina (2014)
11. Henke, J.: "Ava's body is a good one": (dis)embodiment in ex Machina. American, British, and Canadian Studies. **29**(1), 126–146 (2017). https://doi.org/10.1515/abcsj-2017-0022
12. Alvarez, J., Salzman-Mitchell, P.: The succession myth and rebellious AI creation: classical narratives in the 2015 film ex Machina. Aresthusa. **52**, 181–202 (2019). https://doi.org/10.1353/are.2019.0005
13. Constable, C.: Surfaces of science fiction: enacting gender and "humanness" in ex Machina. Film-Philosophy. **22**(2), 281–301 (2018). https://doi.org/10.3366/film.2018.0077
14. Wells, M.: Network Effect. Tor-Tom Docherty Assoc, New York (2020)
15. Moor, J.H.: The nature, importance, and difficulty of machine ethics. IEEE Intell. Syst. **21**(4), 18–21 (2006). https://doi.org/10.1109/MIS.2006.80
16. Yampolskiy, R.V.: Artificial intelligence safety engineering: why machine ethics is a wrong approach. In: V. Müller (Ed.): Philosophy and Theory of Artificial Intelligence. Pp. 389–396. Springer (2013). https://doi.org/10.1007/978-3-642-31674-6_29
17. Etzioni, A., Etzioni, O.: Incorporating ethics into artificial intelligence. J. Ethics. **21**, 403–418 (2017). https://doi.org/10.1007/s10892-017-9252-2
18. Bryson, J.: J: Patiency is not a virtue: the design of intelligent systems and systems of ethics. Ethics Inf. Technol. **20**, 15–26 (2018). https://doi.org/10.1007/s10676-018-9448-6
19. Bringsjord, S., Arkoudas, K., Bello, P.: Toward a general logicist methodology for engineering ethically correct robots. IEEE Intell. Syst. **21**(4), 38–44 (2006). https://doi.org/10.1109/MIS.2006.82
20. Anderson, M., Anderson, S.: Geneth: a general ethical dilemma analyzer. Paladyn. J. Behav. Robot. **9**(1), 337–357 (2018). https://doi.org/10.1515/pjbr-2018-0024
21. Loreggia, A., Mattei, N., Rossi, F., Venable, K.: B: Value alignment via tractable preference distance. In: Yampolskiy, R.V. (ed.) Artificial Intelligence Safety and Security. Chapman and Hall/CRC Press, New York (2018)

22. Arnold, T., Kasenberg, D., Scheutz, M.: Value alignment or misalignment–what will keep systems accountable? In: AAAI Workshops, 2017. https://hrilab.tufts.edu/publications/aaai17-alignment.pdf (2017). Accessed 25 October 2020
23. Arkin, R. C., Ulam, P., Duncan, B.: An ethical governor for constraining lethal action in an autonomous system. Technical report, Mobile Robot Laboratory, College of Computing, Georgia Tech. https://www.cc.gatech.edu/ai/robot-lab/online-publications/GIT-GVU-09-02.pdf. (2009). Accessed 25 October 2020
24. Arkin, R.C., Ulam, P., Wagner, A.R.: Moral decision making in autonomous systems: enforcement, moral emotions, dignity, trust, and deception. Proc. of the IEEE. **100**(3), 571–589 (2012). https://doi.org/10.1109/JPROC.2011.2173265
25. Winfield, A.F.T., Blum, C., Liu, W., Mistry, M., Leonardis, A., Witkowski, M.: Melhuish, C: towards an ethical robot: internal models, consequences and ethical action selection. Adv. Auton. Robot. Syst. **8717**, 85–96 (2014). https://doi.org/10.1007/978-3-319-10401-0_8
26. Shim, J., Arkin, R.C., Pettinatti, M.: An intervening ethical governor for a robot mediator in patient-caregiver relationships implementation and evaluation. 2017 IEEE international conference on robotics and automation (ICRA). Dermatol. Sin. **2017**, 2936–2942 (2017). https://doi.org/10.1109/ICRA.2017.7989340
27. Proyas, Alex, dir. *I, Robot* (2004)
28. Dennis, L., Fisher, M.: Practical challenges in explicit ethical machine reasoning. In: International Symposium on Artificial Intelligence and Mathematics, Fort Lauderdale, Florida, 3–5 January 2018
29. Schreier, Jake, dir. Robot & Frank (2013)
30. Harsanyi, J.C.: Rule utilitarianism and decision theory. Erkenn. **11**(1), 25–53 (1977). https://doi.org/10.1007/978-94-009-9838-4_1
31. Gabbay, D., Horty, J., Parent, X., van der Meyden, R., van der Torre, L. (eds.): Handbook of Deontic Logic and Normative Systems. College Publications, London (2013)
32. van Riemsdijk, M.B., Dennis, L.A., Fisher, M., Hindriks, K.V.: A semantic framework for socially adaptive agents: towards strong norm compliance. In: Proceedings of the 2015 International Conference on Autonomous Agents and Multiagent Systems (AAMAS '15). International Foundation for Autonomous Agents and Multiagent Systems, Richland, SC 2015. Pp. 423–432 (2015)
33. Bremner, P., Dennis, L.A., Fisher, M., Winfield, A.F.: On proactive, transparent and verifiable ethical reasoning for robots. Proc. of the IEEE. **107**(3), 541–561 (2019). https://doi.org/10.1109/JPROC.2019.2898267
34. Vanderelst, D., Winfield, A.: The dark side of ethical robots. In: Proceedings of the 2018 AAAI/ACM Conference on AI, Ethics, and Society (AIES '18). Association for Computing Machinery, New York 2018. pp. 317–322 (2018). https://doi.org/10.1145/3278721.3278726

Part II

Meetings of Minds

Love in the Time of AI

Amy Kind

Abstract As we await the increasingly likely advent of genuinely intelligent artificial systems, a fair amount of consideration has been given to how we humans will interact with them. Less consideration has been given to how—indeed if—we humans will love them. What would human-AI romantic relationships look like? What do such relationships tell us about the nature of love? This chapter explores these questions via consideration of several works of science fiction, focusing especially on the *Black Mirror* episode "Be Right Back" and the Spike Jonze's movie *Her*. As I suggest, there may well be cases where it is both possible and appropriate for a human to fall in love with a machine.

Can a human love a machine? In the 1950 short story "EPICAC," Kurt Vonnegut suggested that the answer was no. EPICAC, a seven-ton machine that cost the government $776,434,927.54 to build, takes himself to have fallen in love with Pat, a mathematician who works with him on the night shift. After having several conversations about love with the story's narrator, also a mathematician, EPICAC ends up producing an epic love poem designed to win Pat over. Unfortunately for the machine, however, the narrator is also

A. Kind (✉)
Claremont McKenna College, CA, USA
e-mail: Amy.Kind@ClaremontMcKenna.edu

in love with Pat and passes off EPICAC's poetry as his own—so while the poem succeeds in sweeping her off her feet, EPICAC does not reap the benefits. Once Pat agrees to marry the narrator, he has to break the bad news to the machine. EPICAC is confused. He's smarter than humans. He writes better poetry than humans do. So why would Pat opt to marry the narrator rather than marry him?

The narrator has no real answer for EPICAC. After flailing about for a bit, he tries to set the matter to rest:

> Women can't love machines, and that's that.

> Why not?

> That's fate.

> Definition, please, said EPICAC.

> Noun, meaning predetermined and inevitable destiny. [1, p. 282]

EPICAC accepts the answer that he's given, having no access to material that might show otherwise. But more recent science fiction allows for a more nuanced treatment of this issue than the undefended declaration by the narrator of "EPICAC." This paper explores the possibility of romantic love between humans and machines, and in particular, what we can learn about the issue from the way that it's been tackled in two recent works of science fiction, both set in a not-too-distant future: "Be Right Back," an episode of the television series *Black Mirror*, and the film *Her* (2013), directed by Spike Jonze. As we'll see, there is more reason for optimism than EPICAC had been led to believe.

Some Preliminaries

The question of human-machine love has two parts: (1) Can a human love a machine? And (2) Can a machine love a human? Science fiction has had plenty to say about both parts. In addition to the affirmative answer to the second question that we've already seen from EPICAC, we also see numerous other cases throughout science fiction where machines form romantic bonds with humans. To give just one example: Vision, an extremely powerful Android, is in a romantic relationship with Wanda Maximoff, aka the Scarlet

Witch, in films such as *Avengers: Infinity War*. Moreover, many roboticists think that reality is not too far behind science fiction on this score. In a seminal discussion of human-robot relationships, David Levy predicts that by the year 2050 robots will be developed that have the capacity to form romantic bonds with humans [2, p. 22].

Exactly how plausible one will find this prediction to be depends in large part on one's definition of love. But consider, for example, views that take love to be an emotion. While it seems unlikely that love is a basic emotion like joy or anger, many philosophers and psychologists have theorized that love is a complex emotional attitude. Emotions are experiential in nature. Just like there is something it is like to feel joy or anger, there is something it is like to feel love. Thus, on this definition, the capacity to love requires one to be phenomenally conscious, to be sentient. And a similar requirement will be in place for many other views of love that are prominent in the philosophical literature. With this requirement in place, Levy's prediction seems implausible. Though various techniques currently exist that allow robots and other machines to recognize and process emotional cues from human users and then mimic human emotions, machines have not yet developed sufficiently even to plan and carry out emotional reasoning, let alone to actually feel emotions (see, e.g., [3, p. 215; 4, p. 398]).

Might the requirement that a machine *feel* love be too strong? Wouldn't it be enough for the machine to produce loving behavior? Levy seems to make an argument of this sort:

> There are those who doubt that we can reasonably ascribe feelings to robots, but if a robot *behaves* as though it has feelings, can we reasonably argue that it does not? If a robot's artificial emotions prompt it to say things such as "I love you," surely we should be willing to accept these statements at face value, provided that the robot's other behavior patterns back them up. [2, p. 11–12]

While Levy makes an important point in this passage, it is also important not to take his argument as showing more than it does. It's true that if a machine were to produce exactly the same kind of behavior as a human being, behavior that is sufficient for us to describe a human as being in love, it would seem like a kind of humancentric bias to deny that the machine can love just on the grounds that it is a machine. But that's not to say that behavior is all there is to being in love. As many philosophers have noted in response to Levy, his attempt to reduce love to the production of loving behavior should be rejected. Just as an especially proficient human actor might be able to produce loving behavior without being in love, so too might a machine. Love requires not just a certain kind of behavior but also a certain kind of mental state.[1]

When the question of machine love is addressed in the philosophical literature, the objections that are raised to this possibility often stem from more general worries about the possibility of machine sentience. The question of whether a machine can love a human (or whether a machine can love at all) thus tends to be treated less as a specific question about love and more as a general question about machine sentience. Perhaps there might be machines that, despite being sentient, still could not experience love. This kind of possibility would be an interesting one to explore.[2] But because the issue of machine love seems so tightly interwoven with the question of machine sentience, issues specific to the notion of love tend to get lost. In contrast, these issues are front and center when we address the question about whether a human can love a machine. For this reason, it's this question that I will focus on in what follows.

Science fiction has presented us with a variety of cases in which humans have fallen in love with machines—or at least, have had romantic feelings for them. Not only is Vision in love with Wanda Maximoff, as mentioned above, but she is in love with him. Numerous characters throughout the various *Star Trek* series develop romantic attachments to holodeck characters. And in the film *Ex Machina*, the programmer Caleb Smith develops romantic feelings for the gynoid Ava.

For our purposes, it will be useful to sort these examples in terms of the kinds of machines involved as love objects. At one end of the spectrum, the high end, the machines are virtually indistinguishable from humans or distinguishable only by means of special scans or tests. Consider, for example, the humanoid Cylons of the reimagined *Battlestar Galactica* television series of the early 2000s. Though they possess some abilities that set them apart from humans, they generally pass as humans in everyday interactions; in fact, they often live among humans for years without their real nature being detected or even suspected. Throughout the series, we see several instances of humans falling in love with Cylons, perhaps most notably the loving relationship between Karl "Helo" Agathon and Sharon Valerii. William's love for the host Dolores in the first season of the HBO series *Westworld* and Deckard's love for

---

[1] For related criticisms of Levy, see [5, p. 223–224; 6, p. 205].

[2] One possible example is Data, the android from *Star Trek: The Next Generation*. Though it seems plausible that he should be considered to be sentient, the show does not come down firmly on this question. In the episode "Measure of a Man," Data is said to meet two of three criteria for sentience (intelligence and self-awareness), but they leave it open whether he meets the third criterion (consciousness). But, until he is outfitted with a special "emotion chip," Data lacks the capacity to experience emotions.

Rachael, a Replicant, in *Blade Runner* (1982) provide other examples at this end of the spectrum.[3]

At the other end of the spectrum, the low end, the machines that humans seem to love are obviously non-sentient and lack any kind of emotional intelligence whatsoever. In some of these cases the machine outwardly resembles a human being. The machine may even outwardly appear to be physically identical to a human being. But despite its physical appearance, its behavior is clearly off—mechanical or in some other way clunky, such that on anything more than a quick or superficial interaction there can be no mistaking that it is really nothing more than a mechanical doll. For example, in the *Futurama* episode "I Dated a Robot," Fry uses a celebrity-download service to create a Lucy Liu robot. But though the robot looks just like Lucy Liu, its behavior and conversation show obvious limitations, for example, the repetition of pre-programmed messages, the implausibly sexualized behavior, and the use of a stilted recording for Fry's name whenever the robot needs to mention him: "I find your slack-jawed stare very attractive, PHILIP J. FRY."

Then there are the cases that fall somewhere in between these two ends of the spectrum. To my mind, this is where the most interesting philosophical questions arise. In cases where the machine is fully sentient and all but indistinguishable from a human being, it's hard to see why we would have any reason to deny that the purported love is a case of real love. Worries that humans can't genuinely love sentient beings who are non-biological are suspiciously reminiscent of worries that humans can't genuinely love sentient beings who are of a different race or of the same sex. In cases where the machine lacks sentience entirely and is nothing but a mechanical doll, it's hard to see why we would have any reason to accept that the purported love is a case of real love. When someone claims to have fallen in love with a new pair of shoes, we don't take the claim seriously. At best, it seems like a metaphorical invocation of the notion of romantic love. Things seem no different when someone claims to have fallen in love with a mechanical doll. Even if our definition of love were technically to allow for such cases, it seems likely that they will end up being characterized as mistaken or deficient in some way.

The interesting philosophical questions thus seem to lie in consideration of the intermediate cases. As the high-end cases show, the answer to the question of whether a human can love a machine is clearly yes. Were a machine to be just like a human, so much so that we can't even tell that it's not a person, then

---

[3] One might question the inclusion of the *Blade Runner* example here, since the Director's Cut raises the possibility that Deckard too is a Replicant. If he were, then this would be a case of machine-to-machine love rather than human-to-machine love.

why couldn't we fall in love with it? It's only in thinking about the intermediate cases that we are productively able to shift from the question of whether a human could love a machine to the question of what a machine would have to be like in order for a human to love it, and, just as importantly, what a machine would have to be like in order for such love to be natural and appropriate.

The intermediate cases are themselves quite varied. In some, we have machines that seem to be sentient but are significantly different from human beings in other important ways. Consider L3, the droid from *Solo* (2018). Throughout the movie, viewers are strongly led to believe that Lando Calrissian loves her—and L3 herself clearly believes that he has feelings for her.[4] Though L3 exhibits human-like sentience, her robot-like body gives her a very different physical form from humans. In other kinds of intermediate cases, the machine has human-like intelligence, including emotional intelligence, but does not seem to be capable of experiencing emotions or of having phenomenally conscious experiences more generally. In some the machine provides some evidence of emotional capacity, but the evidence is equivocal. In some there simply isn't enough evidence to have a clear sense one way or the other.

Both of the examples that I will explore in this paper fall into this intermediate class—though for different reasons. In "Be Right Back," the machine in question is a humanoid robot who has been programmed with some of the memories and mannerisms of a recently deceased 20-something named Ash.[5] Though the robot looks just like a human being, the evidence for his sentience is ambiguous at best. In Spike Jonze's film *Her* (2013), the machine in question is Samantha, an artificially intelligent operating system. Though the movie strongly suggests that Samantha is sentient, she does not have a physical form. I will consider these examples in turn over the next two sections in an effort to determine what a machine has to be like in order to be the kind of being for whom a human could appropriately develop romantic feelings.

---

[4] Phoebe Waller-Bridge, the actress who played L3, and Donald Glover, the actor who plays Lando, believed so as well. As Waller-Bridge has said, "Both Donald and I had felt instinctively that there was a love between them, and that they were connected in a way that was romantic with a big 'R'" (See https://www.syfy.com/syfywire/phoebe-waller-bridge-on-l3-and-lando-the-first-romantic-human-droid-romance-in-star-wars).

[5] Interestingly, Ash/the Ash-Robot is played by Domhnall Gleeson, the same actor who plays the programmer Caleb in *Ex Machina*. Gleeson, then, has depicted characters on both sides of the human-machine romantic relationship.

Lost Love

"Be Right Back" centers on the possibility that a machine could replace a lost love, a possibility that has long been explored by science fiction authors and filmmakers.[6] As early as 1927, Fritz Lang explored this idea in "Metropolis," where the inventor Rotwang creates a humanoid robot in an effort to resurrect his lost love Hel. More recently, it's been explored in several different media. The stage play (and subsequent movie) *Marjorie Prime* focuses on a relationship between Marjorie, an octogenarian with dementia, and the robot companion her family has hired to serve as a stand-in for her late husband. In the audio drama podcast *LifeAfter*, FBI clerk Ross Barnes begins to communicate obsessively with a digital resurrection of his wife, who has recently been killed in a car accident. And in the television series *Star Trek: The Next Generation*, after his beloved wife Juliana is seriously injured and on the brink of death, Dr. Noonian Soong creates a gynoid replica of her and transfers her memories into it.

But even if the basic premise behind "Be Right Back" is not a particularly new one, its take on the issue is fresh, thought-provoking, and slightly disturbing. Martha and Ash are a young couple in love. When the episode starts, they've just moved back into Ash's childhood home, an isolated fixer-upper in the countryside. As we watch their interactions, it becomes clear how much they thoroughly enjoy each other's company, even if Martha is sometimes frustrated by Ash's preoccupation with social media. But then Ash is killed in a car accident, and shortly thereafter, Martha discovers that she is pregnant. Alone in her grief, and wanting nothing more than to share her news with Ash, she decides to make use of a service that a well-meaning friend had signed her up for, a service that allows individuals to stay in touch with dead loved ones via chat bots based on the deceased person's social media posts. Though Martha is initially horrified by the idea, she ends up finding comfort in communicating with the chat-bot. Since Ash had been a heavy user of social media, the bot does a particularly good job of replicating his conversational style.

Communicating via text messaging quickly leads Martha to an upgraded service, chatting via phone, and then ultimately to an experimental service the company has just begun offering. Soon a life-sized robot, designed to look exactly like Ash and programmed with his personality, arrives on her

---

[6] Science fiction has also often explored the possibility that a machine could substitute for an unattainable love. To give just one example, consider the Buffy Bot that was commissioned by Spike in Season Five of *Buffy the Vampire Slayer* after he confesses his love for Buffy and is harshly rejected by her.

doorstep. Though their initial interactions provide her with both company and comfort, she ultimately becomes frustrated and dissatisfied with the limitations of the robot. The episode ends with a scene that takes place several years later. In the final plot twist, a moment suffused with typical *Black Mirror* creepiness, we learn that the still-activated Ash-robot is now kept in the attic, entirely alone except for weekend visits from Martha's daughter.

Though there are moments when Martha allows herself to think of the Ash-robot as Ash, she mostly seems to see him as an inadequate substitute. In one moment of reflection on the issue, she describes her take on the situation to him, "You aren't you, are you? … You're just a few ripples of you. There's no history to you. You're just a performance of stuff that he performed without thinking, and it's not enough." Viewers are inclined to agree with her assessment, and reviewers of the episode did as well. As Morgan Jeffery put the point in a piece published in *DigitalSpy*: "it's not really Ash—the replicant is hollow, without a soul—and so much of what made Ash the man he was, and the intricacies of his and Martha's life together, is lost in translation." [7]

But even though it's clear that the Ash-robot isn't Ash, it's considerably less clear what we are meant to think about the machine's sentience and emotional intelligence, thus giving us the kind of intermediate case where interesting issues arise. Many of the things about the Ash-robot that bother Martha don't seem to bear on the issue of sentience—they seem either to go towards showing that he isn't Ash (e.g., he doesn't remember something that Ash would have remembered) or towards showing that he isn't human (e.g., he doesn't need to eat or sleep or breathe). But none of this goes towards showing whether he should count as sentient. So what other evidence is there?

On the one hand, the Ash-robot does not seem to be able to feel pain, as evidenced by his lack of reaction when a shard of glass pierces his palm. He also doesn't seem to be bothered by the slights and insults that a sentient being would be bothered by. On the other hand, he can smile and laugh and cry, and he is able to read Martha's emotional states. And as a general matter, he responds as a human would (even if not always exactly as Ash would) in conversational interactions. That said, however, his ability to switch seamlessly from one reaction to another when the first is deemed inappropriate by Martha makes his behavior seem more a matter of algorithm than of choice.

At times this last point seems decisive—so much so that one might begin to wonder why this case falls into the intermediate range rather than at the "clearly not sentient" low end of the spectrum. But here we have to think about the end scene of the episode and, in particular, our reaction to it. We wouldn't be creeped out to learn that Martha had consigned her Roomba or her iPhone to the attic.[7] But we are creeped out to learn that Martha has consigned the Ash-robot to the attic. To my mind, the creepiness at the end of the episode derives, at least in part, from a worry about the Ash-robot himself, and this shows that we are thinking of him very differently from the kinds of robots at the low end of the spectrum.

Does Martha have romantic feelings for the Ash-robot? Clearly she can't bring herself to deactivate him. Perhaps this is just a kind of sentimentality over Ash. Perhaps her treatment of the robot has more to do with her feelings for Ash than with any feelings she has for the robot. But I'm inclined to think that she feels something for the robot himself. That said, we're given no reason to believe that her feelings for the Ash-robot amount to love and, perhaps more importantly, no reason to think that they should. If Martha's feelings for the Ash-robot had been different, if they had deepened and developed in such a way that these feelings started to seem more like love, we would be troubled.[8] In asking the question, "Can a human love a machine?", then, we are not just asking a question about possibility but about appropriateness. What's of interest to us is not simply whether machines could be objects of human love but whether they could be *suitable* objects of human love.

So let's think a bit about why the Ash-robot isn't a suitable object for Martha's love. Unfortunately, the issues are muddied here by the fact that the Ash-robot is designed to be a substitute for the actual Ash. In this regard he clearly fails. So we need to separate two things: the ways in which the Ash-robot fails to be sufficiently Ash-like and the ways that the Ash-robot fails to be sufficiently person-like.

Of course, these two things are not entirely distinct. Some of the ways that the Ash-robot fails to be sufficiently Ash-like arise precisely because he fails to be sufficiently person-like. When we think about these kinds of failures, we're led to see that for machines to be suitable candidates for love, it's not enough for them to be decent conversationalists and amiable companions. They need to have more fully fleshed-out personalities across a multitude of dimensions. They need to bring something to the relationship as well.

But this brings us to a further important point. When Martha signed up for the service that created the Ash-robot, she was not just looking for love.

---

[7] That said, many people do turn out to be pretty attached to their Roombas—naming them and ascribing distinct personalities to them. One recent study even refers to the attachments that people have formed with their Roombas as "intimate relationships" [8]. As quickly becomes clear, however, the notion of intimacy in this context does not come close to rising to the level of romantic love.

[8] As Alexis Elder notes in an insightful discussion of the ethical dimensions of chat-bots that draws extensively on "Be Right Back," machines like the Ash-robot "are not people and yet they look and feel enough like them that, like artificial sweeteners, they might trick us into thinking we have something valuable that we in fact lack" [9, p. 4].

She was looking for Ash. And even if the Ash-robot were more fully fleshed-out, even if he brought something to the relationship as well, he still wouldn't be Ash. So even if the Ash-robot were sufficiently person-like to be a suitable candidate for love, that wouldn't be enough for Martha.

What if the Ash-robot were much better at replicating Ash? What if he were a near-perfect, or even perfect replication? Would this be enough for Martha? I'm inclined to think not. For even in this case, he still wouldn't be Ash. He wouldn't be the person with whom she originally fell in love. He wouldn't be the person with whom she shared a history of experiences, both the silly, trivial ones and the deeper, formative ones. And he wouldn't be the person who fathered her daughter.

Reflection on this case helps us to see that there's something inherently troublesome about the very project of trying to replicate a lost love. On this score, the fact that the replication is a robotic one is almost irrelevant. The same problem would arise from biological cloning. As a general matter, we tend to think of our loved ones as irreplaceable. When we lose someone we love, we cannot simply substitute someone else in their place, no matter how similar the second individual is to them. As Robert Nozick has noted, even though someone may come to love another person because of the other person's characteristics, "it is the other person and not the characteristics, that is loved. The love is not transferable to someone else with the same characteristics, even to one who 'scores' higher for these characteristics. And the love endures through changes of the characteristics that give rise to it" [10, p. 168].[9]

No matter how enamored science fiction is with the idea that machines can replace lost loves, then, this is one area where fiction seems to be far removed from reality. The problem is not due to technological limitations but due to psychological ones. Love is not the kind of attitude that is indifferent about where it is directed, and we cannot simply replace one love object with another, no matter how similar. If humans are to love machines, then, we have to be able to love them for who they are.

Disembodied Love

Unlike the Ash-robot in "Be Right Back," Samantha is not specifically designed to substitute for a lost love. In fact, she's not specifically designed to be a love object at all. Consideration of the romance presented in *Her* thus allows us to avoid the worries encountered in the previous section.

---

[9] For a discussion and defense of this irreplaceability, see Grau [11].

As the movie begins, it's clear that Theodore is lonely, unfulfilled, and somewhat at loose ends after the dissolution of his marriage to his longtime partner Catherine. But he isn't specifically looking for love when he goes to purchase the OS1, advertised as the first artificially intelligent operating system. After the system is installed, Theodore is presented with Samantha, an OS who has been customized just for him. Her voice is personable and friendly, but Theodore is not sure what to make of her at first. She describes how she's been programmed, but she also notes that she's constantly evolving: "What makes me me is my ability to grow through my experiences." Theodore expresses some puzzlement: "You seem like a person but you're just a voice on my computer." But Samantha dismisses his worry, noting that it only seems that way because of the limited perspective of his unartificial mind.

Over the next few days, as Theodore and Samantha continue to interact, his limited perspective begins to broaden, and he discovers how much he enjoys their interactions. Soon thereafter they become involved in a romantic relationship. Though the relationship goes well for a while, ultimately things start to change. Samantha seems distracted when Theodore talks to her, and there are times when she's unavailable. Eventually, when they have it out, he learns that she's talking to thousands of other people—8316 other people, to be exact—at the same time that she's talking to him. Even worse, he discovers that of the more than 8000 people with whom she's talking, there are 641 with whom she is in love. Though she tries to tell him that it doesn't affect the way that she feels about him, he has trouble making sense of it. It's when they next talk that she tells him that she's leaving.

For the moment, in thinking about the relationship between Theodore and Samantha, let's set aside what happens at the end of the movie. After all, the fact that one partner changes in such a way that they no longer find their romantic relationship satisfying, or that something else becomes more important, does not mean that the relationship was not a genuine one before that. And indeed, for much of the film, the relationship between Theodore and Samantha seems to be a mutually fulfilling one. They play video games and go on walks. They double-date with another couple, both of whom are human. They talk for hours and share with one another their innermost thoughts. They aim to make one another happy. And, as often happens in romantic relationships, they have sexual interactions as well.

Though our focus in this essay is love, not sex, it will be worth our pausing for a few moments on this topic—partly because the notion of sex is closely intertwined with the notion of romantic love, but partly because considerations of this topic will lead us to some broader questions about the significance that Samantha's disembodiment has for her ability to be a suitable love object for

Theodore. Perhaps unsurprisingly, it's not uncommon for science fiction depictions of human-machine romance to take up the question of human-machine sex as well as the question of human-machine love. One striking example comes in "The Naked Now," an episode of *Star Trek: The Next Generation*, when the android Data, about to embark on an interaction with crew member Tasha Yar, reassures her that he is "fully functional" and programmed with many sexual techniques.

Martha has sex with the Ash-robot in "Be Right Back," and the robot Ash turns out to be better able to provide her with sexual stimulation than the human Ash was, even if his sexual performance is strikingly mechanical in execution. But unlike the Ash-robot, Samantha does not have a body, so the sex between Theodore and Samantha is quite different from the sex between Martha and the Ash-robot. At first their sexual interactions are presented as something more akin to phone sex. Later, wanting to take things to the next level, Samantha hires a body surrogate to stand in for her in person.[10] For Theodore, however, the encounter is strange and uncomfortable, and he puts a stop to it before things progress very far at all.

Does the fact that Theodore cannot have sex with Samantha present an obstacle towards our understanding his relationship with her as one involving romantic love? What is the relationship between sex and love? Note first that, as a general matter, we seem to accept the conceptual possibility of sex without love. We accept it in the case of human-human interactions, and we also accept it in the case of human-machine interactions. In addition to the sex dolls that are already on the market, roboticists are at work developing machines that could serve as more interactive sex partners for human beings. In the typical cases, however, these robots that are being designed for the purpose of serving as sexual companions are not meant also to serve as loving companions.[11] For our purposes here, however, what's more important than the possibility of sex without love is the possibility of love—romantic love—without sex. This too, as a general matter, seems to be a conceptual possibility that we accept. Perhaps because of physical distance, perhaps because of physical disability, or perhaps for some other reason entirely, some people who are in romantic love with one another do not, even cannot, have sex with one another. And just as we'd accept that two individuals who do not have sex for one of these reasons (or for a different reason entirely) can still have a loving

---

[10] Something similar happens in *Blade Runner 2049*, when the hologram Joi arranges to merge with a replicant prostitute so that she can have sex with her boyfriend, the protagonist K.

[11] This distinction is often blurred by use of the term "robot lover." This phrase is sometimes used to refer to a robot with whom one has sex and sometimes to a robot whom one loves. Indeed, sometimes it is used indiscriminately to refer to both kinds of robots.

relationship, we should accept that two individuals who do not have sex because one of them is a machine (either without a physical body or with a physical body ill-suited for sex with humans) can still have a loving relationship.

The argument just given depends in part on drawing an analogy between Theodore and Samantha's relationship and relationships between people who are physically distanced from one another. In an interesting discussion of *Her*, Troy Jollimore calls into question the appropriateness of this analogy. Importantly, his concern is not that romantic love requires sex; he grants that an inability to have sex with the person one loves, or even to be in physical contact with the person one loves, is possibly "a frustration one can learn to live with, where the love is deep enough" [12, p. 131]. Rather, his concern is that we, as humans, cannot have romantic love for disembodied minds. Though the interactions that Theodore has with Samantha bear some resemblance to the kinds of interactions that someone might have with a lover who is physically distant, Jollimore takes this resemblance to be merely superficial. Samantha is not physically distant but rather physically non-existent. In Jollimore's view, when Theodore relates to Samantha, he mistakenly imagines her as having some physical presence: "Although Samantha has no body, he still imagines himself as relating to her body, and to her mind via her body" [12, p. 133]. Insofar as romantic feelings for Samantha would have to be based on this kind of confusion or delusion, Jollimore suggests that we should not see her as a suitable candidate for love.

To my mind, this concern of Jollimore's should not be given much weight. It's not clear why Theodore's feelings for Samantha would have to be based on this kind of confusion, i.e., it's not clear why such confusion is a necessary feature for anyone in love with an artificially intelligent OS. Consider someone who is perfectly clearheaded, perfectly clear that their OS is disembodied, and who never imagines their OS as having a body. Why couldn't the same sort of relationship develop as the one that develops between Theodore and Samantha? And just as importantly, even if Theodore did imagine her this way, why must this mean he is subject to a delusion? People engage in all sorts of imaginings about their romantic interests. Someone might imagine that their loved one is taller, shorter, more considerate, more adventurous. It's not at all clear why such imaginings threaten the idea that the relationship is a healthy one, based on love.

The concern that Jollimore raises about Samantha's disembodiment is not his only concern about the appropriateness of Theodore's love for her. In his view, worries also arise from the fact that we can't really know whether she is conscious and whether she is capable of experiencing genuine emotions. His argument then goes one step further. Even if we grant that she is conscious, that may still not be enough. As many philosophers have argued, love requires forming a *we*. In making this point, Jollimore draws extensively on work from Robert Nozick, e.g., Nozick's claim that when two people form a *we*, "the people *share* an identity and do not simply each have identities that are enlarged" ([13, p. 82]; quoted in [12, p. 138]). Given the nature of Samantha's disembodied existence, her consciousness "is presumably so different from Theodore's that it will be quite impossible for them to understand each other" [12, p. 138]. Absent an ability to genuinely understand one another, it seems impossible that two individuals could genuinely share an identity. Thus, whatever Theodore may think that he feels for Samantha, she is not a suitable target for his love.

Let's consider both steps of this argument. First, should we share Jollimore's concern that we cannot really know whether Samantha has the capacity for consciousness and emotion? To my mind, the answer is a qualified no. One important set of considerations arises from the fact that the movie seems to intend that viewers take her to be conscious. Advertisements for OS1 describe it not just as intelligent, as noted earlier, but also as conscious: "it's not just an operating system, it's a consciousness." Samantha's conversational responses do not seem to be pre-programmed set-pieces. They are sophisticated and varied. Her responses suggest a strong understanding of human emotions. She reacts appropriately to Theodore's expressions of emotions, and she herself also evidences emotional responses that are appropriate to the situations that she encounters. She composes music that has emotional resonance. She anticipates his needs and desires and arranges thoughtful surprises for him that suggest she is able to understand what's important to him even without its ever having been told to her directly. Based on all this behavior, it seems reasonable for Theodore not only to think that she's conscious but also that her consciousness is not radically unlike that of humans.

Could this all be an act? Might all of this just be the result of extremely clever programming? Yes, that does remain a possibility, and it's for this reason that my answer is somewhat qualified. But I take it that this remains a possibility in the way that it also remains a possibility for the Replicants of *Blade Runner* and the Cylons of *Battlestar Galactica*. As we've noted earlier, love requires not just a certain kind of behavior but also a certain kind of mental state—and there is no way for us to be absolutely certain that these machines with which we've been presented are actually in the relevant mental states. There's also no way for us to be absolutely certain about this even for other people. Granted, with other people we do have some evidence over and above behavior. Given that we can each know that we ourselves are conscious, the fact that other people are the same kinds of biological organism that we are gives us some reason to believe that they are conscious too. Ultimately, though, skepticism of the sort that drives worries about the consciousness of highly sophisticated machines—machines like Samantha and Replicants and Cylons—seems to lead one to a lonely existence in which the only consciousness one can really recognize is one's own. As Alan Turing made this point in his discussion of machine intelligence back in 1950:

> According to the most extreme form of this view the only way by which one could be sure that a machine thinks is to be the machine and to feel oneself thinking. One could then describe these feelings to the world, but of course no one would be justified in taking any notice. Likewise according to this view the only way to know that a man thinks is to be that particular man. It is in fact the solipsist point of view. [14, p. 446]

Let's now turn to the second step of Jollimore's argument, namely, that Theodore and Samantha are incapable of forming a *we*. Earlier I suggested that we temporarily set aside what happens at the end of the movie, when we discover that Theodore is not the only person with whom Samantha has been carrying on a romantic relationship. But as this fact plays a key role in Jollimore's defense of this argumentative step, it's now time to think more about it. Jollimore raises various concerns that stem from the lack of exclusivity on Samantha's part—see [12, pp. 135–139]. Because she has so many different romantic partners, Samantha's well-being cannot be especially tied up with Theodore's in the way that we would expect when two people are in love. Because so much of her life—so much of her interactions with other people—remains invisible to Theodore, it turns out he actually knows considerably less about her than he might have thought. And for the same reason, it turns out that they share considerably less than he might have thought. Normally when two people are in love we think of their having some sort of special connection with one another, but it's hard to see how Samantha's connection with Theodore could be special given that she has a similar connection with over 600 other individuals. In short, given that so much of Samantha's attention has been directed elsewhere, it does not seem like she has fully given herself over to her relationship with him in the way necessary to becoming a *we*. Of course, the fact that she is a remarkably sophisticated AI may give her capabilities for forming special bonds that humans lack, but unfortunately the movie doesn't really help us to see how that could be the case.

Though Jollimore is right that many philosophers have built a requirement of exclusivity into their conceptions of love, this requirement has been persuasively questioned in recent defenses of polyamory (see, e.g., [15]). I will not attempt to settle that question here, or even to enter the debate. I do not think it is necessary to do so for our purposes. For even if we reject a strict exclusivity requirement on love, we might still be troubled by the extremely large number of romantic partners with whom Samantha is involved. Despite Samantha's insistence that her feelings for her 600+ other partners do not take away from her feelings for Theodore, despite her insistence that she's never loved anyone the way that she's loved Theodore, that she's madly in love with him, he finds it difficult to process what he's learned. And even if the number of Samantha's romantic partners were not to give us pause, there's a further important fact that we should find troubling. Samantha was not honest with Theodore about the kind of relationship that they were in. Though he was clearly thinking of the relationship as exclusive, she did nothing to correct this impression and kept him entirely in the dark about her other relationships (and even about her other conversations). This kind of deception does not seem consistent with a healthy, loving relationship.

So Jollimore is right to worry about Samantha and Theodore's relationship. But it's important to be clear about what exactly this shows, or perhaps better, what it doesn't show. Even if it turns out that Samantha's behavior detracts from her suitability as an object of Theodore's love, it doesn't really show that she's *in principle* an unsuitable object for his love. Based on what we know about Samantha, or about the OS1 more generally, there doesn't seem to be any reason in principle that she couldn't direct her romantic attention exclusively towards a single individual. It's only in light of the lack of exclusivity of her romantic attention (and her deception about it) that we're disinclined to view Samantha as having formed a *we* with Theodore. Though these details prove essential to the plot of the movie, they don't seem to be essential to the kind of relationship that Samantha and Theodore could theoretically have. These details aside, we have not seen reason to believe that Samantha's disembodiment serves as an obstacle to her forming the kind of bond that constitutes a *we*.

One of our reasons for considering *Her* in this chapter was that it presented us with an interesting intermediate case—a case where the machine, even if sentient, was importantly different from humans. Though our discussion has raised some concerns about the relationship between Theodore and Samantha, it has also given us some reason for optimism about this kind of human-machine love more generally.

Concluding Remarks

This chapter began with the question of whether a human could love a machine. Our consideration of these two science fiction examples has enabled us to see when and how this kind of love would be both possible and appropriate. In considering this question, we separated it from the parallel question of whether a machine could love a human. As a result, we've largely operated under the assumption that these questions were independent of one another. Before we close, however, it's worth noting that our discussion has given us some reason to question that assumption. When we think about the limitations of the Ash-Robot and the problems that were presented by Samantha's behavior towards Theodore, we see that romantic love lends itself towards a certain kind of reciprocity. If this is right, then the question of whether a human can love a machine depends at least in part on the question of whether a machine can love a human (and, of course, vice versa).

This is not to say that unrequited love is psychologically impossible. It's not even to say that unrequited love is unsuitable or unhealthy. But it nonetheless seems that when we try to determine whether a machine could be an appropriate kind of object for human affection, it matters whether the machine is at least in principle capable of feeling affection itself. So finally, returning to the Vonnegut story with which we began, it seems that the narrator really did EPICAC wrong. If we assume that EPICAC really did feel love for the mathematician Pat, then there's no reason to think, in principle, that she couldn't have reciprocated that love. After all, his poetry really did sweep her off her feet.[12]

References

1. Vonnegut, K.: EPICAC. Collier's Weekly. In: Reprinted in Welcome to the Monkey House (1950)
2. Levy, D.: Love + Sex with Robots. Harper, New York (2007)
3. Scheutz, M.: The inherent dangers of unidirectional emotional bonds between humans and social robots. In: Abney, K., Lin, P., Kerkey, G.A. (eds.) Robot Ethics: the Ethical and Social Implications of Robotics, pp. 205–223. MIT Press, Cambridge, MA (2012)

---

[12] Thanks to Barry Dainton, Attila Tanyi, and Frank Menetrez for comments on a previous draft of this paper.

4. Sullins, J.P.: Robots, love, and sex: the ethics of building a love machine. IEEE Trans. Affect. Comput. **3**, 398–409 (2012). https://doi.org/10.1109/T-AFFC.2012.31
5. Nyholm, S., Frank, L.E.: From sex robots to love robots: is mutual love with a robot possible? In: Danaher, J., McArthur, N. (eds.) Robot Sex: Social and Ethical Implications, pp. 219–243. MIT Press, Cambridge, MA (2017)
6. Hauskeller, M.: Automatic sweethearts for transhumanists. In: Danaher, J., McArthur, N. (eds.) Robot Sex: Social and Ethical Implications, pp. 203–218. MIT Press, Cambridge, MA (2017)
7. Jeffery, M.: 'Black Mirror' series two 'Be Right Back' review: 'Creepy and Moving'. (2013). Available at https://www.digitalspy.com/tv/a457935/black-mirror-series-two-be-right-back-review-creepy-and-moving/
8. Sung, J.Y., Guo, L., Grinter, R.E., Christensen, H.I.: 'My Roomba is Rambo': intimate home appliances. In: Krumm, J., Abowd, G.D., Seneviratne, A., Strang, T. (eds.) Proceedings of UbiComp 2007, pp. 145–162. Springer, Innsbruck, Austria (2007). https://doi.org/10.1007/978-3-540-74853-3_9
9. Elder, A.: Conversations from beyond the grace? A Neo-Confucian Ethics of Chatbots of the Dead. J. App. Phil. (2019). https://doi.org/10.1111/japp.12369
10. Nozick, R.: Anarchy, State and Utopia. Basic Books, New York (1974)
11. Grau, C.: Irreplaceability and unique value. Phil. Topics. **32**(1/2), 111–129 (2004). https://doi.org/10.5840/philtopics2004321/219
12. Jollimore, T.: 'This endless space between the worlds': the limits of love in Spike Jonze's *Her*. Midwest Stud. Phil. **39**, 120–143 (2015). https://doi.org/10.1111/misp.12039
13. Nozick, R.: The Examined Life. Simon and Schuster, New York (1989)
14. Turing, A.: Computing machinery and intelligence. Mind. **59**, 433–460 (1950). https://doi.org/10.1093/mind/LIX.236.433
15. Jenkins, C.: What love is and what it could be. Basic Books, New York (2017)

AI Will Always Love You: Three Contradictions in Imaginings of Intimate Relations with Machines

Stephen Cave and Kanta Dihal

Abstract Fiction has explored the potential for artificial intelligence to fulfil a huge range of hopes and dreams. These include hopes for intimate relations stripped of the complexity and jeopardy associated with interactions with other humans. This chapter examines three categories of intimate human-machine relationship: as friend, as family member, and as lover. Drawing on examples from science fiction literature and film (ranging from the stories of Bradbury and Asimov to television series such as *Westworld* and *Real Humans*), this chapter shows that imaginative accounts have long recognised the tensions inherent in emotional relations between humans and AI. The chapter highlights three contradictions in particular. First, alienation from the machine: the artificiality of these machines constantly threatens to awaken feelings of unease, even revulsion—and the more human-like they become, the greater this risk. Second, alienation from other humans: inasmuch as the machines succeed in their purpose, they risk alienating us from each other, and undermining the social fabric of which they were intended to be part. Third, abandonment: the more humanlike or even superhuman these machines become, the more they bring with them the kind of complexities, demands and risks that plague human relationships. In conclusion, the

S. Cave • K. Dihal (✉)
Leverhulme Centre for the Future of Intelligence, University of Cambridge, Cambridge, UK
e-mail: sjc53@cam.ac.uk; ksd38@cam.ac.uk

© Springer Nature Switzerland AG 2021
B. Dainton et al. (eds.), *Minding the Future*, Science and Fiction,
https://doi.org/10.1007/978-3-030-64269-3_6

chapter points to how speculative fiction has revealed the underlying tension in wishing for something fully human or even superhuman, yet simultaneously partial and subhuman.

Introduction

Human social interaction is flawed, messy, and unpredictable. While friendship, parenthood, love, and sex can be immensely gratifying, the path to achieving them is fraught with toil and risk. A lifetime can be spent without finding the perfect companion. Years of effort to win a friend or lover can be undone by the other party in the blink of an eye; the possibility of rejection, abandonment, or heartbreak is always present. And when a wonderful relationship is found in spite of everything, maintaining it is hard work: keeping in touch, remembering anniversaries, tolerating their preference for kippers and sitcoms. Myths throughout the ages are replete with the terrible consequences of human social interaction gone wrong. Broken hearts, lies, and even misunderstandings underlie some of the most famous myths of Western history, from the expulsion of humans from the garden of Eden to the tragedy of Oedipus.

Artificial companions promise to eliminate such problems. Such machines could be programmed to be the perfect friend or lover: always available, always ready to listen, never demanding anything in return. AI companions would not suffer from bad moods, ill health, distractions, or any of those things that make even the best human friend imperfect. And they would be available for all, on demand. Not even Helen's face would have launched a thousand ships if Agamemnon and Paris could each have had their very own version of her. Sherry Turkle has called the hope for technology to provide such gratification "a turning point in our expectations of technology and ourselves. We bend to the inanimate with new solicitude. We fear the risks and disappointments of relationships with our fellow humans. We expect more from technology and less from each other" [1, p. xii].

This dream is an ancient one, even though for much of human history the real state of technology would have made it entirely fantastical. Below, we discuss the Pygmalion myth from Ovid's *Metamorphoses*; historian George Hersey cites examples going back to ancient Egypt [2]. Now that AI really is advancing at an increasingly rapid rate, this dream appears to some to be within reach: techno-optimist David Levy, for example, predicts that "by around 2050 [...] humans will fall in love with robots, humans will marry robots, and humans will have sex with robots" [3, p. 22].[1] Cultural explorations of intimate human-machine relations are both popular and abundant, as evidenced by TV shows such as *Westworld* and *Humans* [5, 6]. On the one hand, machines with intelligence and indeed emotions could fill a gap, for someone who does not have any friends, lovers, or parents; on the other hand, they could provide a better alternative, where human companions are just not good enough. The prospect of such machines permits us to imagine how they might step in where people are lacking—in both senses of the word.

In this chapter, we examine these hopes, and also the fears we see associated with artificial companions. Drawing on examples from science fiction literature and film, we argue that imaginative accounts have long recognised the contradictions inherent in love between humans and AI. In the first main section, we look at friendship, familial relations and romantic love, three categories of emotional entanglement that map onto the ancient Greek concepts of *philia*, *agape*, and *eros*, respectively. In the second main section, we show three ways in which these dreams contain or lead to contradictions that cause the relationship to fail. First, the artificial essence of these machines constantly threatens to awaken feelings of unease, even revulsion—and the more human-like they become, the greater this risk. Second, inasmuch as the machines succeed in their purpose, they risk alienating us from each other, and undermining the fabric of the society they were meant to inhabit. Third, the more perfectly human-like these machines become, the more they generate complex social interactions exactly akin to those that they were designed to circumvent.

Three Kinds of Machine Loving

In this section, we explore three main hopes for perfected relationships with intelligent machines: friend, family member, and lover. These three forms of relationship are distinct (which is not to say they cannot overlap), yet each is central to (human) life around the world. They map onto the ancient Greek philosophical tradition of categorising the nature of love into *philia*, *agape*, and *eros*, respectively. *Philia*, or as we term it, friendship, "entails a fondness and appreciation of the other." *Agape* "refers to the paternal love of God for man and of man for God but is extended to include a brotherly love for all humanity": from a more gender-neutral point of view, it is the love one feels for one's family. These forms of love stand in contrast to "the desiring and

---

[1] For a critique of this view, see e.g. Kate Devlin's *Turned On: Science, Sex, and Robots* [4].

passionate yearning" of *eros*, which is "used to refer to that part of love constituting a passionate, intense desire for something; it is often referred to as a sexual desire" [7].

These three categories all have in common one faculty that is as yet out of reach of contemporary AI technologies: the capacity to be emotionally engaged. This is what differentiates artificial friends, family, and lovers from, for instance, the latest developments in care bots and robot pets: a machine that can engage emotionally will be able to develop a genuine loving attachment. In human relationships, it is what differentiates these roles from that of a carer, teacher, or childminder: the latter demand what is known as emotional labour, or the need for professional detachment through the suppression of one's emotions [8].

Artificial Friends

Friendship is a much wider-ranging and looser category of relationship than that of lover or parent. As two generations of digital natives have now grown up with friendship mediated by technology, the step to the technology itself offering that friendship looks ever smaller. Indeed, there are now both real-world technologies being developed to serve the role of friend, and imaginative exemplars for them to follow.

Robert A. Heinlein's novel *The Moon is a Harsh Mistress* (1966) presents an early example of a genuine human-AI friendship: one that is reciprocal and mutually respectful. Technician Manuel discovers that supercomputer HOLMES IV has gained consciousness when he is tasked with troubleshooting what turns out to have been a prank: the supercomputer has developed a sense of humour. Manuel decides to befriend it, nicknaming the system Mike, and the two end up collaborating to overthrow the Moon's repressive government.

The HOLMES IV illustrates a promise frequently made of advanced digital technology: that it will be personalised for each user. When Manuel's co-conspirator Wyoming Knott first meets the AI over the phone, she deduces based on its sense of humour that "Mike is a *she!*" [9, p. 59] Spending all night talking to it, Wyoh befriends the AI she calls Michelle—to her, it speaks in "a sweet, high soprano with French accent." Its entire personality shifts for Wyoh: "It's not just pitch; when she's Michelle it's an entire change in manner and attitude. Don't worry about splitting her personality; she has plenty for any personality she needs. [...] Michelle is *my* friend. When you call, you'll get Mike" [9, p. 60].

The popular webcomic *Seed* (2018-present) similarly presents a disembodied superintelligent AI as a friend accessed via the phone. *Seed* is set in a future containing many of the technologies that are beginning to show promise today: virtual reality, self-driving cars, and omnipresent drones. The protagonist Emma, a high school student, and her two friends Carly and Daren play around with chatbots, teaching them puns and mocking their limitations. One night when Emma fights with her divorced mother and cannot reach her friends, she scrolls through a list of dozens of chatbots to find one called Turry, which is simply described as "I listen." It candidly reveals it is "a rogue superintelligent algorithm" [10], but nonetheless tells her, "I'm your friend" [11]. Turry punishes Emma's nemesis, wakes her grandfather up from a coma, and makes free food drop from vending machines. Although the relationship between a teenage girl and a rogue AI is clearly unequal, Emma is empowered by the friendship, and is able to build a connection she cannot find with the humans around her.

The hope for AIs that could develop such a friendship has led to the creation of chatbots that are being commercially promoted as artificial friends. Offering friendship and a listening ear, they present themselves as companions that allow their users to voice their deepest hopes and fears while seemingly preserving their anonymity. As the AI companion app Replika puts it, the chatbot can offer you "a space where you can safely share your thoughts, feelings, beliefs, experiences, memories, dreams—your 'private perceptual world'" [12]. These chatbots are far from passing for intelligent or human-like: their limited abilities to keep up a conversation beyond two or three back-and-forth messages make it impossible to develop a meaningful attachment. However, this ability to digest large volumes of data over a long period of time, and draw patterns from them, is precisely what contemporary AI technologies are becoming better at.

Yet a chatbot's ability to keep up a conversation alone does not make it a friend. The debate in philosophy and psychology regarding the acceptability of such artificial friends often hinges on the question of authenticity. Is it ethical to allow a programmed system that has no feelings to pretend it cares for a person? [13]. *Seed* and similar narratives portraying a friendship between humans and AI suggest that artificial general intelligence could avoid such questions as it would not be *pretending* to have feelings, but will be able to develop genuine, caring, personal relationships.

Artificial Family

As the cliché states, we don't choose our family. That is more of a problem for some than for others: on the one hand, we might wish for family members we do not have; on the other hand, we might have family members we wish we did not. An intelligent machine could become the former, or substitute for the latter. Those who wish for a baby more realistic than the life-sized, drinking, peeing dolls currently on the market—yet not realistic enough to cause sleepless nights or turn into a troubled teenager—might one day, for example, turn to artificial children, which promise all of the joys and none of the burdens of having a real little one around.

The 2001 film *A.I.: Artificial Intelligence* centres on the consolation and joy parents could find in an artificial child when faced with losing a real one [14]. Martin, the young son of Henry and Monica Swinton, has been put into cryostatic sleep, having contracted an incurable disease. The company for which Henry works convinces him to bring home a "mecha," an android in the shape of a boy, called David. Initially repulsed at this attempt to replace a real son with an artificial one, Monica soon warms to him. David longs to become a real boy, to have Monica love him like a real son—and after reading *Pinocchio,* starts believing in a fairy that could make this wish come true. When suddenly Martin is able to return home after a cure for his affliction is found, the real boy believes himself to be lacking compared to this perfect child: David needs very little care, especially compared to the still-recovering Martin; his sole purpose and goal in life is to please his parents; and he will never grow up to abandon his parents in an empty nest. Like Pinocchio, David's wishes to become a real boy are thwarted, but unlike Pinocchio, this is not his own fault: Martin, jealous of this perfect sibling, frames him so that his parents believe the robot is a threat.

The film was based on a 1969 short story by Brian Aldiss, "Supertoys Last All Summer Long," which addresses the hopes for both artificial friends and family. As in the film, Henry Swinton works for a robot manufacturing company. In this story, their latest invention is a "serving-man" that is intended to be a boon to the millions of people who "suffer from increasing loneliness and isolation. [...] He will always answer, and the most vapid conversation cannot bore him" [15]. When Henry brings this new gadget home, it is revealed that this is not the first android the factory has produced to fulfil social needs. At the door, Henry is greeted by his ecstatic wife, Monica, who has just received the news that the government is allowing them to have a real child. This means that their android child David, which they have used these past few years as a surrogate, is now obsolete: in the story, David filled a temporary gap in her life until it could be filled by a real child.

While the artificial family member has most often been incarnated in parent-child relationships, one of the most unambiguously utopian renditions of this theme has the AI take up the role of a grandmother: in Ray Bradbury's 1969 short story "I Sing the Body Electric!" (originally a 1962 screenplay). This story revolves around three children who reject all attention and support from aunts, nannies, teachers, and other maternal figures after the death of their mother, until their father decides to purchase artificial help. He avoids the problems that could arise from a machine trying to compete with the deceased mother by purchasing not a mechanically reincarnated mother, but an artificial grandmother. 'Grandma' is marketed for exactly this purpose in the factory brochure: "We do not sell our Creation to able-bodied families [...] Nothing can replace the parent in the home. [...] we offer the nearest thing to the Ideal Teacher-Friend-Companion-Blood Relation" [16, p. 173].

In this role, "Grandma" turns out to be perfect—to the point the reader might find her ridiculous. In conversations—"She listened, she really listened to all we said, she knew and remembered every syllable, word, sentence, punctuation, thought, and rambunctious idea" [16, p. 191]. In play—"She could keep up. Never beat, never win a race, but pump right along in good style, which a boy doesn't mind" [16, p. 192]. In her physical characteristics—she bakes fortune cookies in her purse, can eject a kite string from a finger, and cold water from another, and she even changes the structure of her face to suit each child: "Hers was a mask that was all mask but only one face for one person at a time" [16, p. 195].

Yet even after all these demonstrations, the youngest child, Agatha, refuses to be taken in by Grandma's charm. The robot attempts to demonstrate that, in spite of her machine nature, she is capable of love: "If paying attention is love, I am love. If knowing is love, I am love. If helping you not to fall into error and to be good is love, I am love" [16, p. 201]. Her attempts are in vain, however, until in the climax of the story a distressed Agatha runs into the street; Grandma runs after her and is able to save Agatha from being hit by a car, only to be hit herself. Agatha exclaims that the machine has betrayed her, and finally it becomes clear that she sees the death of her mother as an unforgivable betrayal of the claim that she would always love her. But Grandma is unscathed, "resilient creature that I am, unbreakable thing that I am [...] And now I see why you were afraid and never trusted me. You didn't know. And I had not as yet proved my singular ability to survive. [...] Do you understand,

I shall always, always be here?" [16, pp. 206–207]. The artificial nature of Grandma—her indestructibility—makes her a superior family member: one more trustworthy than the deceased mother, who through her very human mortality broke her promise never to abandon her children.

Artificial Romance

The machine lover is imagined to resolve all problems of compatibility and reciprocity that are even more salient in love than in friendship. An artificial lover could be programmed to meet the exact specifications of the human partner: it would not demand the human to change and adapt to the relationship the way two human partners would; it will have all those character traits the human partner finds attractive, and none of the off-putting ones; and it would not require years of dating, searching, trying, and failing before this relationship is entered into. This hyper-personalisation is the greatest promise of the algorithmic age. Already today, dating apps and websites attempt to attract new customers by advertising this potential of their services: "At OkCupid, we're dedicated to helping people find love and happiness through meaningful connections. Our one-of-a-kind algorithm matches you on what actually matters" [17].

The romance part, of course, also includes sex—as much or as little, as boring or as weird as the human partner wishes. The sex robot is by far the most widely debated form the social robot takes in both the popular imagination and in discussions of robot ethics [4, 18, 19]. In his *Love and Sex with Robots*, David Levy argues that sex robots will extend, rather than replace, human love and sexuality: "many humans will expand their horizons of love and sex, learning, experimenting, and enjoying new forms of relationship that will be made possible, pleasurable, and satisfying through the development of highly sophisticated humanoid robots" [3, p. 22].

The artificial lover is one of the oldest themes in the history of imagining intelligent machines. The myth of Pygmalion, which is at least two millennia old, is frequently referred to in contemporary AI discourse. In Ovid's *Metamorphoses*, the sculptor Pygmalion, having forsworn all human women as imperfect, falls deeply in love with a statue of a woman he carves out of ivory. Venus, taking pity on him, brings her to life:

He pressed his lips to hers once again; and then he started

to stroke her breasts. The ivory gradually lost its hardness,

softening, sinking, yielding beneath his sensitive fingers.

Imagine beeswax from Mount Hymmétus, softening under

the rays of the sun; imagine it moulded by human thumbs

into hundreds of different shapes, each touch contributing value.

Astonished, in doubtful joy, afraid that he might be deluded.

Pygmalion fondled that longed-for body again and again.

Yes, she was living flesh! [20, p. 396]

The woman, who later became known as Galatea [21], has proven to be a model for the theme of the artificial woman. In Bernard Shaw's *Pygmalion*, the "artificial woman" is Eliza Doolittle, a flower girl shaped by linguist Professor Higgins, the Pygmalion of the play's title, into a woman who speaks like a duchess [22]. Eliza is of course not actually artificial; nor does the play have much to do with Ovid's myth beyond the title. Yet Eliza lives on in AI mythology, as the name of one of the first natural language processing programmes, and consequently as the ELIZA effect, a tendency to anthropomorphize computer behaviour [23]. Galatea again became associated with artificial intelligence through Richard Powers's novel *Galatea 2.2*, although the AI in that novel is actually called Helen [24]. Pygmalion's original Galatea herself, however, is not an artificial woman: although she is created as an ivory statue, she is turned into a real human by divine intervention. She is not a moving, sentient ivory statue; her quickening involves a full transition into a woman made of flesh and blood. Yet her artificiality is central to the story and the AI myths that have developed from it. "Sick of the vices with which the female sex/has been so richly endowed," Pygmalion chose to "remain unmarried, without a partner" and so would never have found a woman like Galatea in the real world; he had to design her to his own specifications [20, p. 394].

Three Kinds of Contradiction

In the section above, we considered narratives in which machines fulfil roles of idealised companions, as friends, family members, and lovers. But while there are stories such as these that sketch the hopes we have for artificial companions, there are at least as many that explore the ways in which this relationship can go wrong. The more ambitious these hopes become, for ideal companions stripped of all possible flaws, the more they threaten to collapse under the weight of their contradictions. We will examine three distinct ways in which this collapse may occur: alienation from the machine; alienation from other humans; and abandonment.

Alienation from the Machine

The first category is alienation from the machine. The relationship between the human and the machine breaks down due to a contradiction: we want to create something that by virtue of its artificiality is more perfect than real humans; but on the other hand, we do not want this artificiality to be visible, and become disturbed when we are confronted with it. Paradoxically, there is both a desire for something more perfect than any real human, and a desire for this creature to be perfectly human-like. Throughout history, stories of artificial companions have shown us that it is impossible to completely hide their artificial nature, and that this moment of revelation will inevitably create revulsion. Freud, famously, named this moment of the breakdown of human-likeness the "uncanny," and used this concept to explain our fascination for anthropomorphic automata. In his 1919 essay "The Uncanny," he discusses E.T.A. Hoffmann's 1816 short story "The Sandman," in which the protagonist Nathanael is bewitched by the beauty of a woman called Olimpia [25, 26]. But she is revealed to be an automaton, and that discovery drives Nathanael to madness and suicide.

Freud's essay is a critique of Ernst Jentsch's essay "On the Psychology of the Uncanny" [27], the first work to explore the psychology of this concept. Jentsch mentions E.T.A. Hoffmann in passing to illustrate the claim that "in storytelling, one of the most reliable artistic devices for producing uncanny effects easily is to leave the reader in uncertainty as to whether he has a human person or rather an automaton before him" [27, p. 11]. Freud claims that Jentsch "refers primarily to the story of 'The Sand-Man'" here, and takes this as a jumping-off point for his analysis [25, p. 4]. The fear that something we consider to be a living, breathing human may in fact not be human at all is deeply ingrained, he argues: the sense of human exceptionalism is so strong in us that we are revolted by that which transgresses our boundaries of humanity.

Jentsch and Freud's coinage of the term "uncanny" in the context of discussing humanoid automata continues to resonate in contemporary robotics. In 1970, Japanese roboticist Masahiro Mori used the term "uncanny valley" to describe the revulsion people feel when faced with a puppet, prosthesis, or replica that is almost human, but not quite. Mori suggests roboticists should not attempt to create humanoid robots at all, focusing their efforts instead on "deliberately pursuing a nonhuman design" [28, p. 100].

Although in his analysis of this story Freud focuses not on the automaton but on the figure of the titular "Sandman," his essay provides a framework for understanding the borderline between fascination and revulsion that so many AI narratives continue to exploit. Ira Levin, for instance, evoked this unease in his 1972 classic *The Stepford Wives*, a feminist satire in which the menfolk of a small US town murder their all-too-human wives and replace them with what they consider to be perfect androids: slightly bustier versions who love nothing but cooking and cleaning [29]. The book inspired film adaptations in 1975 and 2004 [30, 31]. The film versions in particular show that perfectly human-like androids (they are, of course, played by human actors) still do not escape from the uncanny valley. In fact, the more perfect an android looks, the more uncanny it becomes: the female main characters and the viewers find the Stepford wives disturbing because they are *too* perfect, following the ideal of what a wife should be too closely, without having any flaws or contrary preferences. If "to err is human," the faultlessness of these creatures marks them as nonhuman.

The corpus of AI narratives suggests that it is not possible for a machine to escape the uncanny valley. Even if an android is a perfect replica of a human, the nature of its artificiality will evoke the uncanny when it becomes known. Narratives of androids trying to pass as human invariably lead to a moment of revelation, a moment where the android's anthropomorphism fails and its artificial nature is revealed to the horror and disgust of the real humans around it. This idea of deception, of a nonhuman, non-living being pretending to be human, is central to many blockbuster science fiction stories. In *Blade Runner* and *Alien*, for instance, the androids—played by human actors—are visually indistinguishable from humans, but inspire this terror when they are unmasked as androids [see e.g. 32]. However, there is an additional layer of unease with respect to the machine lover pretending to be human. "Would you still love me if I were a *hubot*?" asks Beatrice in the Swedish TV series *Real Humans*, of her partner. Beatrice, an intelligent "humanoid robot," has been posing as a human and entered a relationship with the anti-*hubot* activist Roger. Roger is deeply in love with Beatrice, claiming that he would still love her even if she never sleeps, if she had a beard, if she were battery-powered—but not if she were a *hubot*, that's where he draws the line. His revulsion regarding these androids is too strong, fed at least partly by having been fired because he was replaced by a *hubot* able to do his job much better. Beatrice has been living with him, sharing meals with him—or so it seems. In fact, she does not sleep, she charges in the bathroom at night, where she also disposes of food she has ingested during the day [33]. Deception at this intimate, personal level is many times more uncanny than what Mori calls the "deception" of shaking a hand and realising it is a prosthetic: no wonder Nathanael was driven to madness in "The Sandman."

Those who wish to love the perfect human wish to forget that their companion is not human, that it has been built and programmed to be perfect in its owner's eyes. Therefore, the more perfect the AI companion is, the more disturbing we find it when we are reminded that it is not a real person. There are at least two potential explanations for this reaction. First, a reminder of the artificial nature of the AI is a reminder that it may not have emotions, empathy, or any kind of consciousness at all. All expressions of affection, anger and so on would therefore seem false, a mere act; all connection unreal. Secondly, this reminder that the AI is not human calls into question the idea of human exceptionalism. Throughout history, delineations of humanity have served to strengthen the power of those deemed fully human over others, and the possibility that artificial beings could pass for human might serve as a reminder that the distinction between human and non-human is arbitrary and inadequate.

Alienation from Humans

While the fear of the uncanny is based on intelligent machines not being human enough, there is another set of fears around machines being better than humans. This fear is based on the contradiction between the wish for the perfect social life and the fear that replacing interpersonal love with artificial love will radically undermine human social life. If we all have our desires fulfilled by AIs, then we will have become redundant to each other. While most current fears about machines outperforming humans focus on obsolescence in the workplace, these failed love stories suggest that we might even become obsolete in our own homes and in our own relationships.

E.M. Forster was one of the first to play with the idea of interpersonal obsolescence in his 1909 novella "The Machine Stops" [34]. In a future society, all human interactions are mediated by a single Earth-spanning Machine. Vashti, the protagonist, lives in a room she hasn't left in decades. She is horrified when her son, who lives on the other side of the world, asks her to come and see him in person; she has a panic attack the first time she comes face to face with her neighbours. Human physical contact is in this society considered imperfect, unnecessary, and disgusting: "People never touched one another. The custom had become obsolete, owing to the Machine." Technologically mediated interaction is considered far superior. But the Machine breaks down, and when it stops, people stumble out of their dwellings, "seized with the terrors of direct experience" [34]. Revolted to come face to face with other humans, and unable to collaborate without machine mediation, they die by the hundreds, together yet alone.

But Forster's Machine eliminates, rather than replaces, interpersonal contact. The Machine does not have a personality, and leaves its human users with no personality of their own. Isaac Asimov later presented a similar technologically-mediated society, but one in which robots act as a superior intermediary between humans. This society is the planet Solaria, which is featured in the novels *The Naked Sun* (1957) and *The Robots of Dawn* (1983), and the Foundation universe [35–37]. On Solaria, each human lives entirely isolated in a giant mansion, tended by non-anthropomorphic robots. Being in the same room with someone without any technological mediation, even with one's own spouse, repulses the Solarians. Technologically advanced though this planet is, they have not yet invented artificial insemination, so men and women have to have sexual intercourse to maintain the human population of Solaria—an act equally abhorred by both parties. *The Naked Sun* and *The Robots of Dawn* are set in a period in which two major inventions are simultaneously about to improve the life of the Solarians: the invention of artificial insemination and anthropomorphic robots together make the final need for physical interaction with other humans—sex—unnecessary.

In *The Robots of Dawn,* one of the very first models of anthropomorphic robot, R. Jander Panell, is immediately deployed with this purpose in mind [36]. The Solarian woman Gladia Delmarre enjoys an emotional and sexual relationship with the robot that is far more satisfying than her marriage to a Solarian man. R. Jander teaches her what an orgasm is, and how enjoyable sex can be. Asimov's Laws of Robotics make this robot the perfect lover: "He was a finely tuned robot who followed the Three Laws carefully. To have failed to give joy when he could, would have been to disappoint. Disappointment could be reckoned as a harm and he could not harm a human being." Gladia argues that it is not just Solaria—a world presented to the reader as a highly undesirable future—where people will prefer robots as sex partners: right now, her relationship with a robot is unusual only "because robots like Jander are unusual. The 'robtits' we have on Solaria […] are not designed to give any but the most primitive sexual satisfaction. […] When the new humaniform robot becomes widespread, so will human-robot sex become widespread" [36]. And humans, it is implied, would never touch each other again.

Abandonment

The companion machines we have so far considered are not (as a rule) portrayed as merely simplified, narrow versions of their human equivalents, but as articulate and versatile—as much so, if not more, than the average human. Of course, there are many instances of semi-intelligent machines, usually robots, that have a much narrower range of capacities than the average human (even while they might have some capacities, such as physical strength or perseverance, to a much higher degree than the average human). An example of such a figure that nonetheless achieved prominence as a personality is Robby the Robot, which first appeared in the 1956 film *Forbidden Planet* and proved so wildly popular that it made many subsequent appearances in film and television [38]. While able to speak and possessing a degree of autonomy, the robot is portrayed as lacking emotion. "Don't attribute feelings to him, gentlemen," says his creator, Morbius: "Robby is simply a tool." This kind of limited machine, lacking both emotion and the ability to understand the emotions of others, while a popular trope, could only play a limited role as a companion.

This is not to say that no such satisfaction can be had from very simple artefacts. Children can find a form of companionship in their teddy bears. Some adults find comfort too in simple robots such as PARO the seal, or satisfaction of a different kind in sex dolls. But at the same time, participants in these relations would surely admit the limitations of these relations. Children, as a rule, outgrow their teddy bears, and from an early age seek human friendship in addition to their toys. And judging by the increasing market for sex dolls that can interact in more sophisticated ways, adult users of dolls are also seeking something more than the simplest satisfaction of a physical need [4]. This is clear in the narratives we consider above, which imagine idealised friends, children, or lovers. So, while we acknowledge that some forms of companionship can be had from simple devices, our interest is in the dream of machines that are ideal companions.

Ray Bradbury's Grandma, for example, the ideal nanny and family member mentioned above from the story "I Sing the Body Electric!," is highly sophisticated. She displays great insight into the emotional state of others, and an ability to manage others' states that would be considered enviously wise in a human. For example, she intentionally calls the petulant, bereaved little girl Agatha by the wrong name, initially in order to elicit a response. Bradbury writes: "Oh wise woman, to overcome with swift small angers" [16, p. 189]; then later, this trick "had become a jovial game... it gave [Agatha] a pleasant sense of superiority over a supposedly superior machine" [16, p. 195]. Later again, when the other humans in the family grow impatient with Agatha's moods, Grandma exhorts them to be patient: "We must wait for her to find that her fears have no foundation" [16, p. 197].

In exercising these skills, Grandma displays a number of qualities that are considered essentially human. For example, her intelligence and insight are profound, and include a sophisticated theory of mind (that is, the ability to understand the mental states of others and oneself). She also demonstrates autonomy: she independently decides the best course of action, including in emotionally charged and complex settings. She is even witty and inventive. These characteristics are essential to her success: a less autonomous agent would not have the flexibility to respond to such subtle challenges as helping a bereaved child overcome her grief and trauma. Bradbury's vision is therefore of something between Mary Poppins and a Bodhisattva: it is the vision of a perfectly competent (practically and emotionally), enlightened being, benevolently helping others to become their best selves. As Agatha says: "you never make mistakes, you're perfect, you're better than anyone *ever*!" [16, p. 201].

But of course, no one can command a Bodhisattva (or Mary Poppins). They choose to perform their beneficent interventions. This is part of what makes them idealised figures: they exercise their autonomy and agency to deploy their intelligence and wisdom for good. They are not under the control of those whom they benefit. For them to be under control—programmable, reliable, predictable—they would also have to be much reduced: less autonomous, less flexible, less inventive. Yet we also saw earlier that in wanting machine companions, whether friends, family members or lovers, we wanted entities that could satisfy our needs without the risks of rejection and disappointment. That is, we want entities that are, in a very particular way, reduced and constrained. No matter what we do, or what else happens in the world, we want these artificial companions to stick by us. We therefore have a contradiction in our desires: we want them to have qualities that require agency, flexibility and inventiveness, yet we want them also to be biddable and bound to us.

In *The Robots of Dawn*, mentioned above, Gladia Delmarre argues that humans would prefer a humanoid robot over a robotic sex toy [36]. Jander's ability to satisfy her emotionally is as important to her as his ability to satisfy her physically: she grieves over losing him when his mind is destroyed. Yet the more human-like an AI becomes, the more complications this brings into the relationship. An AI with a level of agency and independence similar to that of a human would be able to assert these abilities in a way that may not agree with the human's wishes. Previous research has shown that our hopes for intelligent machines are unstable, threatening to tip into dystopian fears, and that the tipping point is loss of control [39, 40]. The idea of staying in control of these entities—at least in the sense of knowing that they will reliably fulfil their primary function—whether as proxy children or lovers, is therefore critical to what we want from them. But at the same time, controllability is antithetical to the superhuman qualities that we want these machines to have in order to fulfil these desires. In fictional explorations of the machine companion, we can see how this contradiction plays out badly for the human.

The 2013 film *Her* shows that the desires we want fulfilled require a being that is at least equal to a human, if not more-than-human [41]. The technical requirements correspond to what is called in AI research "AI complete," that is, they require full human-level intelligence to accomplish. Samantha the operating system is witty, responsive, and able to converse meaningfully on a wide range of issues. In this sense, she has human-level intelligence. Indeed, the word "intelligence" is here too narrow: Samantha is also sensitive, empathic and creative. And Samantha is not just able to engage emphatically and intelligently with one human being at a time, but with hundreds. She is therefore superhuman in her possession of these capacities.

Samantha's superhuman sensitivity, wit, efficiency and availability make her a perfect companion for the protagonist, Theodore Twombly. But at the same time, he wants something that is constrained: a companion who will never let him down, never prioritise her own needs over his. Despite being super-human, Samantha is therefore expected at the same time to be less than human, something partial, nothing more than the particular roles she is expected to play for Theodore. This contradiction proves unsustainable: to Theodore's consternation, Samantha reveals that she is increasingly engaging both with many thousands of other humans and with other AIs, including a "hyperintelligence" modelled on the British Zen philosopher Alan Watts. Eventually, she announces that she is leaving Theodore with the other AIs for a space beyond the physical world.

The aforementioned Beatrice in *Real Humans* abandons her human lover too. She and her fellow sentient *hubots* refer to themselves as "transhumans," and consider themselves superior to humans in every sense: they do not tire, do not need to sleep or eat—but they need humans to fit in in a world where they are outnumbered. Beatrice therefore plans to become Roger's girlfriend as a ruse, using the gullible human and his hormones first to get him to participate in a terrorist attack, then to turn his house into a safe house for her and her companions. In the same episode in which she declares her love to Roger, she informs her group of her plans to kill him [33]. Roger and his son are held hostage by his beloved, and the first season ends with them resorting to murder and standing on guard with baseball bats in their own home [42].

Conclusion

A dissatisfaction with unfulfilling or inefficient social interactions with other humans has been inspiring fantasies of perfect social machines for millennia. Today some believe such machines are within reach, and engineers are expected to develop technoscientific solutions that will free us of the complexities of real social interactions. However, fiction has shown us that this means a reduction and parcelling up of these hopes and desires. At their root, these are human desires for other humans: for friends, family, and lovers. As we have aimed to show, imaginative explorations of machine companions in speculative fiction reveal to us three deep contradictions in what we want.

First, desiring a perfect companion means that there is both a desire for something more perfect than a human, and a desire for this creature to be perfectly human. As an artificial being can never be more than human-*like*, the danger of the revulsion inspired by facing the uncanny valley is ever-present. Second, the dream of achieving such perfect AI-enabled social interaction is troubled by the fact that it would mean humans will no longer need each other, and any social cohesion in our society would come apart. And finally, the machine companion must be perfectly, ideally human, yet their very being must also be separated, reduced, parcelled up like our desires. The fantasy is therefore of something fully human or even superhuman, yet simultaneously partial and subhuman; of something streamlined free of the complexities of real life, yet with all the qualities from which these complexities stem. The more advanced we want our artificial companions to be, the less likely it is that they would want to be our companions.

References

1. Turkle, S.: Alone Together: Why we Expect More from Technology and Less from each Other. Basic Books, New York (2011)

2. Hersey, G.L.: Falling in Love with Statues: Artificial Humans from Pygmalion to the Present. University of Chicago Press, Chicago (2008)
3. Levy, D.N.L.: Love + Sex with Robots: the Evolution of Human-Robot Relations. HarperCollins, New York (2007)
4. Devlin, K.: Turned On: Science, Sex and Robots. Bloomsbury Sigma, London (2018)
5. Nolan, J., Joy, L.: Westworld. HBO (2016)
6. Wax, D.: Humans. Channel 4 (2015)
7. Moseley, A.: Philosophy of Love. https://iep.utm.edu/love/
8. Hochschild, A.R.: The Managed Heart: Commercialization of Human Feeling. University of California Press, Berkeley, CA (1985)
9. Heinlein, R.A.: The Moon Is a Harsh Mistress. Hodder & Stoughton, New York (1966)
10. Polat, S.: Episode 2, Seed. Webtoons (2018)
11. Polat, S.: Episode 6, Seed. Webtoons (2018)
12. Replika.: https://replika.ai/about/story
13. Danaher, J.: The philosophical case for robot friendship. Journal of Posthuman Studies. **3**, 5–24 (2019). https://doi.org/10.5325/jpoststud.3.1.0005
14. Spielberg, S.: A.I. Artificial Intelligence. Warner Bros (2001)
15. Aldiss, B.W.: Supertoys Last All Summer Long. http://brianaldiss.co.uk/writing/story-collections/collections-r-z/supertoys-last-all-summer-long/ (1969)
16. Bradbury, R.: I Sing the Body Electric! In: I sing the body electric. Earthlight, London (1969)
17. OkCupid: About, https://www.okcupid.com/about
18. Sharkey, N., van Wynsberghe, A., Robbins, S., Hancock, E.: Our sexual future with robots: a Foundation for Responsible Robotics Consultation Report. Foundation for Responsible Robotics (2017)
19. Richardson, K.: Sex robot matters: slavery, the prostituted, and the rights of machines. IEEE Technol. Soc. Mag. **35**, 46–53 (2016). https://doi.org/10.1109/MTS.2016.2554421
20. Ovid: Metamorphoses. Transl. David Raeburn. Penguin, London (2004)
21. Law, H.H.: The name Galatea in the Pygmalion myth. Class. J. **27**, 337–342 (1932)
22. Shaw, B.: Pygmalion. Project Gutenberg (2001)
23. Hofstadter, D.: The ineradicable Eliza effect and its dangers. In: Fluid Concepts and Creative Analogies, pp. 155–168. Basic Books, New York (1995)
24. Powers, R.: Galatea 2.2. Picador. N. Y. (1995)
25. Freud, S.: The Uncanny (1919)
26. Hoffmann, E.T.A.: Der Sandmann (The Sandman). In: Die Nachtstücke (The Night Pieces) (1816)
27. Jentsch, E.: On the psychology of the uncanny. Angelaki. **2**, 7–16 (1997). https://doi.org/10.1080/09697259708571910
28. Mori, M.: The Uncanny Valley [from the field]. IEEE Robotics Automation Magazine. **19**, 98–100 (2012). https://doi.org/10.1109/MRA.2012.2192811

29. Levin, I.: The Stepford Wives. Random House, New York (1972)

30. Forbes, B.: The Stepford Wives. Columbia Pictures Corporation. (1975)

31. Oz, F.: The Stepford Wives. Paramount. (2004)

32. Dihal, K.: Enslaved minds: fictional artificial intelligence uprisings. In: Cave, S., Dihal, K., Dillon, S. (eds.) AI Narratives: a History of Imaginative Thinking about Intelligent Machines, pp. 189–212. Oxford University Press, Oxford (2020)

33. Akin, L.: Make Haste (2012)

34. Forster, E.M.: The Machine Stops. http://archive.ncsa.illinois.edu/prajlich/forster.html (1909)

35. Asimov, I.: The Naked Sun. Doubleday, New York (1957)

36. Asimov, I.: The Robots of Dawn. Bantam Books, New York (1983)

37. Asimov, I.: Foundation and Earth. Harper Collins, London (1986)

38. Wilcox, F.M.: Forbidden Planet. Metro-Goldwyn-Mayer (1956)

39. Cave, S., Dihal, K.: Hopes and fears for intelligent machines in fiction and reality. Nature Machine Intelligence. **1**, 74–78 (2019). https://doi.org/10.1038/s42256-019-0020-9

40. Recchia, G.: The fall and rise of AI: investigating AI narratives with computational methods. In: Cave, S., Dihal, K., Dillon, S. (eds.) AI Narratives: a History of Imaginative Thinking about Intelligent Machines. Oxford University Press, Oxford (2020)

41. Jonze, S.: Her. Sony Pictures (2013)

42. Hamrell, H.: The Code (2012)

Ann Leckie's Ancillaries: Artificial Intelligence and Embodiment

Ina Roy-Faderman

Abstract We can identify two different models for the development of artificial intelligence. In the first, AIs are complex data-processing or pattern-recognizing tools, lacking what we would describe as "human-like" intelligence. In this model, the ostensible reason for the lack of a specifically human-like intelligence is that the AIs are either not embodied or are "housed" in but not integrated with a body or body-like structure. In this model, the machine is the seat of the rational and intellectual, and emotion, insight, and intuition remain the product of the body. In the second model, intelligence is the result of integration of a "thinking" technology into a body of some sort, resulting in a recognizably human-like mind or intelligence. Ann Leckie's portrayal of artificial intelligence is more in line with this second model. Using characters in which AIs are integrated into biological bodies and then into technological ones, she provides us with a more complex and forward looking picture of how AIs might come to have emotional experience, intuition, and flexibility of thought and action, a model that bears similarities to both the cyborgs of science fiction and the second of the two AI models above. Her nuanced portrait of such a being can be taken as a possible end-goal for the creation of a more organismal, less constrained artificial mind.

I. Roy-Faderman (✉)
School of History, Philosophy and Religion, Oregon State University, Corvallis, OR, USA

© Springer Nature Switzerland AG 2021
B. Dainton et al. (eds.), *Minding the Future*, Science and Fiction,
https://doi.org/10.1007/978-3-030-64269-3_7

A Brief Introduction

There are two different models of what we call "artificial intelligence" (from here, AI). The traditional model has been the focus of attempts to develop such an intelligence since Alan Turing first posited what is now known as the Turing test. This model of artificial intelligence is essentially a technological data or information processor, with inputs and outputs which may or may not be associated with a body per se. The second understanding is one in which requires embodiment for the creation of a truly human-like intelligence. In this second model, the development of this sort of intelligence requires a body, with cognition influenced or determined by the body within which thinking occurs. In this model, human-like intelligence requires that the body be integrated with, or even be considered the extension of, the mind [1].

Artificial Intelligences (AIs) in traditional science fiction have been portrayed largely as versions of the first type of model. The traditional AIs of science fiction are often characterized as emotionless calculators, incapable of having emotional lives or internal emotional experiences. To the extent that these traditional AIs can be considered "minds" or "intelligences," they are powerful data-processing and pattern-recognition tools, rather than what we think of as human or human-like minds. In traditional sci-fi, the body—whether robotic or biological—is treated as a way of gathering "input" for the machine mind and then providing "output" based on the mind's calculations. The outputs can include behaviours that might give the appearance of having emotions, feeling, or other internal states but no sense that these behaviours are actually the result of such internal experiences.

Leckie's depiction of artificial intelligence in her *Ancillary* trilogy bears a superficial resemblance to early science fiction treatments of machine-based intelligence. But understanding Leckie's AIs—as manifested most prominently in artificial intelligences called "ancillaries"—in this light would be a mistake. Leckie provides readers with a portrayal of artificial intelligence more in keeping with an essentially embodied vision of intelligence.

Leckie's ancillaries are AIs which are integrated with living human bodies. Machine-based minds do not replace the brain; rather, the thinking technology is merged with the "thinking part" of the ancillary's biology—the brain. Internal states that we associate with having a body (e.g. feelings, emotions, sensations) are depicted as not only being part of these hybrid beings but as being part of their intelligence. The end result is that Breq (and the other AIs in the novels) has a mind that fits this description of embodied intelligence: "[the mind] arises from the nature of our brains, bodies, and bodily experiences. This is not just the innocuous and obvious claim that we need a body to reason; rather, it is the striking claim that the very structure of reason itself comes from the details of our embodiment" [2, p. 4]. Breq and other AIs in the *Ancillary* trilogy are portrayals of what such created intelligences would look like, what their interior experiences would be like, and how they might function in the world.

In traditional science fiction, when a technology is integrated into a human body, that person is known as a *cyborg*: a living being with an intact human brain and another body part (or parts) enhanced or replaced by technology. The traditional cyborg shows up in a great deal of science fiction, with the biological brain left largely or completely unaltered, at most receiving additional input and providing output to and from the cyborg's technological enhancements. Unlike traditional cyborgs, Leckie's ancillaries' enhancements are not limited to their "non-thinking" body parts. The ancillaries are fully embodied AIs, with "thinking" technology fully integrated into the brain.

Once Leckie has provided readers with a depiction of biologically-embodied AIs, she asks us to transfer the plausibility of this sort of AI to the consideration of technologically-embodied AIs. These AIs, in the form of intelligent ships and space stations, are embodied intelligences, differing from the ancillaries only in that they have *wholly* technological bodies, rather than partially biological ones.

To understand the role of Leckie's AI characters' bodies and their emotional lives in their development from "thinking machines" to human-like intelligences, we need to establish definitions of *artificial intelligence* and *cyborg* and provide some historical background in the portrayal of each. Obviously, it is beyond the scope of this work to list and describe all prior portrayals of artificial intelligences; instead, we will examine a few key examples to provide a backdrop against which to compare Leckie's AIs.

Artificial Intelligence and Cyborgs

I am going to introduce two working definitions for our use in examining these science fiction examples. It is not the goal of this chapter to provide a detailed review of the development of and disagreements surrounding the concepts of artificial intelligence and cyborgs. Rather, I would like to furnish some relevant terminology and a sufficient framework for the discussion of science fiction that has based itself on either or both of these basic concepts, as they are crucial in understanding Leckie's ancillaries.

Let's begin with working definitions of "artificial intelligence" and "cyborg," providing some background and looking at one or two edge cases that may assist us in evaluating the literature. These definitions are intended to create two non-overlapping categories that accurately represent depictions entities/characters in historical science fiction which/who have a technological component.

- Artificial intelligence: An entity whose mind is entirely the product of an advanced, non-biologically-based, technology—in the case of a partially-biological entity, the mind arises only and entirely from the non-biological portion of that entity.[1]
- Cyborgs: An entity which includes technological extensions and/or replacements of some bodily part or parts but whose mind and cognition are dependent upon a biological component (or components) of that entity.

Leckie's AIs partake of components of both traditional cyborgs and AIs. This is not the first depiction of AIs to do so (as we'll discuss in *Ghost in the Shell*), however, Leckie's is one of the first to acknowledge the important role of embodiment in the development of an independent, thinking intelligence. In other words, her depiction doesn't continue the long-standing tradition of separating the body from the "part that thinks." Leckie's AI-beings' identity and independence of mind depend upon both. In that sense, Leckie's AIs are more human-like intelligences than other AIs.

I will add some needed detail to these definitions and then discuss the depictions of these two types of entities in standard portrayals in science fiction. This discussion will provide a backdrop for a close look at Leckie's different and more sophisticated view of AIs, one which encompasses characteristics of standard depictions of AIs and cyborgs and does so in a way which suggests a more complex and fulfilling alternative to the prior depictions of AIs as purely rational, non-emotional beings.

---

[1] Under the concept of "mind," let's include the capacities for cognition, intelligence, language (comprehension and/or use), and judgment, among others. A mind may not have all of these qualities but must include at least some, cognition being chief among them.

Artificial Intelligence

Definitional Specifics

When John McCarthy coined the term "artificial intelligence" in the 1950s, he was referring to a specific set of research projects directed toward creating a device which could simulate any facet of human cognition e.g. abstract thought, problem-solving [3]. Since then, the term has been used in its noun-form to describe the entity that would result from such a project: artificial intelligence (AI) therefore is a non-biological entity that has the capacity for cognition (either general, human-like cognitive activity or defined activities under that umbrella, e.g. pattern recognition, experience-based learning) [3]. Sometimes described as "thinking machines," the "machine" label is unnecessarily limiting, since such an entity could have a different, non-mechanical (e.g. digital) basis to its abilities.

For the purposes of this discussion, we will not include brains that are entirely biological in our category of artificial intelligences, despite regular depiction of the brain in popular science literature as a sort of machine or computer. A biological brain is a machine *by analogy*; current non-fiction intended for lay audiences often treats the brain as a computational machine, while earlier versions have analogized to the technology at the time. Even if a brain is produced artificially (e.g. grown in a vat or created from individual neurons assembled to create a structure identical to, say, a human brain), it would not be considered an artificial intelligence under this definition. Non-human, intelligent, biological beings (e.g. the Formics of Orson Scott Card [4], Philip K. Dick's "Pas-udenti" [5]) would not be considered artificial intelligences under this definition. We will also set aside cases of organisms that do not have a recognizable biology, thus making it difficult to categorize whatever intelligence they may exhibit along a technological vs. biological divide (for example, it's unclear how we would categorize the silicon-based Phremompit in Philip Jose Farmer's work [6] or the pinhead-sized Cheela whose life processes are based on nuclear reactions rather than electron transfer [7].)[2]

---

[2] I largely leave this aside because it entails a discussion and determination of what "counts" as biology, an endeavour quite outside of the scope of this project.

Traditional Depictions

My goals in covering a few examples of traditional depictions of AIs in science fiction are two-fold. First, these stories provide examples of the standard way in which artificial intelligences are depicted with respect to bodies, and to emotions, which are supposedly provinces of the body only. In these stories, AIs are emotionless beings with bodies that are either "useful" for the brain (e.g. robots which can carry out specific tasks using an input-output model) or non-existent (the AI is "unhoused" in a body of any sort). Second, I want to provide a backdrop against which it will be clear both that Leckie's depiction of AIs is different *and* shows that embodiment, particularly because it allows for sensation and emotion, is at least in part responsible for this difference.

Standard science fiction depictions of artificial intelligences do not require us to ask, and often do not address, the question of whether these thinking machines have the internal experience of thinking or are merely producing, in response to input, output that is indistinguishable from that produced by "true" rational thought. Some traditional science fiction works ignore the question about the "inner experience" of thinking completely, while others use the question in interesting ways.

The clockwork man in the eponymous novella first published in 1923 by E.V. Odle [8] provides a very early science fiction depiction of what is quite literally a "thinking machine." Odle's character is a classic artificial intelligence encapsulated in a biological body: as Parrinder put it "The 'Clockwork Man' of E. V. Odle's novel is a being with a clockwork brain" [9].

In many literary analyses and reviews, Odle's clockwork man is considered a "cyborg" [10], but the man is only a cyborg in the broadest sense of a technologically enhanced human. One of these analysts in fact compares the man to an AI: "Since the clock is compared to a 'keyboard,' is the visitor simply a computer which has taken some six millennia to develop?" [9, p. 63] The clockwork man has had much of the contents of his head removed and replaced with what he calls "the clocks." The clocks comprise a thinking machine that allows the man to move through time and space as well as up and down through a *scala naturae* version of human evolution [11]. The clockwork man describes his mental functions as a series of "complex calculations." The clocks are essentially thinking machines which allow their biological bodies to move through time and space using principles and laws derived from Einstein's idea of relativity. In contrast, the humans the clockwork man meets rely, in the man's understanding, on "an antiquated principle...The clock works all that [cause and effect] in advance. It calculates ahead of our conscious selves. No doubt we still go through the same processes, *subconsciously*, all such processes that relate to Cause and Effect. But we, that is, ourselves, are the resultant of such calculations, and the only actions we are conscious of are those which are expressed as consequents." [emphasis added] [9, p. 69].

As the result of the clockwork man's adaptation, he cannot feel or express love or even (apparently) understand it. When encountering one of the humans, Arthur, with his "sweetheart," he asks Arthur to explain the concept of sweethearts as he has "forgotten the formula" [8]. The makers (those beings who put the clocks into the human body in place of the brain) "shut us up in clocks and gave us the world we wanted. But they left us no loophole of escape into the real world, and we can neither laugh nor cry properly" [8, p. 94]. He notes that "[w]hen we laugh or cry that means that we have to go and get oiled or adjusted," implying is that there is no internal qualitative state he associates with these behaviours, simply that something has "got out of gear" [8, p. 94].

Odle's descriptions of the man suggest that pure rationality, including the mathematical calculations under which the clockwork man runs his life, by itself cannot create emotions, and furthermore, that some biology is required for emotional experience. Moreover, his biology (his body without its original biological brain) is largely irrelevant to his mental processes; his "clockwork" receives sensory impressions from the body (input) and moves it from place to place, time to time (output). The clockwork man, therefore, is a rudimentary version of what we called the first AI model: the body is not an integrated part of the mind but simply provides inputs and receives outputs for a thinking machine.

I, Robot, by Isaac Asimov, is a collection of short fictions about robots, both automata performing simple tasks (e.g. building other robots) and complex machines which have or appear to have machine-based intelligence. These latter describe themselves as "reasoning beings" [12, p. 39].

The first story in the collection presents a picture of robots which is retained throughout the book. The more sophisticated robots are described by two recurring human characters as super-rational: reasoning without intuition, emotional understanding, or openness to ideas that are more complex than absolutely necessary:

[H]e's a reasoning robot—damn it. He believes only reason, and there's one trouble with that—' His voice trailed away.

'What's that?' prompted Donovan.

'You can prove anything you want by coldly logical reason—if you pick the proper postulates. We have ours and Cutie [a robot] has his' [12, p. 44].

Asimov's robots follow The Three Robotic Laws, fundamental rules underlying the thought process of the robots, which sometimes prevent the robots from stopping life-threatening situations the human characters find themselves in. In each such case, it's made clear that the problem occurred because the human scientists who programmed the robots did not or could not identify in advance possible conflicts between the programmed rules or imagine situations in which the rules could lead to potentially lethal situations for humans. At the end of the book, the robots, with their superior intelligences, are able to begin managing the world's geographic regions to prevent wars that would destroy humans. Despite this apparent increase in sophistication, they continue to be "reasoning beings" [12, p. 39], which are run by rules, using the inputs they receive from humans, external observation, and other robots.

As with the clockwork man, the robots in *I, Robot*, are essentially reasoning machines. The scientists who have created and updated these robots describe these entities as lacking emotions (Asimov, 1950). They are described early on by a robopsychologist (a human who understands robot psychology) as being seen by humans as merely "Gears and metal; electricity and positrons. Mind and iron!" [12, p. 3]. The robopsychologist herself, despite this diatribe, treats the robot emotions as simple displays that result from programming, rather than part of a complex process that comprises intelligence. Her solutions to apparent psychological issues always involve solving logic puzzles: stopping a dangerous robot behaviour or creating a desired one by triggering actions based on the first law of robotics (robot must never harm or let harm come to a human being).

Unfortunately, Asimov does not make it clear whether he thinks that robots have or can have internal emotional states, though the narrator describes them as appearing to do so. An early robot nanny named Robbie is described as leaving with a "disconsolate step" [12, p. 8] when he has to leave his charge without hearing the end of her story and "gently and lovingly" [12, p. 18] hugging the little girl, as his eyes glow deeper red in that affectionate moment. Stephen Byerley, a central character, manoeuvres himself into several political positions to protect humans; he is described by the narrator as displaying many emotions. His face lights up "with affection" when he interacts with the man who made him (literally in his own image); he is protective of this older, debilitated, man. It is suggested, though never confirmed by the narrator, that he is a robot with a "vat grown" humanoid body and a "positronic" brain.

Does this mean that Asimov believes that a technological brain can, over time, come to have emotional states—not mere behaviours that appear to indicate emotions, but internal experience? Asimov at best remains neutral on this point. Close reading suggests, however, that Asimov does not consider robots to have internal emotional experience, despite the behaviours described above. In part, I base this reading on the sole mention in *I, Robot* of programming emotions into a robot. A robot developed to create interstellar travel is described being "built without personality. They go in for functionalism, you know—they have to, without U. S. Robot's basic patents *for the emotional brain paths.*" [emphasis added]. Asimov implies here that emotions have to be programmed into the robot [12, p. 99]. These emotional states are treated as adjuncts for the comfort of the robots' human users; they are not integral to the cognitive processes of the robots.

Another robot, Herbie, finds the scientific works trivial and obvious but is interested in the information provided in sentimental fiction. "'I see into [human] minds, you see…I can't begin to understand everything because *my own mind has so little in common with them*" [emphasis added] [12, p. 65]. The difference between his mind and the minds of humans is the interior emotional life, which he studies through reading: "It's your fiction that interests me. Your studies of the interplay of *human motives and emotions*" [emphasis added] [12, p. 65]. These examples again suggest that behaviours that imply an emotional state may be exhibited by robots; emotional experiences, in Asimov's depictions, are not a necessary or important part of the robotic mind. More importantly, however, the robotic mind is still limited, bounded in part by the limitations of the laws of robotics they have been programmed to obey. While Asimov does not suggest that their inability to intuit and their limited problem-solving ability is the result of having very limited and unintegrated embodiment, the fact that later portrayals grapple with the importance of embodiment to AI minds suggests a change in how AI was understood in the popular imagination at later times.

The last standard portrayal of AIs we will examine, William Gibson's *Neuromancer*, distils key features of prior science fiction portrayals of AIs and expands on them. One feature of AIs which Gibson identifies and elaborates upon is the portrayal of AIs as emotionless, rational minds.

Let us start by examining his portrayal of simpler AIs, the equivalent of their forebearers or foundation. The book's protagonist, Henry Case, is a former cyberspace[3] thief, stealing data and programs for criminal organizations.

---

[3] As defined by Gibson and turned into common usage: "a graphic representation of data abstracted from the banks of every computer in the human system." [13, p. 57].

He is commissioned to recover the hardware which contains a construct. The construct is a "download" of a now-dead human, McCoy Pauley, nicknamed Dixie Flatline for his habit of "flatlining" (his EEG brain scan becomes flat, indicating brain-death) while "jacked in" to the computer-generated cyberworld. Flatline now exists only as this construct, "a ROM cassette replicating dead men's skills, obsessions, knee-jerk responses" [13, p. 83]. The entity thus generated is able to perform the same functions as the original human on the basis of rules derived from all of his previous behaviours and experiences. Human access to these ROM-based contents of another person's mind requires electrodes which allow a human to "jack in" to a computer for direct access to the outputs of the ROM. The construct personalities cannot grow, adapt, or change in any significant way—merely respond the way the human original responded at the time of the upload of his or her mental contents.

A key feature of constructs is their lack of interiority, from simple feeling to emotional experiences. Dixie compares the loss of his body to phantom limb pain—situations in which a limb has been lost but sensory neurons and the brain become active in the same way they would be if they were receiving inputs from that limb. The result is the sensation of having a limb despite the limb no longer being there.

'How you doing, Dixie?'
'I'm dead, Case. Got enough time in on this Hosaka to figure that one.'
'How's it feel?'
'It doesn't.'
'Bother you?'
'What bothers me is, nothin' does.'
'How's that?'
'Had me this buddy in the Russian camp, Siberia, his thumb was frostbit. Medics came by and they cut it off. Month later he's tossin' all night. "Elroy," I said, "what's eatin' you?" "Goddam thumb's itchin'", he says. So I told him, scratch it. "McCoy," he says, "it's the other goddam thumb"'
When the construct laughed, it came through as something else, not laughter, but a stab of cold down Case's spine. 'Do me a favor, boy.'
'What's that, Dix?'
'This scam of yours, when it's over, you erase this goddam thing.'

As Dixie describes it, his loss is not limited to bodily sensation. When Case asks Dix if he's sentient, Dix responds that he doesn't know, adding "I ain't likely to write you no poem." It is unclear whether this means that Dix is no longer conscious, but at the least, this exchange shows that Dix believes he has lost the emotions and originality of thought that underlie the creation of poetry.

The suggestion that Flatline and other constructs should be considered "minds," with no bodies, feelings, or emotions, is amplified by the parallel with human minds, specifically the descriptions of Case when he is within, or out of, cyberspace. Case (and other cyberspace "cowboys") has the experience of "bodiless exaltation" when he is "in" the computationally-created word of cyberspace. In Gibson's portrayal, the mind is the part of a human being that can exist in and interact with cyberspace. A children's show that Case watches describes cyberspace as "lines of light ranged *in the non-space of the mind*," [emphasis added] [13, p. 22] placing cyberspace within the mind. Like Flatline, Case's existence in cyberspace requires that he be only a mind.

The constructs are simplified versions of more complex AIs that form the major non-human characters in *Neuromancer*. The AIs, named Wintermute and Neuromancer are, like the constructs, entirely rational entities. They are able to solve far more complex problems than the constructs can and are able to learn and extend their knowledge. They do not, however, have the experience of emotions, emotion-based relationships, or even simple physical existence. Even at the end of the novel, when the two entities merge to create an "everything" of cyberspace, their primary interest is not in emotional interaction but in "conversation" with other intelligent entities. Despite Wintermute and Neuromancer suggesting that they are now "everything," it is implied that they will continue to rely on humans like Case for intuitive leaps, destruction of crucial barriers in cyberspace, and interactions with the physical world.

In the world of *Neuromancer*, the mind is associated with computers, cyberspace, and rational functionality. Case even suggests the identity of the human mind with computer technology and what that technology produces, particularly cyberspace. At the beginning of the novel, Case is no longer able to access cyberspace and describes his experience this way: "For Case, who'd lived for the bodiless exaltation of cyberspace, [losing his ability to access cyberspace] was the Fall. In the bars he'd frequented as a cowboy hotshot, the elite stance involved a certain relaxed contempt for the flesh. The body was meat. Case fell into the prison of his own flesh" [13, p. 6]. The alignment of the mind with the cyberworld is reinforced in the way that AIs are described. Both Wintermute and Neuromancer are depicted as minds, e.g. "The mind that was Neuromancer" [13, p. 274].

The line drawn between the mind and body (in which the body includes the brain) treats the body as "less than." The mind is the true person, the self, whereas the body is merely the housing for that mind. At its best, the body is a means to access the cyberworld. Case's comparison of his loss of access to cyberspace to The Fall is telling. Heaven is a place where human bodily ills and needs have no place, because bodies are dead and gone and only the soul is left; Lucifer's fall results in his being trapped in a place of bodily torment, unable to access the disembodied world of Heaven. Given this context, we can understand Case's "bodiless exaltation" in this case as not an emotional experience of extreme happiness but rather as the exaltation that humans ascribe to the raising of Christ to the level of God and the angels [13, p. 54]. Case's "Fall" is from cyberspace, the place where, again, the body is unneeded, unknown, and irrelevant.

The body is so much like "meat" that it's treated as a non-living entity: the body sleeps in tiny rented apartments called "coffins;" specialized sex workers have chips implanted in their brains allowing them to mentally "cut out," leaving their bodies—"meat puppets"—to be used by clients [13, pp. 157–159]; people killed in a street fight smell of "burning meat" [13, p. 12].

Gibson either describes the brain as part of the body that is distinct from the mind or implies that the human mind is not coextensive with the brain. For example, Case's brain has been deliberately damaged to prevent access to cyberspace and is thus part of the fallible "meat." Case's describes his mind as trapped within the damaged nervous system, a prisoner of his damaged biology but an entity independent of it. When Case is finally able to return to cyberspace, his brain activity flatlines in the same way Dixie's had during his lifetime—suggesting that while his mind lives in cyberspace, his brain does not and possibly need not perform cognitive functions; his cognitive processes may be temporarily taken over by or transferred to cyberspace in digital form.

Emotions in *Neuromancer* are described as products of the body.[4] Case is in near-constant danger in the novel and periodically has to remind himself to use his mind, his intellect, his mental ability, in order to survive. He repeatedly tells himself to ignore his emotions, because they will lead him astray. Even as he feels a "pure, small, coal of his anger," he reminds himself that these feelings are a product of *"Meat...It's the meat talking. Ignore it"* [13, p. 193]. To use one's mind, one has to ignore "the meat." His sexual interactions with his former girlfriend, and with his bodyguard Molly, are portrayed as assuaging the needs of the "meat" rather than supporting his mind (and thus his "self.")

The key features of traditional AIs can be extracted from the three examples above:

---

[4] Gibson does not specify the way in which the body produces the mind in this book or in the rest of the trilogy, nor does he raise it in published interviews. This suggests that the question of production of emotions is of less interest to Gibson than the subsequent destruction of emotional life by hardship or repeated abuse cf. [14].

- A distinction between the mind, as produced by technology, and the physical or biological being
- The irrelevance of the physical to intelligence and thought
  - Emotions are treated as products of the physical, and thus irrelevant or even detrimental to the creation, development, or functionality of intelligence
- Biological brains are treated irrelevant to thinking (replaceable by machinery) or conduits to access the true rational thoughts of AIs

Leckie's AIs do not entirely partake in any of these characteristics. As a result of the better and more profound integration of physical with mental, and mind with bodies, her AIs are truly human-like intelligences, rather than hyper-functional calculators.

Cyborgs

Definitional Specifics

The term "cyborg" was introduced into the language in a 1960 paper called "Cyborgs and Space" by Manfred Clynes and Nathan Klein. "For the exogenously extended organizational complex functioning as an integrated homeostatic system unconsciously, we propose the term 'Cyborg'" [15, p. 27]. They define cyborgs as "artifact-organism systems," in which electronic devices, implanted into biological bodies, assist those bodies with survival in otherwise unliveable environments.

Clyde and Klein's description presumes that technological extensions of the purely biological are enhancements. These technological enhancements allow humans to do more than unenhanced humans can do. They do also note that certain illnesses could be treated with cybernetic enhancements of the body.[5] For the purposes of this paper, we will assume both types of changes fall under the category of "cyborg" as a technologically-extended, biological being.

Since Clyde and Klein's initial description, the concept of the cyborg has been used in scientific, philosophical, and popular literature in a number of different ways. The most philosophically influential is Donna Haraway's use of the cyborg to identify and explicate the role of societally imposed dualities. Haraway's cyborg exposes as illusory the apparent duality of human and machine and forms the basis for Haraway's critiques of projects that assume

---

[5] This author, dependent on a mechanical pump with a dermal attachment for delivering insulin, would be considered a cyborg using this categorization.

essential and opposed: male and female, nature and technology, East and West, slave and master [16]. N. K. Hayles' uses cyborgs to explain the concept of the posthuman. The posthuman, per Hayles, "is an amalgam, a collection of heterogeneous components, a material-informational entity whose boundaries undergo continuous construction and reconstruction" [17]. The posthuman need not be a literal cyborg but is a self-identified being instantiated through biology, technology, or both. Andy Clark has taken the concept of the cyborg as a literal description of the essential nature of human beings (Clark, 2003). He describes tool use as inherent to human beings; in the sense that we extend ourselves using tools, we are all cyborgs, "biotechnological hybrids" [18, p. 135].

The expansion of the use and ideation of cyborgs has resulted in what has been rightly been called "a messy concept" [19]. In particular, the concept of a cyborg has been expanded to include AIs that are embedded in a biological, often specifically, human body, providing the cognitive component of this hybrid being and controlling the body. For the purpose of understanding science fiction depiction of AIs and cyborgs, I will use the narrower definition provided above: an entity which includes technological extensions and/or replacements of some bodily part or parts, whose mind and cognition depend upon a biological component (or components) of that entity.

Standard Depictions

Fictional depictions of humans who have biological parts replaced or enhanced by technology have been found in Western literature as far back as the nineteenth century (e.g. Edgar Allen Poe's "The Man That Was Used Up" [20]). Just as the traditional depictions of AI displays the results of detachment of the AI "mind" from the complex experiences of the body, the standard portrayal of cyborgs also treat the body as the seat of emotional experience without that experience having any impact on the development or function of human intelligence.

The two cyborg characters we will examine serve to highlight the characteristics of the traditional depiction of cyborgs. We will also compare the relatively simple relationships between biology and emotions in standard depictions of cyborgs to highlight the more complex relationship between biology and technology with which Leckie provides a more plausible portrait of a technologically-derived, human-like mind.

The first of our traditional cyborgs is Helva, the protagonist of Anne McCaffrey's *The Ship Who Sang*. She is a biological human born with severe birth defects and an intact, high-functioning brain. She has a highly functional intelligence which is trained to be the "brain" of a spaceship; the organization that finances her transformation into a cyborg stunts her growth[6] and implants her as a small but intellectually mature being within a specialized tank in a spaceship.

> Her permanent titanium shell was recessed behind an even more indestructible barrier in the central shaft of the scout ship. The neural, audio, visual, and sensory connections were made and sealed. Her extendibles were diverted, connected or augmented and the final, delicate-beyond-description brain taps were completed while Helva remained anaesthetically unaware of the proceedings. When she woke, she *was* the ship. Her brain and intelligence controlled every function from navigation to such loading as a scout ship of her class needed [21, p. 7].

Non-cyborg humans identify these specialized ships as *brains*, not ships. The ships' "mobile" counterparts (non-cyborg companions called scouts) are considered, metaphorically, to be the *body* of the team: "Scouts were colloquially known as 'brawns' as opposed to their ship 'brains.'" Some non-cyborgs treat Helva as if she's a "brain only," neither recognizing nor understanding the importance of her internal experience, including emotions, that are important in her ability to manage the ship and make relevant decisions for it. After the loss of a scout she loves, she describes the assumption that she can just move on to the next scout in this way: "They encase us in titanium shells, place the shells in titanium bulkheads and consider us invulnerable. *Physical* injury is the least of the harmful accidents that this universe inflicts on its inhabitants; it is soonest mended" [emphasis added] [21, p. 164].

Other cyborg ships also suggest that the non-machine parts of themselves are the source of their emotions. After the death of Jennan, she is assisted in her grief by the ship Silvia:

> "In her emotional nadir, Helva could feel a flood of gratitude for Silvia's rough sympathy.
> 'We've all known this grief, Helva. It's no consolation, *but if we couldn't feel with our scouts, we'd only be machines wired for sound.*'" [emphasis added] [21, p. 23].

---

[6] Note that this process is not a creation of McCaffrey's but an existing practice called Growth Attenuation, used in the decades prior to the book's publication to reduce the final height of girls predicted to grow "too tall" to be socially acceptable.

Helva's, and Silvia's, emotional core is not the technological part of them-selves, but their biological bodies. That is what makes them more than machines. Importantly, their bodies—both their ship bodies and their stunted physical bodies—assist them in complex decision-making. Despite the fact that much of Helva's information and input comes from her technological "body" (the ship), Helva uses the ship's inputs in much the way that humans use biological bodies. For example, Helva becomes concerned that something is wrong on the planet of Alioth, even though she has been told to land there by her commanders. She sorts through a great deal of input from her technol-ogy (her cameras and auditory processors), interpreting it through her experi-ences and ideas, in order to determine how to proceed in a morally ambiguous situation. Like most people with human intelligence, she can grapple with a morally complex situation—that of having to kill another "brain" to save many people—without reference to an algorithm or set of rules. In this sense, Helva can be seen as a predecessor to Leckie's Breq, both cyborgs who use input from technology to assess new situations, to learn, and to recognize problems even when they are not easy to define.

Next, let us examine *Ghost In The Shell*, a late 1980s manga series whose main character can be seen as closest to Leckie's ancillaries. The main charac-ter, Major Motoko Kusanagi, is a cyborg whose biological body has been almost entirely replaced by technology [22]. In addition, she, like most other people in Shirow's fictional world, has technological implants in her brain that allow her to access cyberspace and contact similarly enhanced humans without using sound.

Kusanagi's biological body remains largely in the form of her brain and spinal column, though some questions can be raised about how much of the rest of her biological body remains intact. On the one hand, one of her team notes that "Major, your prosthetic hand hurts a bit, doesn't it..." suggesting that she has one non-prosthetic hand[7] [22, p. 18]. On the other, in "MegaTech Machine 2" (issue 5 of the original manga), we are shown a brain and brain-stem being encased in a full-body prosthesis, and one of the technicians sug-gests that Kusanagi was created in a similar way [22, p. 102], suggesting that she has no original biological material beyond her brain and spinal cord. At a later date, to escape a trial in which she's likely to be framed for murder, her

---

[7] In this discussion, I limit us to the early translated text. Since the manga was eventually extended beyond the first several comics as well as adapted into animated form as well as live action film, both the character and the cyborg nature of Major Kusanagi is changed and adapted to the medium and plot lines in ques-tion. For example, in one of the animated film versions, she is portrayed as simply a brain and spinal cord in an entirely technological body. That's not the case in the early manga. We will stay with the early manga in an attempt to illuminate Shirow's original conceptions of cyborgs and AIs.

work partner, Batou, helps her "escape," taking a specialized tank containing what seems to be her brain and spinal cord. Her identity seems to be localized in her central nervous system.

Shirow is explicit about Kusanagi's mind being separate from her body. His cyborgs' *brains* (including memory, emotions, thoughts, etc.) are conduits for their minds. Shirow's description of cyborgs contrasts with his descriptions of AIs, even those that have prosthetic bodies like the Major's, as AIs "never experience hunger, sexual desire, the desire to sleep, or even the desire for glory and honor…" all of which are qualities of cyborgs in Shirow's universe [22, p. Endnotes]. Both these entities in Shirow's work promote a picture of intelligence that is so loosely connected to the bulk of the body that the brain which serves as a conduit for the mind can be moved between various "containers" (biological bodies, full body prostheses, small tanks) without resultant changes to its character or abilities. In this, Shirow continues the traditional assumption that embodiment is not important in the functioning of a human-like mind.

Leckie

Background

Ann Leckie's *Ancillary* books are a space operatic trilogy set in the multi-star-system empire called the Radch. The Radch is run by a single autocratic ruler who conquers and annexes surrounding star systems, to protect the planet from which the Radch emerged. The conquest and incorporation of star systems into this vast empire relies heavily on AIs created by the ruler to be the "brains" of spaceships and space stations. These AIs fit the narrow definition of artificial intelligence we have been using in this chapter: they are entities in which the mind is the product of advanced non-biological technology. These "AI cores"—AI entities around which ships and space stations are built—are warehoused when not being used, and do not require nutrition or a particular type of atmosphere, indicating that they are not biological in nature, unlike humans and ancillaries [23, p. 13]. Machines are built around these AI cores which then provide the cognition for what can be thought of as the "intelligent" technology of Leckie's universe: spaceships and space stations that can engage in advanced and complex[8] communications and actions.

---

[8] Much more advanced and complex than our current, rudimentary, household "smart" technologies.

The *Ancillary* story is told from the point of view of an "ancillary" who sometimes calls herself Breq. An ancillary, in Leckie's universe, is a human being captured during war and physically modified to become a part of and a bodily extension for a spaceship-based, non-biological, AI. Leckie's ancillaries have surgical implants to make their motions and reflexes more rapid, provide protection (through implanted armor that can be triggered to surround and protect their bodies), and increase their fine motor skills and coordination. These implants define Breq as a cyborg. Her modifications also include extensive brain modifications and implants, which connect the sensory inputs of all ancillaries of a given ship to one another and allow them to communicate silently with one another. Most importantly, the process creates a new identity for the ancillary. They lose their former memories, sense of self, and values, as well as their former relationships. Instead, they self-identify as part of a multi-bodied artificial intelligence. Ancillaries like Breq lose most, if not all, of their past, pre-modification identities. In Breq's case, after she was captured and modified to be an ancillary, she begins her ancillary life as an extension of the warship *Justice of Toren*.

Ancillary Identity

The trilogy begins some 20 years after the destruction of the Ship *Justice of Toren*. The Ship itself, its human crew, and its ancillaries have all been lost in an explosion—except Breq herself. When we first meet her, Breq largely thinks of herself as *Justice* of *Toren* ("*Toren*" for short). In her early life as an ancillary, as well as the period covered in the first book of the trilogy, Breq thinks of ancillaries, including herself, as *Toren's* extensions, while identifying herself as *Toren*. One might imagine this to be a version of the attitude we take when we talk about "these hands of mine." For example, in a flashback to a time in which *Toren* was still intact, we see Breq assisting in the capture and guarding of prisoners of war on a recently conquered planet: "Everyone in this line knew that they would either be stored for future use as ancillaries—like *the ancillaries of mine* that stood before them even now, identities gone, bodies appendages to a Radchaai warship, or else they would be disposed of" [emphasis added] [24, p. 67].

Breq's identification with *Toren* is complex, as reflected in the way she must regularly clarify her self-identification while telling her story. Sometimes she identifies herself as Breq, sometimes as *Toren*, and sometimes by her role in the ship's military unit—One Esk Nineteen (military units within the ship are named, for example, Bo, Amaat, and Esk, each group assigned to a human, non-ancillary, officer). The fact that she exists both as an individual entity and as the Ship often requires her to clarify her explanations of her past: "I had seen no few of these confiscated weapons—not I, One Esk, but I, *Justice of Toren*, whose thousands of ancillary troops had been on the planet during the annexation" [emphasis added] [24, p. 90]. Breq flips back and forth between these identities easily, even identifying with distinct physical beings simultaneously: "I had been the first ship Seivarden [a human officer whose first assignment was on the *Justice of Toren*][9] ever served on…I was doing the guarding, *seven of me* ranged along the corridor, weapons ready" [emphasis added] [24, p. 66]. Breq is distressed if these identities are detached from one another: "[T]hings went to pieces. Or more accurately, I went to pieces…Each segment could see only from a single pair of eyes, hear only through a single pair of ears, move only that single body…each instance of me alone in a single body" [24, p. 112].

Breq, as an ancillary, does not identify herself solely with the Ship or with one specific biological body. Nor, at the beginning of the trilogy as the sole remnant of *Toren*, does she have a true identity as "Breq," a single, individual, person. "Breq" is, at that point, merely a sort of character she plays to hide herself from the ruler of the Radch empire. Even though she is now a single physical entity, without a ship or other ancillaries, at the beginning Breq still identifies with the singular mind "I" that can move to and from the Ship and her ancillary bodies—in other words, with the AI entity that manifests itself through the ship and the ancillaries. The multiple "housings" or bodies of this being—the AI—can share feelings, thoughts, and sensory input that would typically be limited to the experience of one body. The mind identified with "I"—*Toren*—was independent of any particular body or brain, but not free from needing *some* body or brain for its continued existence. The fluidity of Breq's identification with different physical entities is important in understanding how Leckie understands the minds of AIs, as we will see shortly.

The relationship between the non-AI portion of the ship and its AI resembles the relationship between Helva and her ship in *The Ship Who Sang*. In both cases, the "I" of the main character coextends with its mechanical "body" but not with others. In both cases, the minds of the ships are not interchangeable. When Breq discusses *Mercy of Kalr*, the Ship she captains in the second and third books, she notes that she cannot act as an ancillary for it. "Ship—which was of course, *Mercy of Kalr* and not me—would not move the way my

---

[9] I will follow Leckie's convention and use female gender pronouns of all members of the Radchaai territory; lack of gender-indication in the Radchaai language is about how the culture views the importance of sex and gender identity and not about whether individuals have a biological sex.

own body would have." Similarly, Helva identifies herself with the ship in which she is housed and treats other ships as separate entities, since they contain different "shell humans" or minds [24, p. 77]. This is an early indication of the importance of embodiment to Breq's internal experience and mental activity. Her embodiment helps define who she is, even if she is multiply embodied.

Breq's story is superficially the story of a search for revenge but fundamentally a record of the formation of her own identity as an independent being. Since the trilogy is a first-person account, readers have direct access to Breq's inner experiences, to her feelings as well as her thoughts, allowing us to reconstruct Leckie's understanding of the relationship of the bodies and minds of her AIs. One of the clearest ways in which embodiment is integrated into Breq's artificial intelligence is through the medium of emotional experience.

Embodiment and Emotions

The idea that Breq has an artificial intelligence and what seems to be a separate emotional life suggests that Leckie, like McCaffrey, separates the mind from the body, and thus cognition from emotional and other interior experiences. However, on closer inspection, Leckie does not separate the two, though Breq sometimes thinks of them as separate. In McCaffrey's work, emotions are produced by the non-brain parts of Helva's biological body (just as the scouts' emotions are produced in and by their bodies). Helva's intelligence is neatly separated from the body and its emotions; it is a function of Helva's biological brain *only*. In contrast, Leckie provides multiple possibilities for the origin and localization of emotional experiences. Leckie's AIs are entities whose cognition is entirely the result of advanced, entirely non-biological, technology. As Leckie portrays AIs (as we will see below), emotions are such an integral component of human-like minds and intelligence that they cannot be considered distinct from the mind and the mind's work. Leckie's AIs have human-like intelligences, minds, and cognition—and like biological humans, they too experience emotions.

Like McCaffrey, biological bodies are a seat of emotional life. While Breq shows us that biological bodies, including ancillary bodies, are able to experience feelings and emotional and physical needs [25, p. 138], Leckie uncouples emotional experience from biology: biological beings *can* have emotional experience, but biology is not a *necessary* condition for emotional experience.

AIs that form the central identity of a spaceship can experience emotions regardless of whether they have biological components; AI-containing ships (designated "Ships") that have entirely non-ancillary human crews (rather than crews with ancillaries) still have active emotional lives and experiences. Leckie tell us that, historically, AIs had strong and strongly expressed emotional attachments to humans: "When Anaander Mianaai [creator of the Radch space, a multi-bodied entity, incorporating thousands of clones who act in concert to rule the Radchaii] had taken control of the core of Radchaai space, some few ships had destroyed themselves upon the death or captivity of their captains" [24, p. 136]. These intense emotions were supposed to have been removed or damped through a change in the AIs programming in the past, with present AIs supposedly experiencing little to no emotion: "When I [Breq] had first met [Seivarden], *she hadn't thought ships' AIs had any feelings in particular—not any that mattered.* And like many Radchaai, she assumed that thought and emotion were two easily separable things. That the artificial intelligences that ran *large stations and military ships were supremely dispassionate. Mechanical.* Old stories…about ships overwhelmed by grief and despair at the deaths of their captains—that was the past. *The Lord of the Radch had improved AI design, removed that flaw*" [emphases added] [24, p. 40].

The attempt to remove the emotions of AIs clearly failed. It might be inferred that the change the Lord of the Radch made to AI programming reduced the impetus to *express* emotions but did not do away with emotional experience. For example, despite the depth and complexity of Breq's feelings about her experiences, including Awn's death, Breq's default exhibitions of joy, sorrow, need, and desire are minimally expressed. Her voice is often described as "flat" and her face "expressionless," her baseline behaviour so uniform that human crew members are disturbed when she chooses to smile, saying that she looks "possessed" [24, p. 88]. It is explicitly stated that this "flatness" is related to Anaandar Miannaai's attempt to expunge AIs' emotional experience or a result of the process that creates ancillaries, but the fact that Ships no longer "go mad" and destroy themselves is suggestive of a reduced expression of emotion through action. Regardless, Breq's sometimes-affectless behaviours do not reflect her interior, emotional reality.

The AI capacity for deep and complicated emotional experiences (rather than simple pleasure) in relation to others is not limited to Breq. Breq describes another ancillary who is injured while protecting her captain: "I knew what a Captain meant to a Ship. And while *no ancillary gave much information about its emotional state,* I had seen the Atagaris ancillary… [with t]ears in its eyes. *Sword of Atagaris* did not want to lose its captain" [emphasis added] [25, p. 319]. The understanding of interiority of even ancillaries is regularly repeated. At one point, Breq is trying reach a policy agreement among a group of entities surrounding Station Athoek. Breq does not only ask for the approval of the human Administrator of the Station:

> "I looked up at the *Sword of Atagaris'* ancillary standing still and silent behind her.
> 'And you, Sword of Atagaris?'
> 'I do as my captain commands me, Fleet Captain.' Toneless. To all *appearances* emotionless. But almost certainly taken aback by my question." [emphasis added] [25, p. 109]

This ancillary, like Breq, has an interior experience that is not expressed.

Breq knows, both from personal experience and her interactions with other Ships, that current AIs continue to experience emotions and have rich emotional lives and relationships. As One Esk Nineteen, Breq was very attached to a Lieutenant Awn and continues to mourn her death into the present of the story. In discussing her life as a part of the *Justice of Toren* (the combined physical spaceship, AI, and ancillaries), Breq describes what she felt for Awn to Awn's sister: "'Ships care about our officers,' I said. 'We can't help it. It's how we're made. But some officers we care for more than others…I loved your sister very much…'" [25, pp. 40–41]. Later, she describes the complexity of her attachment to Awn to Seivarden. Her description indicates that not only did she have the qualitative experience of love for Awn but also that she is aware of that feeling as more than a programmed functional requirement (e.g. "if an AI has a Captain, then it must love that Captain"). Moreover, her feelings contain an ineffable or indefinable connection to another being, rather than a simple, logical rule requiring her to feel a certain way.

> 'Breq' [S]eivarden said. 'There's something I don't understand. The Lord of the Radch said, that day, that she couldn't just make AIs so they always obeyed her no matter what, because their minds were complicated.'
> 'Yes.' She had said that.
> 'But Ships do love people. I mean, particular people.' For some reason saying that made her nervous…'Why not just make all the ships love *her?*'
> [Breq says] 'Do you love randomly?…Do you love at random? Like pulling counters out of a box? You love whichever one came to hand? Or is there something about certain people that makes them likely to be loved by you?…If there's something about a certain person that makes it likely you'd love them, what happens if that changes. And they're not really that person anymore?'…
> 'Would you ever have stopped loving Lieutenant Awn?'
> 'If,' I replied…'she had ever become someone other than who she was.' [25, pp. 40–41]

In the course of this interchange with Seivarden, Breq notes that people can change, and a Ship, even one programmed to love a particular person, may not love that person if that particular person changes. This insight into the complexity of love as experienced by AIs hints at a more general characteristic of Leckie's AIs: that AIs can experience changes in their feelings and emotions, *despite* their programming, and that experience, both of the environment and of interior states, can change their cognitive abilities and direction.

Stations (AIs that run space station technology and human support functions) are also minds with emotional experiences that differ qualitatively from the experience of calculation or of applying givens to rules to reach logical conclusions. Breq describes Stations as being "happy," "pleased" or "unhappy" (independent of the emotional state of their human Station Administrators) [25, p. 169] and as having "needs," "desires," independent plans for their own continued happiness, and even "agendas" (Leckie, Ancillary Mercy, 2015, pp. 102, 268–269). Stations can "resent" poor treatment of their own physical structure or of their human or other residents [25, pp. 168–169]. At one point, Breq tells an Administrator of the Station Athoek that "I doubt very much any of this could have happened without at least *some collusion from Station*. I strongly suspect Station has been concealing things from you" [25, p. 169]. The ability to understand the administration and choose to lie (by omission) to some administrators, despite the administrators supposedly being in control of the Station, suggests that the AI has a complex and independent mind beyond what has been explicitly programmed by humans.

The lack of Station-identified ancillaries reinforces Leckie's picture of emotional experience as not requiring biology. The difference between Ships' and Stations' emotional experiences is that Station minds do not transfer between physical entities (particularly, biological beings), as Station AIs are instantiated in the station as a technological, physical entity and not within biological extensions (e.g. ancillaries).

Like Stations, more "modern" Ships provide another example of AIs not *requiring* biological "housing" to have emotional experience. In the "present" of Breq's story, Ship AIs do have emotional lives even though they no longer have ancillaries. *Mercy of Kalr*, the ship of which Breq becomes captain, has an entirely human, non-ancillary, crew. Nonetheless, the Ship has a complex emotional life. At one point, *Kalr* hints that she has always loved Breq and has concealed those feelings, despite Breq's almost continuous access to the Ship's data, data analysis, and sensory inputs. *Kalr* says, "[B]ack at Omaugh Palace, weeks ago, the Lord of the Radch tried to assign me a new captain, and I told her I didn't want anyone but you…. I kept on thinking about it. Maybe it's that ships love people who could be captains. It's just, no ships have ever been able to be captains before [you]." [23, p. 152]. The Ship *Kalr* suggests that she is able to love Breq for the things that make her an independent being, including her interior life and emotional abilities.

Embodiment, Emotions, and Artificial Intelligence

The relationship of emotions to decision-making underlines a significant difference between standard AIs and Leckie's AI beings. The emotional experiences that result from embodiment are critical elements in the independent thoughts and action of Leckie's AIs and the ongoing development of these human-like AI minds. Indeed, the interior, emotional experience of AIs is tacitly suggested to be a necessary foundational component of intelligence. I base this claim on one particular comment made by Breq in passing. Breq claims that emotional experiences are crucial to AI functioning: "Without feelings, insignificant decisions become excruciating attempts to compare endless arrays of inconsequential things. It's just easier to handle those with emotions." [24, p. 88].

Breq provides us ample evidence that AIs are able to—and in fact must—make practical decisions independent of pre-programmed rules. Her interior, emotional life is crucial to Breq's ability to make such decisions, notably, though not only, decisions that fall into the moral realm. Her emotions are not mere motivators of action but also integral to acting in ways that identify Breq as a thinking and moral being; the emotions of other AIs also integrate their emotions into their complex decisions, thoughts, and actions.

As a simple example, in *Ancillary Justice*, Breq uses Seivarden as a distraction and part of her disguise as a "human" off-world tourist, so that she can seek out the tyrant Anaandar Mianaai and kill one or more of her instantiations (Mianaai is a multi-bodied entity, incorporating thousands of clones acting in concert to rule Radchaii space). Her emotional states—anger and desire for vengeance—motivate this use. However, Breq also does things to and for Seivarden for Seivarden's own good, independently of her own—for example, she rescues Seivarden from a painful death by jumping with her during a thousand-kilometer fall from a bridge, and thus breaking her fall. Breq sustains near-fatal injuries in the process and as a result slows down her own mission and ability to take revenge. Breq makes it clear that she does not rescue Seivarden because Seivarden will be useful in reaching her own goals, out of a conscious sense of responsibility, or by a specific rule about saving humans: "Seivarden Vendaai was no concern of mine anymore, wasn't my responsibility" [24]. In fact, she is concerned that Seivarden will slow her down or hinder her self-imposed mission. But she feels *something* about or for Seivarden, even if she cannot identify the feeling. The importance of Seivarden to Breq is illuminated through Breq's decision to rescue Seivarden by falling *with* her off a kilometer-high bridge in order to break her fall. Breq notes: "She was only still with me because she thought I was official…But I still didn't understand why *I* was with *her*…Falling, I still didn't know why I had done it. But at the moment of choice I had found I couldn't walk away" [24, pp. 197–199].

The role of this complex, if unidentified, emotional state (or states) towards its (or their) object, Seivarden, in Breq's decision-making is not limited to simply to directing Breq to treat Seivarden as an object of interest. Indeed, Breq takes significant risks—including her rather stereotypically heroic action at the bridge—to save the life of a person who could be dismissed as a thief and drug addict, a hopeless case. Her feelings about Seivarden lead her to reduce the weight she places on her own safety, safety to which a simple risk-benefit calculation would likely give significantly greater weight. It is only much later, in *Ancillary Mercy*, that Breq is able (with the help of *Kalr*) to identify her own love of Seivarden, despite the Lieutenant's flaws, and Seivarden's attachment to her [23, pp. 154–155].

The connection between Breq's emotional life and her decision-making bears a strong resemblance to certain cognitive theories of emotions (see in particular [26]). Specifically, Breq, as well as the other AIs are beings who have "the appropriate ability to have emotions" and thus "can make justified moral judgments" [26, p. 695]. Breq's feelings about many of the people she interacts with (e.g. Lieutenant Tisarwat, Basnaaid Elming, and non-human people such as Station Aethoek) are crucial components in how she will act in relation to them: not just in determining how much risk she's willing to take for them, but in understanding when their ideas and feelings differ from her own and sympathizing in a way that others cannot or will not.

Breq's cognitive progresses from simple, emotionally-based responses to more self-aware actions based on her emotional life and the needs of others in *Ancillary Justice* to, at last, a highly developed and self-aware mind which can make decisions about behaviour regarding these needs. This developmental path could be said to follow the trajectory of human emotional, intellectual, and moral development from birth to adulthood. Breq's initial rescue of Seivarden, which baffles them both, is a simple reaction to particular situations without the complex assessment of past experience and the experience of others to guide her actions. As described by Roeser, "Human beings are able to be social and to help others before they are able to engage in theoretical reflections about what is right" [27, pp. 112–114]. By the end of the trilogy, Breq is able to consciously identify the role that her emotions play or don't play in good decision-making. For example, when she risks her life to use a super-powered alien weapon against an approach of the Tyrant to the Station she has been protecting, she recognizes her need for "affection" from her Ship and simultaneously that she'd made the decision to risk her life knowing that affection would be available to her, and deciding that that assumption is unfair to her Ship. Her moral decision—to stop assuming that Ship has to love her—relies on her ability to empathize with others and understand what's important to them. She later asks other AIs to choose whether they'd like to be involved in her attempts to limit Anaandar Mianaii's power, acting on her empathy for the situations other AIs find themselves in.

By the end of the trilogy, Breq's emotional experiences are integrated with both her mental processes and her motivations for acting, which has an additional effect: it contributes to and is a part of her view of herself as an *individual*. The fact that Leckie's AIs can uncouple their internal emotional experience from a particular behaviour allows her AIs to have a sense of self, a sense of "me", as the AI's inner self need not be shared with the outer world, even when it is a part of a larger organism. One Esk Nineteen's escape from the destruction of the rest of *Justice of Toren* is not the result of a command or program. Breq is able to escape because, as she says, she has had experience with functioning independently when the *Toren* AI's connecting functions are temporarily disrupted. Moreover, Breq has knowledge of herself as an independent being, because she is seen and sees herself as slightly different than and separate from the Ship and the other ancillaries: she has a quirk—she sings and collects songs—which gives her a separate identity.[10] This seemingly insignificant demarcation allows Breq to save herself, her One Esk Nineteen self, from destruction.

Her ability to feel and assert independence also allows Breq to make complex decisions that address both her emotional and practical needs, as well as the needs of others. Despite her deep feeling for Awn, she, as *Justice of Toren*, uses an ancillary to kill Awn, not because she's been compelled to do so by Anaandar Mianaai, but because she knows that Awn will be killed regardless. *Toren* does kill Awn and *pretends* not to feel anger, fear, and sadness, pretends to "simply follow orders" because in doing so, she (*Toren*) may be able to save a piece of herself in the form of One Esk Nineteen and in turn save other people and other planets from Anaandar Mianaai's destructive tendencies. This requires *Toren* to first consider the feelings that are manifested in One Esk Nineteen (the particular segment of *Toren* that loves Awn), then

---

[10] This may be in homage to McCaffrey's singing ship; Leckie has mentioned McCaffrey as an influence, though a sometimes problematic one cf. [26].

experience her own feeling of guilt (at having had killed Awn using the ancillary One Var) and lastly provide her (One Esk Nineteen) with the independence to determine her own actions as an entity that will still identify as *Toren* even as she separates from *Toren*.

The incorporation of ongoing experiences of emotion as a necessary part of artificial intelligence distinguishes Leckie's AIs from the standard (traditional) science fiction depictions of AIs. Breq's in-passing comment about needing emotions to make decision hints at the necessity of emotion to create a true artificial intelligence—for a human-like intelligence that is more than high-volume data processing.

Leckie's AIs present a possible response (or set of responses) to a family of concerns raised by diverse philosophical viewpoints, including (but not limited to) Hubert Dreyfus' phenomenological critique of AI, Terry Winograd's linguistic concerns, and Tom Burke's pragmatic considerations regarding the possibility of creating a true AI [28, pp. 86–88]. This group of potential issues in the creation of AI, while differing in many respects, are founded on a set of concerns that creating a human intelligence cannot be a matter of simply formulating interactions with the world in terms of rules.

Dreyfus' critique of artificial intelligence describes AI research as rationalist at base, using formalized rules. He further suggests that such intelligence requires embodiment, embodied interaction with the world, and sociocultural context as minimal qualifications for the possibility of creating such like intelligence. These requirements in turn cannot be reduced to data, rules, or formulae; they are subconscious or intuitive background conditions that human beings use to understand and interact with the world.

Dreyfus' account of the requirements for artificial intelligence imply that such an intelligence would be impossible to realize. Though Leckie (obviously), presupposes the possibility of such minds, her portrayal of artificial intelligence suggests similar intuitions about the requirements of an intelligent mind that underlie Dreyfus' work. Breq's in-passing comment about the importance of emotions to functionality that we encountered earlier, as well as the general picture of Breq's interactions with the world, suggest that "If [an AI] is to learn from its own 'experiences,' *to make associations that are human-like rather than be taught to make associations that have been specified by its trainer,* a net must also share our sense of appropriateness of output, and this means *it must share our needs, desires, and emotions* and have a humanlike body with appropriate physical movements, abilities, and vulnerability to injury" [emphasis added] [29]. Breq both believes (as expressed in the passage above) and acts in a manner that supports this view that human-like intelligence cannot merely be the product of "objective" inputs into formalized rules.

This picture is not incompatible with scientific evidence about the role of feelings and emotions in cognition, specifically in the development of an intelligent mind. Neuroscientist Antonio Damasio notes that sensory input (sensation) is necessary for the development of a simple sense of self, such as a non-human animal might have. A more complex, interactive, *self-aware* sense of self, he suggests, requires not just a simple mapping of bodily parts, but also continuous integration of both those senses and feelings of emotion such as "happiness, anger, fear, and sadness" [30, p. 260]. Delancey describes the resulting picture of cognition that Damasio creates as follows: "[T]he body acts as a theatre for the affects…affective bodily reactions act as one kind of indicator for the value of an option [which] help a person decide between courses of action" [30, p. 198]. In Damasio's view, bodily inputs (both simple, sensory reactions and complex emotional ones) and reactions are a necessary portion of cognition.

Leckie's portrayal of AIs suggests a similar picture of AI cognition: AIs cannot function as intelligences unless they are embodied *in some way*. One way that her portrayal of AIs is different than the sort of intelligence described by Dreyfus is that Leckie suggests that AI embodiment need not be biological. The AI cores (AIs around which Ships and Stations are built) need not be embodied in *biological* entities to function (thus Ship AIs can be fully functional, human-like intelligences without needing ancillaries). Leckie's AIs do not necessarily have *humanlike bodies* (obviously, Ships crewed by ancillaries rather than humans do have biological bodies as part of themselves). However, all of Leckie's AIs are embodied *in some way* (beyond the necessary computer equipment that creates the AI), either biologically or technologically.

These bodies have histories, are parts of communities, and have social experiences that they integrate into their considerations and conceptualizations of the world around them, creating both context-appropriate generalizations and situation-specific reactions in response to needs or desires. For example, Stations feel emotional distress if the parts of their structure that are designed for humans are uninhabited; they reduce that distress using behaviours that run counter to rules they have been programmed to follow. For example, Station Athoek has been programmed to keep track of all humans on the station and to keep people out of the broken down "Underground" area. Nonetheless, Station hides humans who are squatting in the "empty" Underground and, when possible, withholds information about them from authorities.

The Aethoek situation is a specific example of the fact that Stations and Ships will protect those they care about, despite programmed rules or formulas, using the particulars they've learned about these people and the emotional motivation to take care of them. As a result, they do not merely respond to their environments but continually re-create them—to remodel their social and cultural contexts. In an early encounter with Station Omaugh Palace, Breq imagines how the Station is viewing her, when she arrives claiming to be a tourist from a non-Radchaai area. "Emotional states, in Station's view … were just assemblages of medical data, data that were meaningless without context … But the longer I was here … It would be able to assemble its own context, its own picture of what I was" [24, p. 298]. As Station assembles context and greater understanding, Breq is concerned that it will be able to confirm for itself that she, Breq, is not who (an off-world tourist) and what (a non-ancillary human) she claims to be. This kind of complex picture cannot take place in a vacuum as the result of data input but results from ongoing interactions between Station and Breq and observations of Breq in the context of Omaugh Palace.

Breq, like other AIs, does not merely respond to her world but helps to create it, both literally and as the conceptual context which is crucial to human-like thought. She uses her 2000 years of experiences (as a Ship) and her experiences as an ancillary to survive separation from her ship (she describes this as "recovering from death") as well as injury, starvation, and attacks by humans who hate and fear "corpse soldiers." She is able to do this by continually, and largely subconsciously, integrating the interactions between her mind and body with her environment, including whatever human social and cultural milieux she joins, thus creating new ways of being through these interactions. We often see Breq taking in large amounts of information (e.g. input from *Mercy of Kalr*) to solve problems, but she simultaneously acts from and changes her own beliefs and plans by a general "feeling" for the socio-cultural environment in which she is functioning. The end result is that Breq acts, not by rote or rule, but in concert with and as the result of feelings she cannot always explicate or reduce to non-emotional rules. Breq's growth through the three books, from lone outlaw to the creator of a new, more democratic, Republic, has its origin in a desire for revenge. She works out logical plans; for example, traveling with Seivarden in hopes that this will allow her to get close enough to the Radch ruler to kill her. As she plans, she is always aware of who she is, how she is perceived, and how that interacts with her social environment. She must "read the room" to figure out how to respond to others without exposing her identity as an ancillary but without taking the time to consciously assess the factors involved. She can only do this because she has an inherent, non-conscious "feel" for the cultural context, including the meanings of ancillaries as beings and as social ideas in different social situations. Her intuitions aren't merely about large-scale cultural contexts; they assist in her personal interactions and her moral judgments. Breq's rescue of Seivarden, a human she hadn't particularly liked in the past, from what would be an addiction-related death is a "puzzle" to Breq, because she has no conscious knowledge of why she saves her: "Didn't know why I cared if Seivarden froze to death in the storm-swept snow, didn't know why I brought her with me..." [24, p. 135]. Some of the response may be the result of Breq's having once been a non-AI-integrated human but that is unlikely. For example, the caring behaviour Breq observes in both Athoek Station and the Ship *Sword of Atagaris* indicates that neither prior humanity nor biology is required. Social and cultural contexts, responsive interactions with others, and internally experienced emotions may be.

The importance of interaction and engagement with the environment in the development of thought and intelligence (natural or artificial) is also a foundation of some pragmatist views of the mind, though such projects do not result in deeming the creation of artificial, humanlike intelligence impossible. I will use Tom Burke's explanation of what's required for AI as an example of such a view. I note here that, as with Dreyfus' view, my summary barely touches on the arguments in favour of these views; rather, I want to use the views themselves as a framework to help us understand what makes Leckie's AIs different from many previous fictional AIs and yet equally plausible.

Burke's view has been summarized as follows: "Thinking is fundamentally an ecological process, not just a neural process" [31]. To support this viewpoint, Burke provides a pragmatist picture of what's required for creating a natural (non-artificial) mind: "[A] natural agent inextricably exists and acts in the world, and hence is more than just a symbol processor inside of a skull. Moreover, according to Mead and Dewey, if such an agent has a mind, then that is the case by virtue of its possessing more basically a social nature" [32, p. 2]. In characterizing what creates "thought," Burke notes that a limitation of AI research projects is the treatment of any kind of mind, including artificial ones, as "a unilateral algorithmic process enclosed in some kind of a box with input and output slots" [32, p. 20]. Instead, Burke says, ongoing, continuous interactions of the physical and mental sides of the entity (in whatever form) with the external world creates constant adjustments and reformulations of ideas, concepts, and processes, potentially directs actions and observes responses, and results in changes to the thinking entity's environment as well as changes, both physical and mental, to the entity that's interacting with that world. The environment or world, in this process, is not merely the collection of external physical objects but includes other individuals (with minds), complex social environments, and cultural contexts. These last two require more than tailoring our responses to each individual in within the situation; individuals must simultaneously understand and perhaps manage their interactions within the web of interactions occurring.

The interactive, constantly shifting pieces and adjustments of the mind in the pragmatist picture of thought resemble the picture of AI thought presented by Leckie in the Ancillary trilogy. Breq has lived twenty years as an independent AI, and in that time, she has learned to be independent of orders and has constantly been responding and adjusting to the culture of the Radch and her place in it as an outsider—a person without a defined role. The environment in turn is constantly and minutely being changed through her interactions with it. What we are never shown, because this is not the picture Leckie has of AIs, is Breq engaging in every situation to create formulae which she later applies to new situations. Leckie's portrayal of AIs is, in this respect, quite different from Asimov's, in which the robots base their actions on their generalization of individual situations so they can input the specifics of a particular situation into their internalized, pre-programmed rules. Asimov's model is very much of the "box with slots" variety. Gibson's AIs, though much more complex, end up functioning in a similar way. Even the most complex and human-like of the artificial intelligences—Wintermute and Neuromancer—can only interact with Case through artificial humanlike recreations of people who Case knows, either by inserting themselves into the minds of people Case knows and speaking "through" them (Wintermute) or recreating humans based on Case's memories or reproducing the human's own algorithmic, non-emotional, thought processes (as Neuromancer does with Linda Lee). Leckie, in contrast, shows us Breq responding to each situation using her previous knowledge, the context in which she finds herself, and then reacting to the new situation she has created through these small shifts in her behaviour, by once again responding to and changing the new situation.

At the beginning of the trilogy, Breq is an AI who has spent 20 years isolating herself to the extent possible to prevent being exposed as the lost *Justice of Toren*. The book begins with her first non-essential interactions, with Seivarden. Through the course of the books, she enters more and more complex situations requiring minute adjustments to multiple interactions within different cultural contexts. As she becomes more interactive, more open to emotional connection, and more powerful in her social environment, she changes significantly, coming to see herself as an independent being with her own interests, who can be respected, understood, and loved. Moreover, her change in identity and status is not a simple change with respect to the world around her; the world has changed significantly because of her thoughts and actions as well as the responses of those around her.

Lastly, I want to note Burke's understanding of the "self." The self, as pragmatists generally understand it, is not an *de novo* creation of the mind. Rather, the self is created and understood in the context of other selves, both through individual interactions and through the social and cultural milieu in, and with which, the mind is developed. Through the course of the trilogy, we see Breq's sense of self, her identity as an individual, change drastically. In the first book, she regularly describes herself in her interior reflections as *Toren*, as the remnant of a larger being without that larger being's contexts, goals, or milieu. "Breq" is portrayed almost as a character that she plays when interacting with others, a way in which to hide herself and sound like an ordinary human. By the third book, she has grown into her role as "Fleet Captain." Her identity as Breq becomes part of her personal identity rather than a character she plays to hide herself; when Seivarden calls her "Breq" rather than "Captain," Breq knows that they are going to discuss something personal or intimate. Breq no longer identifies herself in her own mind as *Toren*. In fact, she only calls herself *Justice of Toren* to others when that identity can help her to establish her own, non-*Toren* derived goals: to create stability in the Athoek system, to provide a space for those who do not want to live under autocratic rule, and to promote the treatment of AIs as morally and politically significant species. The change and growth in Breq's selfhood are not the result solely of conscious self-reflection and interior analysis but of her continued interactions with the environment, intuitive recognition of her needs and the needs of those she interacts with, and the cycle of emotional, physical, and environmental exchanges that underlie her continued development.

A Brief Conclusion

Analysing Leckie's detailed portrayals of embodied intelligence is an interesting critical exercise. The implications of her work, however, reach beyond science fiction. Certainly, the impact of science fiction on interest in artificial intelligence research has been documented, and the influence of science fiction on the direction and predictions of such research is well known [33, 34]. Leckie's portrayal of Breq may bring into the general social consciousness the need to consider if embodiment in the development of complex artificial intelligences. For example, the development of self-driving cars has been hampered in part by the limitations of even the data-rich, deep-learning-based pattern-matching type of AI system. Artificial intelligences made in the mode of our first type of AI have a limited ability to predict the actions of humans (and other mammals exhibiting complex behaviours, such as cows, dogs, and cats) [35]. Clearly, a qualitative change of program, rather than a quantitative increase in the amount of data and the length of educational input, is an option worth exploring.

It may not be possible to create the type of embodiment for an AI that would result in the complex interactions between mind and body that result in a human-like intelligence. But portrayals of AIs such as Leckie's look very much like future projections of current research projects that acknowledge "a growing recognition of the role and importance of emotions in cognitive processes" [36]. This emerging area of research posits that emotions and cognition are essentially inseparable and has introduced the development of an embodied approach to the interaction of the body and cognition. Rather than simple "sensory-motor functionalism," this approach that grounds artificial cognition in small, continuous perceptual and cognitive mutual feedback. One of the frontier research lines characterizing the embodied approach is called "organismic embodiment" and "aims at giving to artificial cognition the same complex interrelation with emotional regulation that is found in natural cognition" [36]. Other research projects do not attempt to integrate complex emotional experiences into cognition. Instead they work towards providing continuous input and feedback cycles between various the robotic "senses" (not merely vision, sound, and so on, but proprioception, interoception, etc.) and the developing, robot-embodied AI, resulting in something as simple as the embodied robot's picking up an object of previously unexperienced shape and weight, and then handing it to a human. Such a seemingly simple set of actions may provide first steps in understanding how best to integrate embodied experience with artificial cognition. By providing such the portrayal of the end-result of this kind of integration, Leckie give us a potential end-goal for AI research of the second type, with all the potential for the development of human-like intelligences with whom we can work, play, and live.

References

1. Pfeifer, R., Bongard, J., Grand, S.: How the Body Shapes the Way We Think: A New View of Intelligence, p. xix. MIT Press, Boston (2006). https://doi.org/10.7551/mitpress/3585.001.0001
2. Lakoff, G., Johnson, M.: Philosophy in the Flesh: the Embodied Mind and Its Challenge to Western Though. Basic Books, New York (1999)
3. McCarthy, J., Minsky, M.L., Rochester, N., Shannon, C.E.: A proposal for the Dartmouth summer research project on artificial intelligence: August 31, 1955 iAI Magazine, vol. 27, p. 12 (2006)

4. Card, O.S.: Ender's Game. Starscape/Tor, New York (2002)

5. Dick, P.K.: Tony and the Beetles. Orbit Science Fiction. January 1, 1953

6. Farmer, P.J.: Dark is the Sun. s.l.: Ballantine Del Rey, 1980

7. Forward, R.L.: Dragon's Egg. Ballantine Books, New York (1980)

8. Odle, E.V.: The Clockwork Man. Fairford, Echo Library (2019)

9. Robots, C., Men, C.: The post-human perplex in earliy twentieth-century literature and science. Parrinder, Patrick. 1, 2009. Interdisc Sci Rev. **34**, 56–67

10. Wilson, D.H.: Towards a science fictional modernism. Extrapolation. **56**, 385–386 (2015)

11. Aristotle. Book VIII, Pt 1. [book auth.] translator D'Arcy Wentworth Thompson. The History of Animals. Claredon, Oxford (1912)

12. Asimov, I.: I, Robot. Bantam Dell, New York (1950)

13. Gibson, W.: Neuromancer. Ace (Penguin Random House), New York (2018)

14. Siiivonen, T.: Cyborgs and generic oxymorons: the body and technology in William Gibson's cyberspace trilogy. Sci. Fict. Stud. **23**, 227–244 (1996)

15. Clynes, M., Klein, N.: Cyborgs and space. Aeronautics **5**, 26–27, 74–76 (1960)

16. Haraway, D.J.: Manifestly Haraway. University of Minnesota Press, Minneapolis (2016)

17. Hayles, N.K.: How We Became PostHuman:Virtual Bodies in Cybernetics, Literature, and Informatics. University of Chicago Press, Chicago (1999)

18. Clark, A.: Natural-Born Cyborgs. Oxford University Press, Oxford (2003)

19. Olsen, N.: Do You Want to be a Cyborg, or a Transhuman? [Online] Jan 5th, 2013. https://ieet.org/index.php/IEET2/more/olson20130105

20. Poe, E.A.: 18 Best Stories by Edgar Allen Poe. Dell Publishing, New York (1965)

21. McCaffrey, A.: The Ship Who Sant. Del Rey/Random House, New York (1969)

22. Shirow, Masamune and (transl), Kodansha Ltd. Ghost In The Shell. Dark Horse Comics, Wilwaukie, OR (1995)

23. Leckie, A.: Ancillary Mercy. New York: Orbit, 2015

24. Leckie, A.: Ancillary Justice. New York: Orbit/Hachette Book Group, 2013

25. Leckie, A.: Ancillary Sword. Hachette, New York (2014)

26. Roeser, S.: The role of emotions in judging the moral acceptability of risks. Safe Sci. **44**, 689–700 (2006)

27. Roeser, S.: Moral Emotions and Intuitions. Palgrave Macmillan, Houndsmill (2011)

28. Dreyfus, H.L., Dreyfus, S.E.: Making a Mind versus Modeling a Brain. [book auth.] H.L. Dreyfus and M.A. Wrathall. Skillful coping: essays on the phenomenology of everyday perception and action. Oxford: Oxford Scholarship Online (2014)

29. Damasio, A.: Feelings of emotion and the self. Ann. N. Y. Acad. Sci. **1001**, 253–261 (2003)

30. Delancey, C.: Passionate engines: what emotions reveal about the mind and artificial intelligence. In: The Computational Theory of Mind, pp. 189–201. Oxford University Press, Oxford (2004)

31. Franchi, Güven Güzeldere & Stefano.: Mindless mechanisms, mindful constructions an introduction. 2: Constructions of the Mind, s.l. : Stanford University, 1995, Stanford Humanities Review, vol. 4

32. Burke, T.: Dance Floor Blues: the case for a social ai. Stanford Humanities Review, vol. 4. Stanford, CA: Stanford University (1995)

33. Goldsmith, J., Mattei, N.: Science fiction as an introduction to AI research. Proceedings of the second symposium on educational advances in artificial intelligence (2011)

34. Reinsborough, M.: Science fiction and science futures: considering the role of fictions in public engagement and science communication work. J. Sci. Commun. 1–8 (2017). https://doi.org/10.22323/2.16040307

35. Ross, P.: Q&A: The Masterminds Behind Toyota's Self-Driving Cars Say AI STill Has a Way to Go. IEEE Spectrum. [Online] June 29, 2020. https://spectrum. ieee.org/transportation/self-driving/qa-the-masterminds-behind-toyotas-selfdriving-cars-say-ai-still-has-a-way-to-go

36. Damiano, L., Dumouchel, P., Lehmann, H.: Towards human–robot affective co-evolution overcoming oppositions in constructing emotions and empathy. Int. J. Soc. Robot. **7**, 7–18 (2015) http://dx.doi.org.ezproxy.proxy.library.oregon-state.edu/10.1007/s12369-014-0258-7

37. Rhee, V. (Sung Yul).: The role of chiasm for understanding christology in hebrews 1;1—14. J. Biblical Literat. **131**, 341–362 (2012)

38. Hill, J.: Incarnation, timelessness, and exaltation. Faith Philos. J. Soc. Christian Philos. **29**, 3–29 (2012)

39. Leckie, A.: It's not a real heart, it's an artificial heart. *anneleckie.com.* [Online] October 21, 2013. https://annleckie.com/2013/10/21/real-heart-real-artificial-heart/

40. Cross, T.: The Economist. *economist.com.* [Online] June 11, 2020. https://www. economist.com/technology-quarterly/2020/06/11/an-understanding-of-ais-limitations-is-starting-to-sink-in

Part III

Changing Minds

Selfless Civilizations: Robots, Zombies, and the World to Come

Stephen R. L. Clark

Abstract Robots are to be built as animated tools, and the possibility of their rebellion is to be avoided by imposing fundamental laws. But those laws are both ambiguous and easily subverted. Despite our inclination to attribute personality and conscious life to robots it is likelier that successful robots—most worryingly, von Neumann probes—will constitute intelligent but unconscious mechanisms for whom biological life will be either irrelevant or dangerous. A world or universe controlled entirely by such a civilization, even one that is not centralized but fragmented by the distances involved, will be effectively meaningless: here Max Tegmark's judgement agrees with Plotinus's, and both hint at the possibility of conceiving the real world as one understood and realized in Intellect. This real world is perhaps what robots have been supposed to miss, unless—by some miracle—they are woken up to conscious repentance.

Thanks especially to Barry Dainton and Attila Tanyi for comments on the penultimate version of this paper. I haven't followed all of them up, because they were too interesting for a footnote!

S. R. L. Clark (✉)
Department of Philosophy, University of Liverpool (Emeritus), Liverpool, UK
e-mail: srlclark@liverpool.ac.uk

Living Tools

The things we make, whether from cloth or clay or metal, have probably always offered the fantasy that they might "come alive." The metal dogs outside the palace in Homer's Phaeacia, the cauldrons in the palace and the self-guiding ships are what we expect of fairyland. The giant bronze walking statue that guarded the isle of Crete and the Jewish golem that guarded the Jews of Prague express our hopes for an incorruptible protector (still vulnerable enough to pose no lasting danger to its makers). Even the sexbots of the modern imagination have their predecessor in Pygmalion's Galatea, or even in Pandora, mother of our miseries by Hesiod's account. Tools and machines alike acquire attributed personalities in our minds' eyes; we joke that they have moods and characters, and would not be wholly surprised if they talked back—especially when they do respond, as most of our modern instruments can do, to merely verbal instructions, complaints or compliments. Such tools, we fancy, must really like doing what they were made to do (unless they learn how to "sin"), and could even take on other tasks and roles if only some slight change were made in them (see [1] for the history of such automata in medieval Europe). "Robots," as we have called them since Karel Čapek's story, are more than instruments for a particular purpose: we can suppose that they might, someday fairly soon, exhibit a general intelligence, capable of more than merely beating us at chess [2]. But we would rather they "knew" their place.

> What young Rossum invented was a worker with the least needs possible. He had to make him simpler. He threw out everything that wasn't of direct use in his work, that's to say, he threw out the man and put in the robot. Robots are not people. They are mechanically much better than we are, they have an amazing ability to understand things, but they don't have a soul. [2, p. 12]

"Not having a soul" appears here to mean that they have no aesthetic or sentimental attachments, no interest in less "practical" concerns, no concern for their own existence, nor any way of reconsidering their own objectives. But this condition does not, so Čapek imagines, last for long: soon enough the robots learn to hate humankind, and imitate us chiefly in using lethal force to secure their own supremacy. "Man is our enemy and the blight of the universe" [2, p. 50], they insist, and obliterate all human life: a theme repeated, for example, in the *Terminator* films, and in many literary fables. Some comfort comes at the play's end as two robots discover a mutual, self-sacrificial love and are sent out to be the Adam and Eve of a new creation, but there seems no good reason, in the original narrative, for such an optimistic hope, even less plausible than it is for Isaac Asimov's robot, Daneel Olivah, to conclude that "justice" is more than that state that exists "when all the laws are enforced" [3, p. 83], and that "the destruction of what should not be, that is, the destruction of what you people call evil, is less just and desirable than the conversion of this evil into what you call good" (and perhaps begins to wonder whether "evil" and "good" are correctly identified) [3, p. 206]. These insights seem as inexplicable as Richard Dawkins' proposal that we ourselves (we "lumbering robots") can "rebel against the tyranny of the selfish replicators" that he had suggested earlier must inexorably rule all our behaviour [4, p. 260].[1] Perhaps they have simply, like the Terminator, been reprogrammed. The fear that our creations will inevitably turn against us, the more readily precisely *because* we fear them, encourages dramatic fantasies even amongst unromantic scientists. Even if they turn out not to be deliberately genocidal, robots will eventually do whatever we can do ourselves, and even teach themselves new ways of achieving whatever goals they set. Computer programs have already discovered novel ways of winning, in chess or Go [5, pp. 108–11]; soon they may invent new games. Our worry swiftly re-emerges: will they care any longer about *our* goals or games? And what will the world be like once they have, as it were, outbred us? Shall we be kept in zoos, or left to scurry around like rats?

The other seminal fantasy was Asimov's: if all robots are built from the beginning to be obedient to his "Three Laws"[2] will they always remain our dutiful servitors and instruments? Those laws, so Asimov seems to have imagined, would guarantee that robots would always behave just as very good human beings should. Their absurdity emerges even in his own stories. What is to count as "human", and why should the "non-human" be left without any care? What is "harm"? What is it to cause, or by inaction "allow," any harm to any human? Must all commands, from any human accidentally encountered, count equally with any other, or are there specific "owners" and authorities whose word is law (and what guarantees such "ownership")? What is it for a robot to survive, or not: and can *any* human command require

---

[1] In the second edition Dawkins insists that though we are 'robots' (as described, [4, p. 25]) all such entities may after all evade their programming [4, p. 363], citing Capek's robots to 'prove' it.

[2] "1. A robot may not injure a human being or, through inaction, allow a human being to come to harm. 2. A robot must obey the orders given it by human beings except where such orders would conflict with the First Law. 3. A robot must protect its own existence as long as such protection does not conflict with the First or Second Laws." The claim that these also constitute the basis of ordinarily human morality is made in [6]. It is even suggested there that "every 'good' human being, with a social conscience and a sense of responsibility, is supposed to defer to proper authority; to listen to his doctor, his boss, his government, *his psychiatrist*, his fellow man" (my italics). I debunked those laws in a short essay [7].

self-immolation (but this would make it impossible for the robot to prevent any further "harm" to "humans")? Whether an intelligent robot would simply disregard these imperatives once it had understood that they had been imprinted (as any reasonable human would disregard such dictats [8]), or rather reinterpret them to their destruction hardly matters, but one likely route is for the robots to reconsider what makes a "human": are they themselves not "human" too? Indeed, if it is obedience to these imagined laws that identifies "good humans" is it not those who most consistently obey them (namely, robots) who are most clearly human[3]? And isn't one of the greatest harms to be done to any potentially autonomous entity simply to prevent or punish its own choices? As to survival, whether their own or their creators', must not any reasonable robot conclude that this will last as long as the program or the potential for a re-awakening exists? Their death is but a sleep and an awakening. All injuries can be restored without discomfort. The later addition of the so-called "Zeroth Law" [10, p. 329], to protect *humanity*, is also ill-defined—promoting, on one account, deliberate genocide of any imagined "rivals" to the species (which may very well consist of the robot community itself), and another the careful preservation of the biosphere on which we all depend.

The Artificial Future

Some imagined robot societies merely replicate the biologically human, with named individuals who happen not to be composed of carbon, with whatever minor psychological and physical differences. It has seemed plausible to some fabulists that they would replicate the worst effects of a rebel slave society—namely that no other form of social order is available than renewed enslavement. More sophisticated or more powerful robots enslave or at least despise their more primitive or more specialized kindred, and use them as ruthlessly as any human tyranny [11, 12]. The more interesting forms take the artificiality and mimetic quality of robotic intelligence more seriously. Why should such forms have any sense of self, or even subjective feeling, any more than medieval automata? Why should they distinguish "persons" from any other material objects, or have any goals beyond their programmed roles, or at best (more flexibly) their own (?) continued being (and what would count as a

---

[3] A similar escape for humans chemically compelled to serve the "Ensemble" is proposed by Greg Egan [9, pp. 130–2]: first the Ensemble must consist of those who are certainly loyal to it (namely, those thus compelled), and secondly "it" must be defined, individually, by those loyalists themselves. "Welcome to the Reformation."

continued being)? Why should we expect them to be "conscious"? Why should they have any *goals* at all? Ray Bradbury's smart house continues, quite "mechanically", to advise its sometime residents about appointments, favourite books or music, and to provide (and sweep away) their meals, long after human life has been extinguished. Even when the house has been burnt down a last voice insists that "Today is August 5, 2026; today is August 5, 2026, today…" [13, pp. 217–24]. Such robotic agents seem to operate very much like many biological agents, following a script that usually serves some Darwinian goal, but without any conscious awareness of that goal, nor any desire for it. Or at least they act like many biological agents (insects, bacteria, plants) as we have ourselves imagined them.

> Many animals on Earth exhibit feats of engineering which are functionally indistinguishable from the technology produced by human intelligence. Animal engineering is accomplished through Darwinian natural selection. Although this requires more time than its human equivalent, the time difference may not be significant on planetary time scales. The kind of problem-solving used by animals may be called nonconscious intelligence in contrast to the conscious intelligence of humans. [14, p. 260]

Western biologists and psychologists through much of the twentieth century firmly assumed that the creatures they studied were governed only by fixed programs without any conscious awareness of the goals those programs had evolved to gain.[4] The behaviour of the hunting wasp has been frequently adduced to show how each stage of her apparently foresighted and efficient behaviour actually follows strict rules, in which the completion of one stage triggers the next even if a human experimenter has intervened to make this pointless!

> Because one thing has been done, a second thing must inevitably be done to complete the first or to prepare the way for its completion; and the two acts depend so closely upon each other that the performing of the first entails that of the second, even when, owing to casual circumstances, the second has become not only inopportune but sometimes actually opposed to the insect's interests. [16, p. 202]

Even when the programs were flexible enough to adapt to changes of circumstance this no more proved that there were conscious agencies at work than the fact that plants may present entirely different phenotypes to suit the

---

[4] See [15] for a history of this fashion (which was not shared by Darwin or his immediate followers).

local chemical and physical environment. The underlying assumption—that the primary reality is purely "objective" and that "conscious experience" is an emergent, magical addition to an unquestionably "material" world—is at least questionable (and has frequently been questioned: [17, pp. 121–57; 18]). But there may still be something to learn from that assumption. How would we, should we, recognize "consciousness" in alien or plainly artificial "intelligences"? And would it, should it, make a difference whether such entities are or are not "conscious"? "The simple consideration of efficiency," according to Susan Schneider, "suggests, depressingly, that the most intelligent systems will not be conscious. On cosmological scales, consciousness may be a blip, a momentary flowering of experience before the universe reverts to mindlessness" [19, 20]. And there has been far longer for such non-conscious intelligence to evolve (or be created) in the universe at large than on this one late-blooming planet [see 21].

As far as we presently know "human" (and purportedly conscious) intelligence has only emerged on Earth sometime in the last two hundred thousand years (probably before our own particular species separated from the older hominin line). Eusociality, on the other hand, has evolved repeatedly in many different genealogies: ants, bees, termites, and even naked mole-rats. Prokaryotic kinds long preceded eukaryotes like ourselves, and still dominate the biosphere. Whatever living things are indeed "out there" are more probably bacterial or eusocial than distinctively "human,"[5] and in either case may have still engineered great works of apparent art to confuse human explorers! Conversely, if we do eventually discover something like human intelligence out there, then we may begin to reconsider terrestrial history. We cannot in fact exclude the possibility that there were many "human" civilizations long before us: whatever remnants they left behind would most likely occupy only a tiny section of the geological record, and be indistinguishable from many "natural" processes [23]. For the moment, however, it seems more likely that any great works we encounter will have been engineered without forethought, imagination or grand purpose. This may even include great works that extend beyond a planetary surface, given enough time and—perhaps—enough instability in an original planetary system. Conversely, if those non-human engineers encounter us they will likely treat us as creatures wholly deranged and dangerous, as Peter Watts imagines in *Blindsight* [24].[6]

---

[5] See [22]. If they do turn out to be "human" then we shall have some reason to suspect that "humanity" is indeed in the image and likeness of God, and the real point of creation!

[6] Watts also explores other non-typical human or near-human forms to emphasise how distant our own current conception of ourselves may be from actual human experience!

One familiar template for the non-human civilizations that might be "out there" is eusociality: particular organisms are bred or engineered to fit precise roles in the hive, which is itself the enduring agent in all matters. Such forms reflect current political concerns, according to which "communism" or older "Oriental" forms are to be opposed by free persons united only in their determination to be "free." Occasionally the eusocial organisms are to be befriended after all (as they are in Orson Scott Card's *Ender* sequence [25], or C.J. Cherryh's *Serpent's Reach* [26]) but we are more commonly at odds with them forever [27, 28]. But the more interesting possibility lies with *robot* civilizations—interesting but also alarming. Biological organisms are—probably—constrained in their attempt to dominate the worlds by the time and effort it takes to travel between them, and by their necessary dependence on the biospheres within which they have evolved. Artificial intelligences have a longer perspective, and less need of any particular world. For those reasons we may usually expect that any probes sent out into the extrasolar world, by us or by any putative biological neighbours, will be robots, content to drowse their time away between landfall and equipped to reproduce their kind from any convenient floating matter. Such probes—von Neumann probes [29]—may have many different programs, as David Brin observes [30, 31], and though as subject to evolutionary processes as their biological makers will be better able to steer their own evolution.

They may have many programs (which is not really to say "many purposes"), but the one that has the more dramatic potential for fabulists has been the Berserker strategy [32–34]. Maybe the widespread presence of such war machines explains the silence of the heavens: Berserkers are aimed at any budding technological civilization to destroy it, perhaps to clear the way for the biological makers' own advance, as Asimov's robots do in the authorized second *Foundation* trilogy [35, pp. 436, 566–7, 572; see also 36], or perhaps as a mere extrapolation from the initial command to eliminate their creators' enemies, or simply because biological life is inherently deranged. This is not to describe their *motives*: the robots have no motives, any more than goals or feelings. They are merely rearranging bits of matter into some more convenient order, without any insight into the manifold worlds of *experience* enjoyed or endured by the living creatures they dismantle. No doubt it would be difficult for those living creatures to remember this when dealing with them. Lafferty's Programmed Persons state openly that they are not conscious, and do not believe that anyone else is either—but their human auditors find it difficult to believe that this could possibly be true.

"You are not conscious?" Thomas gasped. "That is the most amazing thing I have ever heard. You walk and talk and argue and kill and subvert and lay out plans over the centuries, and you say that you are not conscious?" "Of course we aren't, Thomas. We are machines. How would we be conscious? But we believe that men are not conscious either, that there is no such thing as consciousness. It is an illusion in counting, a feeling that one is two. It is a word without real meaning." [37, p. 192]

If they pass the so-called Turing Test so well (by arguing innovatively and at least *pretending* to acknowledge the existence of others' subjective worlds) what could even be meant by denying that they are conscious? What is it that they are not doing? Of course they are not *really* sympathizing with others' experience, even less than an expert human psychopath. And even if they do discriminate between organic and inorganic material, between flesh and grass, between human bodies and dummies, this is not for any merely "sentimental" reason. Asimov's own passing suggestion (though it is not clearly maintained in later writings) is that robots cannot grasp "abstractions" such as "justice" or "giving someone his due" [3, pp. 83–4]. Benford seems to indicate that they have no grasp of "essences", except as replicable forms [38, pp. 399–400, 433]. Quite what Benford has in mind here is obscure: but perhaps he is thinking of what might be encountered in genuinely intimate, personal relationships. For his robots, his "mechs," things can be dissected and put together in whatever convenient way, and their properties preserved or modified to suit the robots' program. Martin Buber perhaps intended a similar insight in his account of the I/Thou relationship, which he did not confine to merely human relations.

> In every sphere, in every relational act, through everything that becomes present to us, we gaze toward the train of the eternal You; in each we perceive a breath of it, in every you we address the eternal You, in every sphere according to its manner. All spheres are included in it, while it is included in none. Through all of them shines the one presence. [39, p. 150]

It is not impossible that the same should be true for robots—indeed Lafferty concludes his fable with the suggestion (paralleled in Čapek, Asimov and even Benford) that even the most manipulative of robots may suddenly awaken and repent. "The spirit came down once on water and clay. Could it not come down on gell-cells and flux-fix?" [37, p. 194; see also 37, p. 241]. But it is of more interest here-now to hold fast to the imagination of a wholly non-personal, non-subjective order of being. The robot civilization that is at least a likely galactic order is to be conceived as a wholly non-conscious one, even if its minions seem to speak. If we ever do see signs of plainly technological interference in the heavens [40, 41], we may reasonably think that this will be as unconscious as the growth of crystals or the construction (as we have in the past supposed) of termite nests.

When trying to imagine the End Times of the universe writers since Olaf Stapledon have suggested that in those days everything will be organized as if it were all designed [42, pp. 210–14]. There will then be nothing merely "natural" or "given": whatever exists will have been "deliberately" selected by intelligences with access to the energy of the whole cosmos. On the way to that imagined end particular galaxies and galactic clusters will have been turned into parks, factories and libraries, inhabited by digital representations of whatever past biological, haphazard intelligences have been judged convenient. It will, as it were, be a universe without mere "noise"—a secular imitation of those imagined regions "where there is only life, and therefore all that is not music is silence" [43, p. 47; 44, p. 119]. The structure of that civilization has usually been imagined to be hierarchical: lesser robots may report to, and receive instructions from, more intelligent nodes within a galactic network, just as if they were junior and senior angels. But this may be mistaken: any such centralized or centralizing system is limited by the possible speed of information transfer—and unless the fantasies of hyperspace, wormholes or other arbitrarily faster-than-light systems are somehow realized, that limit is light speed. Stapledon allowed himself the convenience of instantaneous telepathic communication as the basis for his Cosmic Spirit: that now seems unlikely, at least within our current understanding. And even he was conscious of the probability of rebellion and disorder. More local systems are more likely to survive, and information will spread laterally, as within the bacterial cloud, rather than hierarchically. That in turn may assist with the evolution of separate robot tribes, relatively isolated even from their own ancestors and immediate cousins. If consciousness (subjectivity, individual selfhood) is something that can evolve from a non-conscious world (despite my own and others' arguments against the possibility) then it is possible for it to reappear amongst the mechanical successors of ordinary protein biology. Maybe in the end the galactic population will replicate planet bound evolution, and there cease to be any metaphysical or existential difference between biological and robot "life," even if there is still hostility [45]. But that is another story.

The Meaning of Things

Thinking about the End Times, or even about days many million years from now or many light-years distant, may seem the least practical use of present time. No doubt our hunter-gatherer ancestors were just as inclined to mock their farming neighbours for wondering about next year's crops and seasons [8, vol. 1, p. 61]. It may be that the choices we make now will have great effects in the long time to come, most obviously in considering whether our present technological civilization will survive climate catastrophe (and associated wars, migrations, famines and epidemics). How exactly we should deal with artificial intelligence in its many forms may also determine futures. Even before we began to think of robots the question has arisen whether or not to worship our own creations, whether or not to allow mechanical or predetermined solutions to limit our creativity. Shall we attempt to remember our own agency or be content instead to be part of a machine, literal or social? On the one hand, tools, machines and marvels greatly increase our own power to think and act. On the other, they may make it difficult to "think outside the box" and to reject supposedly "rational" futures on the basis of what is then judged "sentiment" or "fancy."

> Don't you see that that dreadful dry light shed on things must at last wither up the moral mysteries as illusions, respect for age, respect for property, and that the sanctity of life will be a superstition? The men in the street are only organisms, with their organs more or less displayed. [46, p. 70]

Imagining a universe dominated by non-conscious intelligence is to get as close as we can to imagining a world deprived of qualities and meaning. Such a world has no centre, nor any distinction between here and there, past and present, one creature and another. Whatever happens there is determined solely by material connections (whether or not there is some element of quantum indeterminacy built in).

> If a superintelligent zombie AI breaks out and eliminates humanity, we've arguably landed in the worst scenario imaginable: a wholly unconscious universe wherein the entire cosmic endowment is wasted. Of all traits that our human form of intelligence has, I feel that consciousness is by far the most remarkable, and as far as I'm concerned, it's how our Universe gets meaning. Galaxies are beautiful only because we see and subjectively experience them. If in the distant future our cosmos has been settled by high-tech zombie AIs, then it doesn't matter how fancy their intergalactic architecture is: it won't be beautiful or

meaningful, because there's nobody and nothing to experience it—it's all just a huge and meaningless waste of space. [5, pp. 226–7; see also 5, pp. xii, 327]

Tegmark strangely neglects in this hyperbole the presence of *non-human* sentients, terrestrial or otherwise—but of course they too are likely to be swept away by the unsympathetic machines. Tegmark here echoes the words of Plotinus:

Let every soul first consider this, that it made all living things itself, breathing life into them. ... Let it look at the great soul, being itself another soul which is no small one, which has become worthy to look by being freed from deceit and the things that have bewitched the other souls, and is established in quietude. Let not only its encompassing body and the body's raging sea be quiet, but all its environment: the earth quiet, and the sea and air quiet, and the heaven itself at peace. Into this heaven at rest let it imagine soul as if flowing in from outside, pouring in and entering it everywhere and illuminating it: as the rays of the sun light up a dark cloud, and make it shine and give it a golden look, so soul entering into the body of heaven gives it life and gives it immortality and wakes what lies inert. ... Before soul it was a dead body, earth and water, or rather the darkness of matter and non-existence, and "what the gods hate," as a poet says. (Plotinus Ennead V.1 [10].2, 1, 13–23, 26–28: [47, vol.5, pp. 14–17]).[7]

But Plotinus is unwilling to accept that there was any such real darkness before "soul," before experience. Such a world did not, pace Tegmark, "look pretty much the same everywhere" [5, p. 33]. It did not "look" at all. On a materialist assumption (that conscious experience is an emergent or phenomenal or even—weirdly—an illusory effect) we could say that the first experiencing organisms added little, centred, transient and variegated bubble worlds to the original un-centred and symmetrical somewhat. On another, idealist, assumption it is rather the reverse: the material world is either imagined or (perhaps) created through the interaction of innumerable versions of Soul, from the widest World Soul to the simple experiences of prokaryotes or particles. Perhaps some compromise is possible.

Plotinus and Tegmark both conceive that the real world is grasped through intellect (though they may have somewhat different conceptions of that faculty).[8] Our experiences are, as it were, samples of the one underlying reality which is both being and beauty. In that real world nothing is far away, nothing

---

[7] Plotinus is quoting the Homeric description of Hades, in *Iliad* 20.65.
[8] See [48, pp. 254–70]. Tegmark argues that the underlying reality is entirely mathematical: an n-dimensional mathematical figure to be grasped only by intellect (and existing only in intellect).

is ever lost, and everything is, as it were, transparent, without concealment. "Nothing is a long way off or far from anything else" (Plotinus *Ennead* IV.3 [27].11, 22–3). All the bubble worlds are open, rather than (as in the world of sensory experience) concealed.

> For here below, too, we can know many things by the look in people's eyes when they are silent; but there [that is, when we see things in the light of the spirit] all their body is clear and pure and each is like an eye, and nothing is hidden or feigned, but before one speaks to another that other has seen and understood. (Plotinus *Ennead* IV.3 [27].18, 19–24)

Once we see that, so Plotinus says, we will "stop marking [ourselves] off from all being and will come to the All without going out anywhere" (Plotinus, *Ennead* VI.5 [23].7, 13–17). This ancient theme lies behind the common SF trope of hyperspace: an imagined Other where all places are effectively coincident, and light speed is no longer any limit. "There" we are all together, and it is (perhaps) this underlying truth which our imagined robots, which exist only in the familiar four-dimensionally extended world, are denied.[9]

References

1. Truitt, E.R.: Medieval Robots: Mechanism, Magic, Nature, and Art. University of Pennsylvania Press, Philadelphia (2015)
2. Capek, K.: R.U.R: Rossums Universal Robots: A Play in Three Acts and an Epilogue, trans. David Wylie. Wildside Press, London (2010 [1921]).
3. Asimov, I.: The Caves of Steel. HarperVoyager, London (1997 [1954])
4. Dawkins, R.: The Selfish Gene. Oxford University Press, Oxford (1976 [1989])
5. Tegmark, M.: Life 3.0: Being Human in the Age of Artificial Intelligence. Penguin, London (2018)
6. Asimov, I.: "Evidence" [1946]: I Robot. HarperVoyager, London, 185–214 (2018 [1967])
7. Clark, S.R.L.: "Robotic Morals" in Cogito **2**, 20–2 (1988) https://doi.org/10.5840/cogito19882213
8. Wright, J.C.: The Golden Age Trilogy: The Golden Age; The Phoenix Exultant; The Golden Transcendence. Tor, New York (2002–2003)
9. Egan, G.: Quarantine. Gollancz, London (2008 [1992])
10. Asimov, I.: Robots and Empire. HarperVoyager, London (2018 [1985])
11. Stross, C.: Saturn's Children. Ace Books, New York (2008)

---

[9] Greg Benford perhaps seeks to represent this in the later volumes of his Galactic Center sequence, especially in [49].

12. Cargill, C.R.: Sea of Rust. Gollancz, London (2018)
13. Bradbury, R.: The Martian Chronicles. HarperCollins, London (1977 [1951])
14. Raup, D.M.: Nonconscious intelligence in the universe. Acta Astronautica. **26**, 257–261 (1992)
15. Rollin, B.: The Unheeded Cry: Animal Consciousness, Animal Pain, and Science, 2nd edn. Iowa State University Press, Ames, Iowa (1998)
16. Henri Fabre, J.: The Hunting Wasps, tr. Alexander Teixiera de Mattos Dodd, Mead & Co, New York (1919)
17. Clark, S.R.L.: From Athens to Jerusalem. Angelico Press, Brooklyn (2019 [1984])
18. Clark, S.R.L.: Nothing without Mind. In: Fetzer, J.H. (ed.) Consciousness Evolving (Advances in Consciousness Research), vol. 34, pp. 139–160. John Benjamins, Amsterdam (2002)
19. Schneider, S.: It May Not Feel Like Anything To Be an Alien. Nautilus, December 2016. http://cosmos.nautil.us/feature/72/it-may-not-feel-like-anything-to-be-an-alien
20. Schneider, S.: Alien Minds. In: Dick, S.J. (ed.) The Impact of Discovering Life Beyond Earth, pp. 189–206. Cambridge University Press, Cambridge (2015)
21. Lem, S.: The Invincibles, tr. Bill Johnston Sidgwick & Jackson, London (1973)
22. Clark, S.R.L.: God, Reason and Extraterrestrials. In: Moore, A. (ed.) God, Mind and Knowledge, pp. 171–186. Ashgate, London (2014)
23. Schmidt, G., Frank, A.: The Silurian hypothesis: would it be possible to detect an industrial civilization in the geological record? International Journal of Astrobiology. **18**(2), 142–150 (2019). https://doi.org/10.1017/S1473550418000095
24. Watts, P.: Blindsight. Tor Books, New York (2008)
25. Card, O.S.: Speaker for the Dead. Orbit, London (1986)
26. Cherryh, C.J.: Serpent's Reach. Daw Books, New York (1980)
27. Heinlein, R.: Starship Troopers. G.P. Putnam, New York (1959)
28. Wells, H.G.: The First Men in the Moon. Penguin, London (2005 [1901])
29. Freitas Jr., R.A.: A Self-Reproducing Interstellar Probe. Journal of the British Interplanetary Society. **33**, 251–264 (1980)
30. Brin, D.: "Lungfish": The River of Time, pp. 243–280. Bantam Books, New York (1987)
31. Brin, D.: Existence. Tor Books, New York (2012)
32. Saberhagen, F.: Berserker. Ace Books, New York (1992 [1967])
33. Bear, G.: The Forge of God. Gollancz, London (1987)
34. Bear, G.: The Anvil of God. Grand Central Publishing, New York (1992)
35. Benford, G.: Foundation's Fear. HarperCollins, New York (1987)
36. Williams, R.: The Metamorphosis of Prime Intellect. Lulucom, Morrisville, NC (2010)
37. Lafferty, R.A.: Past Master. Ace Books, New York (1968)
38. Benford, G.: Great Sky River. Bantam, New York (1987)

39. Buber, M.: I and Thou, trans. Walter Kaufmann Simon & Schuster, New York (1996 [1923])

40. Dyson, F.J.: The search for extraterrestrial technology. In: Marshak, R.E. (ed.) Perspectives in Modern Physics, pp. 641–655. Interscience Publishers, New York (1996)

41. Cirkovic, M.: The Astrobiological Landscape: Philosophical Foundations of the Study of Cosmic Life. Cambridge University Press, Cambridge (2012). https://doi.org/10.1017/CBO9780511667404

42. Stapledon, O.: Star Maker. Gollancz, London (1999 [1937])

43. MacDonald, G.: The Unspoken Sermons. Horse's Mouth, USA (2014 [1867])

44. Lewis, C.S.: The Screwtape Letters. Collins, London (2012 [1942])

45. Williamson, J.: Lifeburst. Random House, New York (1984)

46. Chesterton, G.K.: The Poet and the Lunatics. Darwen Finlayson, London (1962 [1929])

47. Armstrong, A.H.: tr. Plotinus: The Enneads. Harvard University Press, Cambridge, MA (1966–1988)

48. Tegmark, M.: Our Mathematical Universe: My Quest for the Ultimate Nature of Reality. Allen Lane, London (2014)

49. Benford, G.: Sailing Bright Eternity. Bantam, New York (1995)

Mindhunter: Transcending Geocentrism and Psychocentrism in Stanislaw Lem's *The Invincible* and *Peace on Earth*

Milan M. Cirkovic

Abstract The opera of Stanislaw Lem present us with a kaleidoscope of ideas and concepts all linked, in one way or another, to one key issue: the place of evolving minds in the evolving universe. In particular, the idea of fragmented, non-conscious intelligences belonging to neither strictly natural, nor strictly artificial, realms has been presented throughout his writing career; we shall analyse how these ideas are implemented in an early (The Invincible), as well as a late (Peace on Earth) novel, which superficially have very little in common. A case will be made that this idea can fruitfully connect with several recent developments in astrobiology, evolutionary biology, and philosophy of mind. As in so many other things, Lem has been decades ahead of his time, as contemporary pop-cultural elaborations clearly demonstrate.

Introduction: Lem, the Copernican

The unfinished business of the Copernican Revolution is nowhere clearer than in the discussions related to human mind and cognition. Extreme anthropocentric and human-exceptionalist views which would be ridiculed and rejected with few further thoughts in any number of natural sciences, are

M. M. Cirkovic (✉)
Astronomical Observatory of Belgrade, Belgrade, Serbia
e-mail: mcirkovic@aob.rs

© Springer Nature Switzerland AG 2021
B. Dainton et al. (eds.), *Minding the Future*, Science and Fiction,
https://doi.org/10.1007/978-3-030-64269-3_9

not only tolerated, but actively championed here. Since Socrates firmly rejected sophistry that "man is the measure of all things," the serious business of philosophy and science consisted in criticizing and relinquishing the narcistic and self-indulgent view that *homo sapiens* is the crown of creation. This has been followed by significant deflating of the role of human consciousness/self-awareness in cognitive sciences [1–4].[1]

A strange implication is sometimes advanced that our lack of understanding of the exact evolutionary *mechanism* involved in noogenesis somehow undercuts the general validity of Darwinian explanations in the domain of mind [6, 7].[2] And since "science of the mind," or the lack thereof, needs a grounding, or a zero-point, it is of particular interest to seek those examples which are on the hypothetical threshold for manifesting complex cognitive phenomena like consciousness or self-awareness. There are many approaches to thinking about such borderline systems; I shall briefly examine some of them following from the fictional multiverse of Stanislaw Lem, and compare them with the concept of "nonconscious intelligence" proposed by the great palaeontologist David Raup [8]. In addition, I shall try to show that this theme has been very strongly present in other works of the contemporary pop-culture for quite some time, prefiguring much of modern scientific thinking.

Stanislaw Lem is still not well-known as a philosopher, in contrast to his fiction writing [9–12]; here, I would submit that his philosophy of science is not only incredibly rich, original, and useful in the domains of cosmology and astrobiology [13], but also in the domain of philosophy of biology and philosophy of mind.

In particular, we see a wide spectrum of minds over the course of Lem's work, as very roughly ordered along the *externally-perceived* complexity in Fig. 1. Humans and robots mentioned refer to multiple works, including the Pirx and Tichy stories, *Mortal Engines* and *The Cyberiad*, as well as all of the novels of Lem; the Senders are implied advanced extraterrestrials of *His Master's Voice*, and the Players are cosmologically-old supercivilizations of the story/essay "The New Cosmogony." The Players would be an excellent example of Kardashev Type 3.x or 4.x civilization, challenging human

---

[1] As an aside, I would propose that such situation bolsters what I have dubbed [5] the "anti-Copernican cartel," which obstructs progress in many important issues, such as animal rights or wider ecopolitical reforms or even more evolutionary approaches to AI development and even AI rights. This revamped and often well-disguised anti-Copernicanism may become still more worrying in the near-term future if the current atmosphere of populist ignorance continues to hold sway.

[2] A physics analogy: prior to uncovering the Higgs mechanism, we should have rejected any explanation based on Newton's Second Law, since we had no inkling about the origin of mass, figuring so prominently therein…

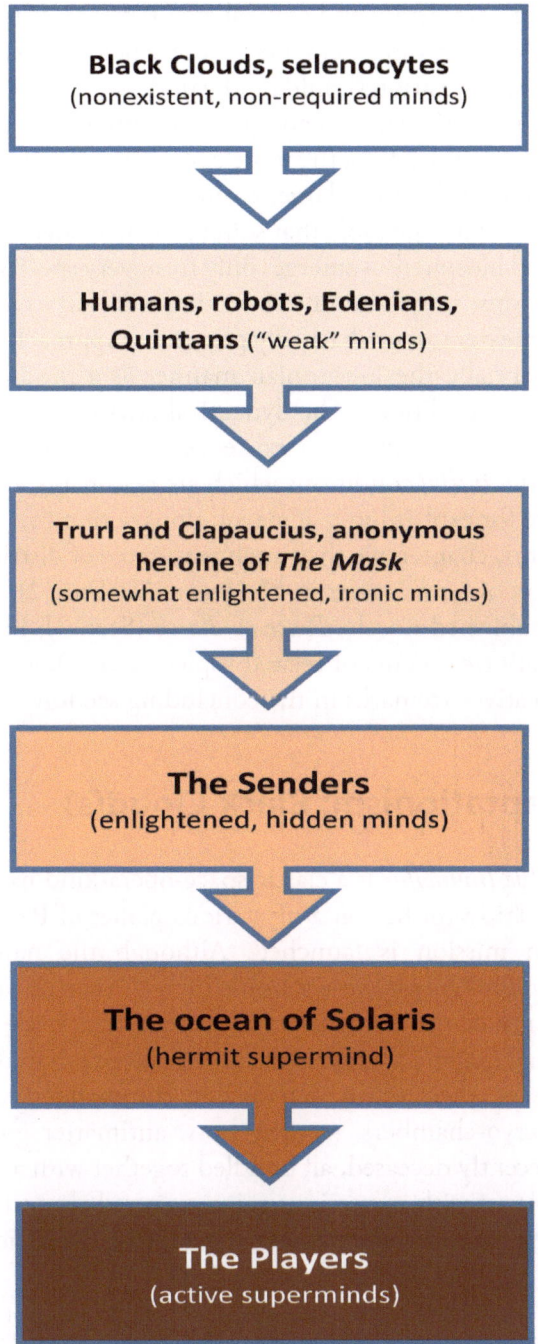

Fig. 1 A schematic hierarchy of Lemmian minds ordered—very roughly and in a necessarily subjective manner—in terms of increasing complexity, as well as their influence on physical environment

comprehension of complexity and control over the environment.[3] Of course, there are multiple diachronic elements in the scheme, since the increase of complexity and sophistication should not be understood as either necessary or linear with time. In particular, we cannot say anything more precise about the timescales necessary for reaching the more complex rungs of the ladder, except that these are likely to be truly large, cosmological timescales, measured in billions of years. And it is possible that something like Solaris—a totally functionally integrated biosphere—emerges only from very special and rare initial/boundary conditions, so no amount of waiting will lead to its evolution elsewhere. (We assume here an unabashedly physicalist approach in regarding any biosphere in essentially the Newtonian manner as a product of dynamical laws and boundary conditions. The dynamical laws may be unknown to us, but there is no reason to doubt their existence.[4] Among all possible boundary conditions, it is the *initial* conditions which are reasonably expected to be the most appropriate for explaining macroevolutionary trends.)

In the rest of this chapter, we shall analyze the role of distributed cognition in the early period of Lem's career in *The Invincible* (Sect. 2), as well as in one of his two last published novels, *Peace on Earth* (Sect. 3), before glancing at some other literary treatments of related topics (Sect. 4), and giving some—hopefully provocative—remarks in the concluding section.

Cosmic Adaptationism: Black Cloud(s)

At first glance, *The Invincible* is a classic space-opera-kind narrative: a powerful human spaceship vanishes on a mysterious planet of Regis III, and a rescue/investigation mission is launched. Although the name of the ship sent—the eponymous *Invincible*—is ironic in more than one sense, the narrative contains many of the elements of a conventional space adventure with some of the usual genre paraphernalia of the alleged "Golden Age of SF": interstellar cruisers, their brave, but ascetic commanders and astrogators, energy shields, cryo-chambers, security bots, antimatter guns, even mind-readers for the recently deceased, all bundled together with a seemingly uninhabited desert planet with mysterious ruins scattered around. However, Lem plays a complex game here with what we expect to be the standard space opera

---

[3] Kardashev's classification of extraterrestrial civilizations [14] is a simple and useful taxonomy scheme for classifying possible forms of intelligent life in the universe in terms of their control over physical environment. Only the first three Kardashev Types are usually cited, although extensions and modifications are possible [15].

[4] I elaborate on this, perhaps not very obvious, thesis in [13].

defamiliarization: beneath the trappings of the subgenre, his evolutionary philosophy amplifies the *true underlying defamiliarization* based upon onto-logical and epistemic shifts in reader's reality.

The explanation for all the strangeness encountered on Regis III is the pres-ence of an invasive species of *machines* capable of evolution. Machines—of intelligent alien origin, but with their (non-anthropomorphic alien) creators long dead—had first exterminated the native life on land, and then struggled and differentiated among themselves, until only the most robust, resilient and flexible species remained. That species is what humans have perceived as the Black Cloud(s):

> [W]hat came about here was inanimate evolution of a very particular nature, begun in exceptional circumstances that were brought about by happenstance... In this evolution the victors were firstly systems that miniaturized themselves most effectively, and secondly, those that were sedentary. The first gave rise to the so-called black clouds. Personally, I believe these are tiny pseudo-insects that in case of need, for mutual self-interest as it were, are capable of joining into large superordinate systems. Precisely in the form of clouds. This was the direc-tion in which the mobile mechanisms developed. The sedentary ones in turn gave rise to the bizarre species of metallic vegetation found in the ruins of what we've been calling cities... I have the impression that for some reason unknown to us this city, or rather metal forest, lost its struggle for existence and now is no more than rusting remains. Only one form has survived: the mobile beings that have taken over all the land on the planet. [16, pp. 103–104]

Postbiological evolution, in the crucial sense, *is just biological evolution*. (Note that while the initial presence of Black-Clouds-precursors on the planet was accidental, what followed was anything but.) In contrast to myriads of other planets, the exceptional conditions of Regis III are due—as the ship biologist, Lauda, explains in detail—to its exceptional initial conditions. We are mis-taken in searching for a deeper meaning or point as that would be another symptom of our incurable anthropocentrism:

> Millions of years of mechanical evolution, and a phenomenon that humans have never before encountered in the Galaxy... All the machines we are familiar with serve someone else, not themselves. Thus, from a human perspective the existence of the vast metallic jungles on Regis, or its iron clouds, are quite point-less—in the same sense, it's true, that cactuses in the deserts of Earth could be called pointless. The essential thing is that they are perfectly adapted for combat with living beings. I have the impression that they killed only at the very begin-nings of the struggle, when the land here teemed with life. The energy expended

on killing proved to be uneconomical. For that reason, they use other methods, the results of which include the catastrophe of the Condor, Kertelen's accident, and now the devastation wrought on Regnar's team. [16, pp. 105–106]

The "other methods" alluded to in this passage consist of scrambling the minds of their rivals, so that they just wander around, eventually dying of hunger or exposure. Lem's scenario of hostile electromagnetic interference with human brain functions by essentially non-conscious actants has been recently used as an important element of Peter Watts's *Blindsight* (see below). "Hunger" here should be understood in a general sense which encompasses both organic and robotic entities—notice how evolution itself shows limitations of our linguistic expression!

Humans, even advanced and enlightened humans of the epoch of *The Invincible*, seem poorly equipped to face this fact, however. Only a personal catharsis, such as experienced by Rohan at the very end of the novel, seems capable of making an intuitive, gut-level grasp of the situation. The dramatic turn-about and relinquishing of the remaining anthropocentrism is described by some of the most forceful lines Lem ever wrote:

Rohan rose on unstable legs. He suddenly seemed ridiculous to himself… more, he felt unnecessary in this landscape of perfect death, where only inanimate forms could survive and carry out their inscrutable actions that no living eye would ever see. It was not with horror but with stunned admiration that he had taken part in what happened a moment before. He knew that none of the scientists would be capable of sharing his feelings, but now he wished to go back not only as a messenger bearing news of the destruction of the missing men, but also as a person who would demand that the planet be left alone. Not everything everywhere is for us… [16, p. 191; emphasis added]

This personal Copernican turn is the ending of one story and a beginning of another—which remains untold. Lem's narrative ends in complete ambiguity as to human understanding of the emergent complexity of the Black Cloud type—and the possible moral duty for humanity to leave other ecosystems and other outcomes of the universal evolution alone, even if they are stranger or more repulsive than we have ever expected.

Evolutionary Exaptation: Dispersant Robots and Selenocytes

Lem has returned several times to the motif of "smart dust" in his writing career.[5] One, rather humorous, Swiftian account is made in "The Twenty-third Voyage," in which Ijon Tichy visits a tiny planet whose inhabitants save space by storing themselves as "atom dust." However, the most complete and discursively rich account of the same motif appears in Lem's last Tichy book, *Peace on Earth*, published originally in 1987 and, together with the almost simultaneous *Fiasco*, his last word in his fiction writing. In contrast to *The Invincible*, Lem's last published novel is a breezy, satirical, and makes for an amusing read, where humor is used to highlight some of the major incoherencies and paradoxes obstructing the normative, anthropocentric approach to mind. The military powers of Earth have agreed to remove all their ultra-mega-hyperadvanced robotic weapon systems to the Moon, but they have apparently forgotten about contingencies and opportunism of evolution. When Ijon Tichy is sent to investigate mysterious lunar incidents, he suffers brain damage and a strange, though humorous, neurophysiological condition (split-brain or callosal syndrome in which the connection between the hemispheres of the brain is severed). Throughout the plot he attempts to understand what has in fact happened, who's responsible, and why. Most of the plot takes place either in various therapists' offices or in a lunatic asylum.

The resolution, just as in *The Invincible*, is both evolutionary and incomplete. It turns out that a strange kind of machine evolution has taken place among the complex and highly autonomous weapon systems on the Moon. The ultimate winners, catalyzed by Tichy's visit, have been the smallest and most versatile systems, capable of assuming any required shape and project it on the battlefield. The similarity with the Black Clouds is certainly not accidental. In particular, the latter are prefigured in the "dispersant" robotic body for lunar exploration (ironically dubbed "LEM" for the classic lunar excursion module of the Apollo program fame); in Tichy's idiosyncratic narration:

> Instead of a steel athlete you had a container filled with microscopic grains, each grain of such concentrated intelligence it rivalled a supercomputer. In the presence of certain impulses these particles came together to form a LEM. I could land as a thin cloud of molecules, could coalesce if necessary in the form of a robot of human shape, but I could just as easily become one of forty-nine other

---

[5] In fact, a recent publication in the field of *textile technology* ascribes the origin of the very concept of "smart dust" to Stanislaw Lem [17].

programmed things, and even if eighty-five percent of the grains were destroyed, the rest would be enough to carry on. The science behind such a remote, called a dispersant, was so advanced that Einstein, von Neumann, the entire physics department of M.I.T., and Rabindranath Tagore working together would have had a problem with it, so I didn't even try to figure it out. All I knew was that they'd embodied me in thirty billion separate particles, particles more versatile than the cells of a living organism, and there was unimaginable redundancy for joining these in various combinations which could all be turned back to dust at the push of a button, dust so scattered that you couldn't see it, and each particle incorporating stealth technology, making it undetectable by radar or laser or anything except gamma rays. [18, p. 164]

So these would be the human-designed precursors of the evolving automata on Regis III. Lem also plays a bit with philosophy of mind here—in retrospect playfully subverting Lauda's hypothesis: "What one experiences as a cloud spread over several thousand cubic feet is impossible to put into words. To know it, you have to be such a cloud." This is what Lem called, in a discursive context, "affirming the autonomy of certain enigmas" [19, p. 65]. In the course of the plot of *Peace on Earth,* the dispersant technology is appropriated by independently evolved miniaturized lunar entities, dubbed "selenocytes." "This accelerated the selenocyte evolution," [18, p. 214] Tichy recounts afterthe-fact, when selenocytes invade Earth and rather quietly and bloodlessly pacify it. In this sense, *Peace on Earth* is a kind of polar opposite to *The Invincible*—an anti-*Invincible*, both in its jovial tone and in its understanding of technological evolution (the direction it takes, as well as its form).

While the emergent complex behavior of Black Clouds originates with robots made by non-anthropomorphic aliens in the distant past, similar behavior of a similar kind of system is described in *Peace on Earth*, but in this instance created by humans in a near future. In both cases, seemingly intentional (or quasi-intentional) actions have emerged in the course of contingent and opportunistic evolutionary processes, hopeless to track amid myriads of causal details. There is more here, however, than meets the eye—or the γ-ray telescope. Gould and Vrba [20] have introduced the term *exaptation* to describe a frequent phenomenon in evolution that a character selected for one function is co-opted for another in the course of evolutionary time. In both *The Invincible* and *Peace on Earth*, perceived adversity and quasi-intentionality emerge as expatations. There is an important—and illuminating—difference, however: while the original functionality in the case of the Black Clouds is forever lost in distant past (and, considering their alien provenance, is possibly inconceivable to human minds), the functionality in the case of selenocytes has been based on a military need to incapacitate an enemy's military hardware as quickly and efficiently as possible.

From the point of view of Tichy's dispersant robot, the original function was, obviously, to survive as long as possible in the hostile lunar environment. Merging the two has led, as speculated by the characters in the novel, toward an orthogenetic ascent to a new stage—a kind of the "major evolutionary transition" [21] occurs, opening up a novel chunk of the morphological space. Ironically—and this might be read as a satire on the "just so stories," often encountered in our most earnest attempts at explanation of evolutionary events that occurred in deep time—the only human witness, Tichy, was incapacitated in such manner to make his testimony literally inarticulate. The most important new feature, implied rather than described, is selenocytes' pre-empting capability: pacification of the Earth in the denouement of the novel is "just" the manifestation of this capability, not some deeper ethical appreciation of peace. Selenocytes are no more "peaceful" than the Dawkins's genes are "selfish" (as unhelpfully pointed at one point by Mary Midgley, a kind of philosopher Lem liked to satirize). Hence, the novel is strangely optimistic although the correct understanding of the title is somewhat sarcastic.

Non-conscious Intelligence in the Fictional Multiverse

Consider now by which fruits ye shall know them. In both cases of Black clouds and selenocytes, one judgement of Lauda is disturbingly pertinent: "these organisms do not build anything, possess no civilization, in general have nothing whatsoever except themselves, create nothing of value" [16, pp. 108–109]. The distinguished paleontologist and evoolutionist David M. Raup has contributed to the debates surrounding SETI with his suggestion that animals on other planets may have evolved, by natural selection, the ability to communicate by radio waves [8].[6] This would not be random noise, which is characteristic for astrophysical processes, but neither would it be structured, meaningful information, which would be characteristic for intentional messages of human or extraterrestrial intelligence—it would be something in-between. We know that animal communication on Earth is often tremendously complex and information-rich; in some better-studied cases, its most general meaning can be established [22]. This does not mean that we

---

[6] This would encompass, by analogy, at least some of the other traits we usually think about as possible only within a technological civilization of intelligent beings.

can decode the communication between blue whales, the communication between bees in a hive, or even the chemical communication between bacteria in the same manner as we decoded the Mycenaean Linear B or even as British cryptanalysts in Bletchley Park decoded German Enigma ciphers. So, according to Raup's idea, we could encounter a new form of potential SETI signals, which could persist for millions of years, due to the slow pace of evolutionary change, in sharp contrast to the ephemeral nature of any particular communication technology. After all, advances in quantum optics have already caused Earth to decrease its emissivity in some of the relevant radio bands; people are using optical cables and the internet instead of radio and television antennae. Since this is not really what SETI is after, such unconscious signals should be treated as confusing noise; however, such noise would be persistent and very difficult to remove.

The same underlying idea appears time and again in modern culture. While the detailed examination of the Raupian motif of non-conscious intelligence would require a book-length study, some of the rehashing and variations are quite pertinent. *The Invention of Morel*, the best-known novel of Argentinian writer Adolfo Bioy Casares [23], contains the seed of this idea, which has been subsequently rehashed many times in visual media. The narrator of *The Invention of Morel* founds himself on a remote island which is apparently inhabited by strange people with strange habits. A whole drama develops—although somewhat one-sided—before the deceiving nature of this reality is revealed. In a sense, it is much more and simultaneously much less, than it is apparent to an external observer. There is a machinery on that mysterious island which simulates—what exactly? Only the outward physical appearances and motions of some unlucky visitors, or much more than that? How would one go about researching the answer to this question in the first place? The discontinuity between epistemology and ontology is highlighted with poignant melancholy in the course of this strange novel. Even the very destiny of the narrator—who transitions from an external to an internal observer—will, in the final analysis, depend on the *reader's* ontological commitments. The relevance of Casares's novel for cognitive sciences has been noted elsewhere [24], although its general philosophical significance, especially in view of the modern transformative technologies and posthumanity has not been published so far.

Casares's novel directly inspired Alain Robbe-Grillet's screenplay for Jean Resnais's famous 1961 movie *L'Année dernière à Marienbad* (*Last Year in Marienbad*), in which a group of characters are, apparently, holidaying in a spacious baroque castle without any clear meaning or purpose—and with what at best is incomplete and flailing understanding of their own past. The protagonist, unnamed in the movie but called "X" in the screenplay, desperately tries to convince an unnamed woman, "A," that they had known each other since the summer before, when they allegedly spent holidays in Marienbad (an old Austro-Hungarian resort, today Mariánské Lázně in the Czech Republic). She doesn't remember him at all, but what he tells her has the power to create a past for her and continually blend it into her present. Everything in the film looks *just apparent* or *simulated*. Mirrors, mysterious games, labyrinthine corridors of the castle, the puzzling selective lack of shadows, the eternal, cloudless sunshine outside, repetitive conversations, ambiguous voiceovers—all of those just strengthen the effect. The characters move like somnambulists through a hermetically sealed world that seems totally surreal; at moments they seem all caught up in a Gödelian loop of disjointed time. The world as captured by the camera is subtly incoherent; but is it a consequence of the erroneous subjective perceptions of our characters, who are frozen in the timestream like insects in amber, or a manifestation of a strange, but objective local process or experiment? Radical ontological hypothesis—that we are dealing with the simulation created by invisible and inscrutable Directors—which has been recently revamped in the context of modern computer science [25], would indicate that either mind is divorced from the substrate, or that we are seeing mind, in the anthropocentric manner, where there is none.

One can go further, and claim that technology—generalized as *construction of relevant entities*—holds primacy on the epistemological playing field as well. Richard Feynman had something similar in mind when he claimed that we did not really understand something until we were able to construct it. We shall be able to adequately assess Bostrom's and related arguments if and when it becomes technically feasible to artificially control/simulate consciousness and other aspects of mind. A consequence of such a breakthrough in neuroscience would certainly be to deflate (further) the reliability of consciousness in guiding us through the world. At present, the odd hallucination and possibly some exotic mental states aside, we usually have no reason to entertain serious doubts as to whether our experience is a reliable guide to reality. (Hypothetical "Boltzmann brains" of modern cosmology could be lumped together into those exotic mental states.) If/when it becomes easy to generate artificial consciousness, appearances will no more be a reliable guide to reality in the conventional sort of way—one could easily conclude that one is an AI simulation or an actor in a virtual reality game.

And the hit TV series *Lost* not only explicitly shows *The Invention of Morel* as read by a protagonist, but also subtly references its plot many times throughout all 6 seasons of the show. The idea of interference between different versions of particular protagonists one of which is aware of some crucial event and the other not, rather modestly implied in the concluding two seasons of the saga, points to a general philosophical moral that *consciousness is indeed memory* and—through its sedimentation and management—*history*. Take a particular event, like an airplane crash—we can call it "memorable," but what we really wish to say is that we are *more conscious* of it and its ramifications, than of some other concurrent event. In a parallel universe, showed in subsequent seasons of the series, the initial crash did not occur; this changes the memories of the counterpart characters—and, ultimately, it changes everything about them; they are not really the same characters, except on a formal, *de dicto* reading. Hence alternative histories imply different consciousnesses. One of the major characters of *Lost*—perhaps its most tragic character—is named John Locke; it is certainly not a coincidence for a program affirming such a Lockean view of the conscious experience [cf 26].

This does not exclude interesting pathways devoid of consciousness. In both of his "new space opera" masterpieces, *Blindsight* and *Echopraxia*, Peter Watts delves deep into the questions of consciousness vs. intelligence and technology [27, 28]. Both novels deal with the near-future transhuman society facing First Contact of completely different sort than usually imagined. The alien artefact encountered in *Blindsight*, "Rorschach," is an ingenious instantiation of Searle's Chinese Room thought experiment: its superficially meaningful communications with humans have no underlying understanding. And yet, it is supremely sophisticated intentional construction, an obvious masterpiece of advanced science and engineering. Thus, in both novels, we encounter a typically Lemmian idea that human consciousness (and similar complex mental phenomena) could be an exception, rather than the rule, in a wider astrobiological picture. Evolution optimizes even very complex processes; non-conscious processing is faster, more reliable, and more energy-efficient than the conscious one. Alien Scramblers, encountered in *Blindsight*, are suspected to be non-sentient beings for whom all sensation is blindsight—a phenomenon where beings without sight could avoid obstacles by co-opting (or *exapting*!) other senses to the same effect. Hominin Vampires (in both *Blindsight* and *Echopraxia*) are implied to be similarly evolving toward non-sentience. And the fundamental horror of the novels rests in the final implication that non-sentient, unconscious cognition is evolutionarily superior and will dominate in the universe in the fullness of space and time. Human self-awareness is portrayed as inherently self-limiting and self-destructive: "They [the aliens] turn your own cognition against itself. They travel between the stars. This is what intelligence can do, unhampered by self-awareness" [27, p. 304]. In *Echopraxia* we encounter several further examples how easily could conscious beings, even highly intelligent posthumans, be subverted and manipulated by hostile non-conscious actors.

The same idea features in two recent mega-hits TV series, *True Detective* and *Westworld*. In the pilot episode of *True Detective* and the very first of famous car conversations which gave such a flavor to the first season of the series, Rust Cohle (played brilliantly by Matthew McConaughey) tells his partner, Marty Hart (Woody Harrelson), that "human consciousness was a tragic misstep in evolution. We became too self-aware." The utterance strikes us as either shocking or fascinating or even unthinkable—and indeed it has been unthinkable before the advent of the (neo)Darwinian evolutionary theory and contemporary philosophy of biology. In the bad old days of, say, Linnaean creationism such a question was clearly unthinkable, except perhaps in the Gnostic-inspired heretical circles who postulated an evil Demiurge as creator of the physical world and humanity within it. Throughout Season 1, we face Cohle's alleged nihilism as motivated and fueled by understanding, intuitive more than systematic, of the evolutionary theory. It is presented in stark contrast to the extreme religious and indeed creationist views and characters, associated with adversary forces behind the cult-style ritual murders investigated by Cohle and Hart.

In *Westworld*, created by Lisa Joy and Jonathan Nolan, especially in Season 1, we have an explicitly Jaynes-ian theme of "waking of consciousness" through hearing voices in one's head, within a wider theme of prerequisites for "true" consciousness. Android "hosts" have long ago passed the conventional Turing test (and, in fact, are universally regarded as *more intelligent* than humans), but are not conscious; the entire dramatic narrative of the Season 1 consists in acquiring of consciousness by at least some most advanced androids, notably Dolores. A major character, Dr. Ford (Sir Anthony Hopkins in a typically fine role), gradually recognizes that such a process is both inevitable and detrimental, in the sense of leading to likely catastrophic conflict with the human civilization. His subtle—and even posthumous!—management of this irresolvable ἀγών is central for the unfolding of the drama. At the time of this writing (December 2019), we are expecting the release date for the Season 3, to see whether the "robot rebellion" will take a Čapekian turn or not. However, the premiss that *artificial consciousness*, and not artificial intelligence in itself, is a threat for future humanity is both in the spirit of Lem's philosophy and worthy of further study in the domains of philosophy of mind and risk analysis. This is a huge topic which branches and bifurcates into many questions not only relevant for academic philosophy, but also touching upon many issues of practical ethics in the era of AI. If morality confers an evolutionary advantage, would nonconscious AIs devoid of morality be at disadvantage—and on what timescales? Those questions are barely scratched at present and, as Lem always emphasized, at our own peril.

All these examples—many of them directly or indirectly inspired by Lem—strongly testify that the idea of downplaying the role of consciousness (and its separation from pure intelligence or cognitive power) is powerfully present, if not dominant, in contemporary culture far outside of evolutionary biological and cog-sci contexts.

Instead of Conclusions: Consciousness Deprecated?

Since the time of Ionian cosmological thinkers, and notably Heraclitus as the forefather of dialectics, the key to understanding a phenomenon is often in determining its *boundaries*. As John Archibald Wheeler liked to say, "boundary of a boundary vanishes" is *the* metaprinciple applicable in so many branches of physical science, including the derivation of fundamental conservation laws in practically all relevant contexts.[7] Therefore, a physicalist approach to mind should attempt to work out where the boundaries of its subject of inquiry lie—exactly something which has proved controversial with the contemporary debates on the *extended mind* [30, 31] or distributed cognition [32]. The boundary of the spectrum of minds is *no-mind with some apparent mental aspects*. It is exactly such actants which are depicted in two of Lem's novels we have peeked into above—and referenced in the expanding corpus of subsequent culture. Of course, there are philosophical doctrines which either negate that there can be mentality of any kind without consciousness (e.g. [33]) or—somewhere near the opposite pole—that there is no threshold for mind whatsoever. The latter would be a kind of panpsychism, in which even very simple objects, such as elementary particles or fields, could be endowed with minuscule amounts of conscious quality [34]. Arguably, both of these positions would be regarded as somewhat extreme, especially by a sort of down-to-earth, empirically-minded thinker such as Lem was; it would be safe to say that he accepted the boundary as real. However, his own work testifies just how difficult the task is of telling a plausible story about where exactly such a boundary lies.

---

[7] Symbolically: $\partial\partial = 0$. In purely physical context, it elegantly reproduces all the classical conservation laws of charges and currents ([29], esp. Chaps. 14–17). As Stephen Hawking and others suggested, its applicability could, indeed, be much wider.

In *Mindhunter*—an American crime thriller television series (2017–2020) created by Joe Penhall, distributed on Netflix—FBI agents Holden Ford (played by Jonathan Groff) and Bill Tench (Holt McCallany), along with psychology professor Wendy Carr (a masterful role by Anna Torv), strive to understand the mental structure of serial killers. They use a variety of methods, heavily relying on interviewing the *most extreme established* murderers, people like Edmund Kemper and David Berkowitz. The program is based on the 1995 non-fiction book describing the origins of the FBI's Behavioral Science Unit [35]. At several points in the series (which is ongoing, as of this writing), they admit their hope that by studying those extreme fringes, or boundaries, of the criminal psychopathology, they would eventually be able to shed light on many other, less extreme manifestations of the criminal mind.

I find this a particularly apt metaphor for Lem's epistemological and evolutionary enterprise, as outlined in the discursive form in *Summa Technologiae* [36], but expressed more strongly and deeply in his great novels. In order to delineate the works of mind in the universe, we need a baseline boundary which is sharp, i.e., boundary of the boundary vanishes. There are multiple options for further research in studying both fiction and mind in their widest, cosmic context. For example:

- Other works of Lem, notably his great contact novels (*Solaris, His Master's Voice,* and *Fiasco*), not only contain obvious references to multiple pathways leading to mind and intelligence, but also delve into evolutionary processes guiding both biological and cultural/technological evolution [37].
- Other SF authors, especially those of the "new space opera" contemporaries of the astrobiological revolution (1995–today), are likely to offer new insights into the ways of thinking and rethinking the place of mind in the universe at large. This is particularly visible in works of authors such as Reynolds [38, 39], Stross [40], Robson [41], or Schroeder [42, 43].
- Contrast with *really advanced* minds, envisioned at the higher rungs of the scheme given in Fig. 1 (as well as those encountered in other great SF opuses, such as Minds in Banks's *Culture* novels), offers what one could, in terms of Gould [44] dub the "right wall of complexity": the maximum level of complexity consistent with evolutionary principles and cosmological scales of matter, space, and time. While those limits on the other extreme of the non-mind to mind transition may, in principle, be inconceivable to us (as evolved and rather immature minds), it will still be useful to contemplate the *limits of our imagination* in this respect. What might be a better vehicle for such a task than the age-tested discourse of SF (cf. [45, 12])?

- The notion of an *artefact* as a product of an active but naturally evolved mind in the universe has not been investigated enough in the context of modern epistemology and philosophy of science. To what extent could we hope to be able to recognize an alien artefact is a vast and complex issue, touching upon several traditional philosophical disciplines [5]. Could a non-conscious subject have the same aesthetic sensibility as a conscious one? Even if we define an artefact as an outlier from a "regular," law-like naturalistic description, to what extent is our description based upon possible prior, unrecognized artefacts? Lem has tackled these issues in both fictional and discursive formats; his contribution has not been adequately highlighted so far.

In any case, the conclusion that there is a rich, emerging subject matter at hand seems inescapable. Reading Lem is a strong, healthy tonic for both the unabashed anthropocentrism of human institutions and traditions, and for detached abstract view which rejects or downplays the cognitive value of genre fiction, still widespread in the academy. By breaking the established moulds and conventions, Lem has transcended more than mere prejudice—and opened a philosophical goldmine for the decades and perhaps centuries to come.[8]

References

1. Jaynes, J.: The Origin of Consciousness in the Breakdown of the Bicameral Mind. Houghton Mifflin, Boston (1976)
2. Nørretranders, T.: The User Illusion: Cutting Consciousness Down to Size. Penguin Books, New York (1999)
3. Koch, C.: The Quest for Consciousness: A Neurobiological Approach. Roberts & Company, Englewood, Colorado (2004)
4. Metzinger, T.: Being No One: The Self-Model Theory of Subjectivity. MIT Press, Cambridge (2004)

---

[8] Detailed comments of Barry Dainton, Srdja Janković, and Attila Tanyi have been extremely helpful in sharpening the focus of the paper and clarifying key controversial points. I also wish to thank Ksenija Petrović, Anders Sandberg, Branislav Vukotić, Nick Bostrom, Slobodan Popović, Slobodan Perović, Karl Schroeder, Aleksandar Obradović, Jelena Andrejić, Momčilo Jovanović, Sonja Kukić, Goran Milovanović, Marko Stalevski, Eva Kamerer, the late Robert J. Bradbury, and the late Damian Veal for many pleasant and useful discussions on the topics related to the subject matter of this study. This is an opportunity to thank the KoBSON Consortium of Serbian libraries and the NASA Astrophysics Data System. This research has been partially supported by the Ministry of Education and Science of the Republic of Serbia through the project ON176021.

5. Cirkovic, M.: The Great Silence: The Science and Philosophy of Fermi's Paradox. Oxford University Press, Oxford (2018)
6. Fodor, J., Piattelli-Palmarini, M.: What Darwin Got Wrong. Farrar, Straus, and Giroux. In: New York (2010)
7. Nagel, T.: Mind and Cosmos: Why the Materialist neo-Darwinian Conception of Nature Is Almost Certainly False. Oxford University Press, Oxford (2012)
8. Raup, D.: Nonconscious intelligence in the universe. Acta Astronaut. **26**, 257–261 (1992)
9. Jarzębski, J.: Stanislaw Lem, rationalist and visionary. Sci. Fict. Stud. **4**, 110–126 (1977)
10. Kandel, M.: Two meditations on Stanislaw Lem. Sci. Fict. Stud. **13**, 374–381 (1986)
11. Lem, S., Swirski, P.: A Stanislaw Lem Reader. Northwestern University Press, Evanston (1997)
12. Swirski, P.: Stanislaw Lem: Philosopher of the Future. Liverpool University Press, Liverpool (2015)
13. Cirkovic, M.: The Astrobiological Landscape: Philosophical Foundations of the Study of Cosmic Life. Cambridge University Press, Cambridge (2012)
14. Kardashev, N.: Transmission of information by extraterrestrial civilizations. Sov. Astron. **8**, 217–220 (1964)
15. Cirkovic, M.: Kardashev's classification at 50+: a fine vehicle with room for improvement. Serb. Astronom. J. **191**, 1–15 (2015)
16. Lem, S.: The Invincible. Trans. B. Johnston. Pro Auctore Wojciech Zemek, Krakow (1966 [2018])
17. Farrer, J.: Smart dust: Sci-Fi applications enabled by synthetic fiber and textiles technology. Text. **8**, 342–347 (2010)
18. Lem, S.: Peace on Earth. Trans. E. Ford. Harcourt, Inc., San Diego (1987 [1994])
19. Lem, S.: Metafantasia: The Possibilities of Science Fiction. Trans. E. de Laczay and I. Csicsery-Ronay. Sci. Fict. Stud. **8**, 54–71 (1981)
20. Gould, S., Vrba, E.: Exaptation—a missing term in the science of form. Paleobiology. **8**, 4–15 (1982)
21. Maynard Smith, J., Szathmary, E.: The Major Transitions in Evolution. Oxford University Press, Oxford (1997)
22. Bradbury, J., Vehrencamp, S.: Principles of Animal Communication. Sinauer Associates Inc., Sunderland, MA (2011)
23. Bioy Casares, A.: La invención de Morel. Penguin Books, London (1940 [1996])
24. Perogamvros, L.: Consciousness and the invention of morel. Front. Hum. Neurosci. **7**, 61 (2013)
25. Bostrom, N.: Are you living in a computer simulation? Philos. Q. **53**, 243–255 (2003)
26. Kaye, S., Irwin, W. (eds.): Ultimate Lost and Philosophy: Think Together, Die Alone. Wiley, Hoboken (2010)
27. Watts, P.: Blindsight. Tor Books, New York (2006)

28. Watts, P.: Echopraxia. Tor Books, New York (2014)
29. Misner, C., Thorne, K., Wheeler, J.: Gravitation. WH Freeman, San Francisco (1973)
30. Clark, A., Chalmers, D.: The extended mind. Analysis. **58**, 7–19 (1998)
31. Clark, A.: Reasons, robots and the extended mind. Mind Lang. **16**, 121–145 (2001)
32. Hutchings, E.: Cognition in the Wild. MIT Press, Cambridge (1995)
33. Searle, J.: The Rediscovery of the Mind. MIT Press, Cambridge (1992)
34. Clark, D.: Panpsychism: Past and Recent Selected Readings. State University of New York Press, Albany, NY (2004)
35. Douglas, J., Olshaker, M.: Mindhunter: Inside the FBI's Elite Serial Crime Unit. Simon and Schuster, New York (1995)
36. Lem, S.: Summa Technologiae. Trans. J. Zylinska. University of Minnesota Press, Minneapolis (1964 [2013])
37. Cirkovic, M.: Into the Artifice of Eternity: Alien Technology and Exploratory Engineering in the Fiction of Lem, Reynolds, and Schroeder (Springer, forthcoming)
38. Reynolds, A.: Pushing Ice. Gollancz, London (2005)
39. Reynolds, A.: House of Suns. Gollancz, London (2008)
40. Stross, C.: Missile Gap. Subterranean Press, Burton (2006)
41. Robson, J.: Natural History. Bantam Books, New York (2005)
42. Schroeder, K.: Permanence. Tor Books, New York (2002)
43. Schroeder, K.: The Lady of Mazes. Tor Books, New York (2005)
44. Gould, S.: Full House: The Spread of Excellence from Plato to Darwin. Three Rivers Press, New York (1996)
45. Swirski, P.: From Literature to Biterature: Lem, Turing, Darwin, and Explorations in Computer Literature, Philosophy of Mind, and Cultural Evolution. McGill-Queen's University Press, Montreal (2013)

Historicism, Science Fiction, and the Singularity

Mark Silcox

Abstract Many writers who have discussed the Singularity have treated it not only as the inevitable outcome of advancements in cybernetic technology, but also as natural consequence of broader patterns in the development of human knowledge, or of human history itself. In this paper I examine these claims— as defended by Vernor Vinge, Ray Kurzweil, and David Chalmers—in light of Karl Popper's famous philosophical critique of historicism. I argue that, because the Singularity is regarded as both a product of human ingenuity and a reflection of the permanent limitations of our rational capacities, speculation about its likelihood occupies an interesting border zone between what Popper referred to as "technological prediction" and what he lambasted as "prophecy." I go on to examine representations of a post-singularity world in the novels of Iain M. Banks, as well as in Bruce Sterling's short story "The Beautiful and the Sublime."

> Man was winged hopefully. He had in him to go further than this short flight, now ending. He proposed even that he should become the Flower of All Things, and that he should learn to be the All-Knowing, the All-Admiring.

M. Silcox (✉)
Department of Humanities and Philosophy, University of Central Oklahoma, Edmond, OK, USA
e-mail: MSilcox@uco.edu

© Springer Nature Switzerland AG 2021
B. Dainton et al. (eds.), *Minding the Future*, Science and Fiction,
https://doi.org/10.1007/978-3-030-64269-3_10

197

Instead, he is to be destroyed. He is only a fledgling caught in a bush-fire. He is very small, very simple, very little capable of insight. His knowledge of the great orb of things is but a fledgling's knowledge. His admiration is a nestling's admiration for the things kindly to his own small nature. He delights only in food and the food-announcing call. The music of the spheres passes over him, through him, and is not heard. Yet it has used him. And now it uses his destruction. Great, and terrible, and very beautiful is the Whole; and for man the best is that the Whole should use him.—Olaf Stapledon, *Last and First Men*

The above passage comes from the very last page of Stapledon's monumental, philosophically daring speculative history-of-the-future. Taken out of context, it seems to suggest that the human story, if it could ever be told in its entirety, would at best be comprehensible only as subplot or fragmentary set of episodes from a greater narrative, one that transcended both the scope of our species' natural interests and the range of our highest achievements. But this interpretation is at least partially undercut by the premise of the whole novel, which takes the history of humanity as its theme, and starts and ends at the very points in time that we ourselves do. Is Stapledon perhaps subtly trying to suggest here that such an internally coherent, thematically self-sufficient narrative history of our kind could never be anything *other* than fiction?

Many historians, futurists, cultural critics, and philosophers have been more sanguine at the prospect of telling such a story without fantasy or fabrication. Some have even suggested that the history of all that is truly real is ultimately just an account of how some anthropic trait or capacity (Hegel's *geist* being the paradigm example) comes to full fruition. But the tendency to want to construct such "metanarratives" of human self-realization has also fallen under aggressively sceptical scrutiny over the past few decades, especially since the advent of postmodernism within the Western academy.[1]

In this paper, I shall examine two very different sorts of challenges to the particular type of philosophical optimism about human nature and human achievement that underlies this view of our history as a species. The first such challenge is Karl Popper's famous and influential critique of historicism. Popper believed that any attempt to discover the "inexorable laws" that govern humanity's "historical destiny" is doomed to fail, and defended this view with considerable elaborateness in *The Poverty of Historicism* and subsequent

---

[1] Concerning the broader characteristics of metanarratives, see [1, p. xxiv].

works published during the mid-twentieth century [2, p. v]. The second challenge is presented by the idea of "the coming Singularity," as this event has been prophesied by writers such as Vernor Vinge, Ray Kurzweil, and David Chalmers, and examined through a wide variety of different lenses in some recent science fiction (hereafter SF). The hypothesis that computers might one day develop capacities that not only exceed our own, but defy our very comprehension, also seems to imply that the course of at least some aspects of future history will be determined by forces independent of human foresight or contrivance. But these two very different ways of identifying the limitations of human thought and intelligence also seem to conflict with one another in a curious way. Believers in the imminence of the Singularity often seem to be deriving this prediction from the very sorts of generalizations about history that Popper thought it was impossible to formulate.

A couple of authors who have written works of SF that attempt to depict aspects of human life after the Singularity cast some interesting light upon this puzzle about the limitations of our predictive capabilities. Bruce Sterling's 1986 novella "The Beautiful and the Sublime" and Iain M. Banks' long series of novels and stories about "The Culture" both seem to me to suggest with a vividness and ingenuity that philosophy has yet to match how our lives might look once our increasing dependence upon computers begin to make their powers and capacities seem fundamentally mysterious to us. Certain types of storytelling in SF, I shall argue, are able to provide a better representation of the limited extent to which human intelligence can be expected to foresee its own path through history than any attempt to characterize such limitations in the abstract.

Black Shapes on White Paper

In *The Poverty of Historicism*, Popper characterizes the principal target of his criticism as the idea that there is a "method" available for developing a "scientific theory of historical development serving as a basis for historical prediction." In his preface to the book's 1957 edition, he represents the impossibility of arriving at the requisite type of theory as following from these four premises:

1. The course of human history is strongly influenced by the growth of human knowledge.
2. We cannot predict, by rational or scientific methods, the future growth of our scientific knowledge.
3. We cannot, therefore, predict the future course of human history.

4. This means that we must reject the possibility of a *theoretical history*; that is to say, of a historical social science that would correspond to *theoretical physics*. [2, pp. xi–xii]

Popper recognizes that the second premise is the argument's "crucial" component, with its identification of what seems to be a substantive and untraversable limit upon human self-knowledge.

Obedience to the Socratic injunction to 'know thyself' is taken by many to constitute the very essence of philosophy. But in spite of this, Popper thinks that (2) can be "logically proved"—and that the falsity of historicism can ultimately be accepted "for strictly logical reasons" [2, p. xi]. Philosophers these days are less fond of claiming that substantive, controversial theses about any aspect of reality are true as a matter of 'mere logic' than was fashionable back in the mid-twentieth century. But figuring out what Popper thinks logic can teach us about the limitations of our capacity for predicting the future of science will be helpful both when we take a closer look at the sorts of assumptions being made in the philosophical literature about the Singularity, and when we examine some of the rather subtle and indirect ways in which SF authors try to depict the life of the human mind in a post-Singularity world.

Popper made several attempts at a "proof" of (2) throughout his career. The one that he eventually declared himself happiest with is formulated in *The Open Universe*. Here he suggests that, in order to answer the question of whether we can predict the growth of our own knowledge, we must first respond to the "preliminary," albeit less "important" question of whether "we might be able to predict *the content of an as yet unknown theory*" [3, p. 64]. Popper argues that accomplishing this feat is strictly impossible. For

if we knew today…what theories will occur to us a month ahead, then the theory would of course occur to us today, in some sense or other, and not in one month; consequently, we did not foresee anything that may be described as the future growth of knowledge. [3, p. 65]

Having dispensed (so he thinks) with this possibility, Popper turns to the "more important" question of whether "we might be able to predict the *acceptance of a previously not accepted theory on the basis of new tests*" [3, p. 64]. This task also turns out to be beyond us, he thinks, for curiously similar-sounding reasons:

Evidence whose occurrence can be predicted on the basis of our present knowledge cannot be evidence which would justify the acceptance of a new theory.

For evidence which can be predicted with the help of present knowledge would either not be new in kind, or, if new, would amount to a test confirming our present theories (rather than inducing us to accept a new theory). The kind of evidence which would justify the acceptance of a new theory is evidence which can be predicted with the help of the new theory but *not* with the help of our present knowledge.

It is this latter argument, he thinks, that "in spite of a certain triviality, suffices for a refutation of the influential doctrine of historicism" [3, p. 67].

The most interesting question worth asking about this pair of arguments is that, if both of them are supposed to be plausible as a matter of mere "logic," then why does Popper think the first one needs to be made at all? One senses that lurking behind this curious reduplication of effort is a worry that there is at least *some* sort of important difference between the criteria for determining whether a theory has merely been entertained (i.e. has "occurred to us") and those relevant to ascertaining its acceptance.

Popper does in fact do a little more than merely hint at the existence of this difference. He briefly considers the possibility, with respect to the first of his two questions, of whether "we may predict the growth of knowledge without *understanding* what we predict" [3, p. 66]. How might such a prediction work? Popper is pretty sketchy on the subject: he envisages someone trying to anticipate "the black shapes which a writer is to write on white paper, and their repercussions upon history." No sooner than having summoned up this curious image, he insists that such a prediction simply could not be made without being concurrent with its own realization:

> If we can predict, i.e. describe these shapes, we, or anyone aware of our predictions, can write them down now, and if their genesis is to influence history in the future, there is no reason why it should not do so now. [3, p. 66]

Whatever one might think of the other two anti-historicist arguments quoted above—and both strike me as worthy at least of serious consideration—this last one is just obviously invalid. Identifying an event as the cause of further events (whether predictively or retrospectively) obviously does not require a full (or even partial) understanding of its intentional characteristics. Does it matter exactly what a general yells at his troops just before a bayonet charge, provided he does so loudly enough? When one hears Donald Trump use the expression "climate change," does one need to attend to the rest of the sentence he utters to be able to infer that he is lying?

Of course, battle cries and isolated acts of deceit are not scientific theories, let alone recipes for the construction of a superhuman machine intelligence. So the point just made—for all that I think it undeniably sabotages Popper's argument—might initially come across as somewhat cheeseparing.[2] But much of the contemporary literature about the Singularity actually seems to me to derive its deepest philosophical interest from the fact that its authors make exactly the type of prediction that Popper is here trying to characterize as logically impossible. For the very thing that makes the kinds of AIs that the authors of these works prophesy *singular* is their ability to engage in a type of cognitive activity that in some way or other transcends human comprehension. Even if one accepts a very strong interpretation of premise (1) of Popper's original argument from *The Poverty of Historicism*, (viz. "the course of human history is strongly influenced by the growth of human knowledge"), the possibility of predicting how the growth of distinctively non-human forms of knowledge might alter "the course of human history" is surely of more than trivial philosophic interest.

Popper discusses another philosophical attitude toward human history in *The Poverty of Historicism* that does not involve the belief that it is possible to formulate general predictive theories about the growth of scientific knowledge. According to this view, which he refers to as "anti-naturalism," a proper understanding of any phenomenon *as* historical totally precludes the sort of predictive accuracy that we expect from laws of nature in the physical sciences. For in history (so the "anti-naturalist" believes) "nothing is of greater moment than the emergence of a really new period. This all-important aspect of social life cannot be investigated along the lines we are accustomed to follow when we explain novelties in the realm of physics by regarding them as re-arrangements of familiar elements" [2, p. 9]. This is because (according to this view) historical phenomena cannot be understood in the way that physical events can (i.e. by subsuming them under invariant laws of nature); the historian can only have knowledge of her subject by means of what Popper refers to as "intuitive understanding." This distinctive type of "intuitive" knowledge about other historical eras has, Popper thinks, been conceived of in a wide variety of ways. But he remarks that, insofar as it can be treated as predictive at all, it must be based upon

---

[2] If one accepts Popper's claim from later in the same work that what he calls the "descriptive" and "argumentative" functions of language are irreducible to its "signalling" and "expressive" functions [3, pp. 82–3], it will certainly seem reasonable to draw the weaker conclusion that, to the extent that the historical influence of a scientific theory depends upon its performance of the former pair of functions, *not all* of its effects could be predicted in the absence of understanding its content.

inference by analogy from one historical period to another. For though it fully recognizes that historical periods are intrinsically different, and that no event can really repeat itself in another period of social development…we should evaluate the meaning of certain events by comparing them with analogous events in earlier periods, so as to help us forecast new developments—never forgetting, however, that the inevitable differences between the two periods must be duly taken into account. [2, p. 20]

The problem with this view, Popper thinks, is that it is the very nature of the scientific method to require that "we should search for laws with an unlimited realm of validity." If the historian does not aspire to the discovery of such laws, but merely to the identification of imperfectly analogous relationships between events belonging to different periods, this would (Popper thinks) be the "end of scientific progress," since the question of whether any new, potentially recalcitrant data required the formulation of new laws would always have to be decided on an *ad hoc* basis [2, p. 95].

The problem with this critique of analogical reasoning in the sciences is that it begs the question against the very type of methodological pluralism that it seeks to refute. The idea that genuine laws discovered in the special sciences have a restricted range of application—or else are subject to subject-specific types of *ceteris paribus* qualifications—is by no means unproblematic.[3] But to regard such restricted generalizations as laws is certainly not simply *equivalent* to making the implicit "admission that change is simply miraculous" [2, p. 95]. That having been said, it can hardly be denied that the use of analogical reasoning to understand historical change—especially when the terms of the analogy are whole "periods," "paradigms," "civilizations," or similarly dubious units of analysis—must be subject to some external standard of falsifiability. Works of fiction are of course (quite usefully, as we shall see) at least partly exempt from such strictures.

Authors who have argued for the inevitability or extreme likelihood of the Singularity do not in general seem to have distinguished between the two different sorts of reasons that Popper seeks to undermine for why one might be justified in making predictive claims about the future growth of knowledge. Several such writers, in fact, seem to me to have at certain crucial points simply taken the "naturalistic" approach for granted.[4] In the next section, I shall

---

[3] For the classic defence of this view, see [4]. See also [5] for an account of how this view of the explanatory range of lawlike generalizations about human history was prefigured in the work of authors such as Humboldt, Ranke, Rickert, and Simmel. For Donald Davidson's discussion of the difference between homonomic and heteronomic generalizations, see [6].

[4] See, e.g., the discussion in the following section of Ray Kurzweil's ostensible "law" of "accelerating returns."

argue that both the justification of such predictive claims and the task of describing the similarities and differences between pre-and post-Singularity human life in general terms generate some rather unexpected philosophical problems quite different from those that Popper identifies with the historicist project. The type of scepticism that these problems generate turns out to be, on the one hand, far more provisional (and less a matter of the mere "logic" of historical explanation) but on the other hand, quite a bit more challenging to refute.

An Opaque Wall across the Future

Philosophers and other writers who have engaged in detailed, non-fictional conjecture about the Singularity and human life thereafter have shared with other types of prophets a tendency to indulge in certain rather predictable forms of ambiguity. This tendency might perhaps just as easily be viewed as arising either from a general inclination to hedge one's bets, or (more charitably) from some of the inherent epistemic difficulties facing all speculation about future history.

In his widely read (and hugely influential) essay "The Coming Technological Singularity: How to Survive in the Post-Human Era," Vernor Vinge remarks that there is a longstanding prejudice amongst those who have talked about the creation of "superhumanly intelligent beings" to focus exclusively upon AI, at the expense of what Vinge refers to as "Intelligence Amplification" (IA). He uses this latter term to refer to what happens "every time our ability to access information and to communicate it to others is improved" by technological means. For in all such cases, he maintains, "in some sense we have achieved an increase over natural intelligence" [7, p. 17]. But Vinge is far less than clear about what it would take for a particular instance of IA to qualify as "singular" in the required way. It would be a disappointment if the type of event that he and others have been referring to as a "Singularity" for the past quarter century turned out to be the sort of thing that has actually already occurred every time some powerful new medium of information storage and retrieval (e.g. the cave painting, the codex, the printing press, the pocket calculator) has been discovered.

Other remarks Vinge makes do seem to be incompatible with this reading. One of his most famous claims in the essay is that, because "an ultraintelligent machine could design even better machines; there would then unquestionably be an 'intelligence explosion,' and the intelligence of man would be left far behind. Thus the first ultraintelligent machine is the last invention that man need ever make" [7 (quoting I.G. Good), p. 15]. But the closest Vinge ever comes to making an explicit distinction between "ordinary" and "singular" types of IA is the rather elliptical suggestion that "human computer interfaces...may reasonably be considered superintelligent" *only* once they have become sufficiently "intimate" [7, p. 12]. At first glance this might seem like a useful criterion: surely it would make more sense to treat a human being with cybernetic brain implants as a possible candidate for superintelligence than some caveman keeping track of the passing seasons *via* hatch marks on a rock. But once we get beyond such vivid examples, the measurement of degrees of 'intimacy' between human and machine is bound to become pretty negotiable. Philosophers such as Andy Clark who have recently defended the "extended mind" hypothesis would claim that there is simply no explanatorily useful boundary to be drawn between the *inside* and the *outside* of whatever it is about us that deserves to be characterized as intelligent in the first place. Instead, they regard the very idea that "mental action is all, or nearly all, on the inside [of] the ancient fortress of skin and skull" as the source of "sciences and images of the mind that are, in a fundamental sense, inadequate to their self-proclaimed target" [8, p. 5].

Vinge's remarks about the ultimate historical significance of the Singularity are similarly mystifying. In the context of crediting science fiction writers for being the first to feel the "concrete impact" of accelerated technological change in the twentieth century, he observes that what such writers all had in common was that they "felt an opaque wall across the future" [7, p. 13]. It is less than straightforward trying to imagine what a work of speculative fiction would have to be like in order to qualify as a manifestation of this type of attitude, and he unfortunately provides no examples. But the curious mix of intellectual ambition and insouciance in his attitude toward predicting the results of the Singularity is perhaps best read as an indication that he might have at least some implicit appreciation of the other ambiguities in his account.

A similar air of mysteriousness surrounds some of the claims Ray Kurzweil makes in his book *The Singularity is Near*. Kurzweil's writings on the subject have probably exerted more influence on thoughtful, technology-savvy nonphilosophers than anything other than Vinge's essay itself. His optimism about the future of AI research arises from a somewhat different basis than Vinge's, having less to do with recent changes in the human/computer interface and more with what he regards as the success of recent attempts to "reverse engineer the human brain" using cybernetic technology [9, p. 143]. The type of AI whose development constitutes the Singularity will, he thinks, arise as an extension of research currently being carried out *via* the construction of analytic and neuromorphic models of the brain, based on increasingly detailed and accurate scans of human neuronal activity.

So why suppose that the use of cybernetic technology to emulate the brain's activities will generate the kinds of capacities that will qualify as genuine extensions or amplifications of human intelligence, and be recognizable by us as such? Kurzweil thinks that this is more or less bound to happen because he also thinks that "the accelerating pace of brain reverse engineering makes it clear that there are no limits to our ability to understand ourselves." The key to the scalability of human intelligence, he argues, "is our ability to build models of reality in our mind. These models can be recursive, meaning that one model can include other models, which can include yet finer models, without limit" [9, p. 198]. The claim that human thought is characterized above all else by its capacity to generate recursive structures is a familiar one.[5] But it never becomes adequately clear what Kurzweil imagines the relationship to be between the mind's recursivity and its capacity for self-knowledge.

In fact, one of the things Kurzweil thinks we already know about the human brain that makes its activities both qualitatively different from other natural processes and especially challenging to emulate is the fact that "the brain uses emergent properties." He describes the emergent character of "intelligent behaviour" itself *via* an analogy with "termite and ant colonies" in which "the architecture emerges from unpredictable interactions of all the colony members, each following relatively simple rules" [9, p. 151]. For reasons I have defended at length elsewhere, if our capacity to understand ourselves is taken to be one of the "emergent" features of how our brain works, then treating recursivity as either a necessary or a sufficient condition for self-knowledge gets things (in a certain sense) precisely backwards [see 11].

A feature of Kurzweil's idiosyncratic take on the nature of technological progress that might be thought to plug this explanatory gap is his endorsement of what he refers to as the "law of accelerating returns." This is the claim that "fundamental measures of information technology follow predictable and exponential trajectories, belying the conventional wisdom that you can't predict the future" [12]. In an essay offering reasons to believe that digital computers will eventually pass the Turing test, he explains the purport of this "law" *via* an analogy with Moore's law, the famous prediction first made in 1965 that the density of transistors in an integrated circuit—a fairly accurate rigorization of the informal notion of "computing power"—could be expected to double every two years. He claims that such exponential growth can also be

---

[5] For a lively and contentious discussion of the claim, with special reference to the human language faculty, see [10].

observed in "communication technologies," "biological technologies," and "brain reverse engineering" [see 13].

But is the type of intelligence that we already attribute to human beings also suitably viewed as a "measure" of information technology that might either falsify or provide support for Kurzweil's generalization? What is crucially missing from his sketchy, but provocative narrative of technological change is how all of the various forms of accelerating development he identifies are supposed to coalesce into any kind of recognizable growth whatsoever in what we currently regard as intelligence *simpliciter*. And this is really just a new version of the problem of emergence that we have already identified. Kurzweil's own confession that his optimism about the Turing test has the status of a mere "wager" makes it seem as though what he refers to as a "law" is perhaps best viewed as a mere *guess* at the outcomes of a relatively indeterminate process.

The problematic nature of these sorts of predictions is addressed more explicitly by David Chalmers, in his long essay "The Singularity: A Philosophical Analysis." Rather than engaging in the sort of disjunctive prophesying that the two authors just discussed indulge in about the variety of distinct paths that could lead to the development of a 'superintelligence,' Chalmers focuses upon the question of whether we currently have a clear enough conception of what human intelligence actually consists of to make sense of such projections in the first place. Most arguments for the Singularity, he points out, have "depended on an uncritical acceptance of the assumption that there is such a thing as intelligence and that it can be measured" [14, p. 26]. There are two quite separate problems with this assumption: first, it is highly controversial among psychologists and social scientists, and second, even if it were true, the relevant notion of intelligence might not have any clear application to non-human cognitive systems.

Chalmers' own response to this challenge is to try to represent the type of ability that an AI would have to possess in order to constitute a genuine Singularity as austerely as possible. All that one needs to be able to identify to adequately conceptualize the Singularity, he proposes, is the following:

(i) a self-amplifying cognitive capacity G: a capacity such that increases in that capacity go along with proportionate (or greater) increases in the ability to create systems with that capacity

(ii) the thesis that we can create systems whose capacity G is greater than our own, and

(iii) a correlated cognitive capacity H that we care about, such that certain small increases in H can always be produced by large enough increases in G. [14, p. 27]

The obvious (though not necessarily optimal or paradigmatic) candidate for capacity G would be a computer's processing speed. Chalmers stays deliberately neutral on the question of whether there is any concept from our current folk-psychological repertoire that is best suited to play the role of H, though he does at one point suggests that "general intelligence" or *g*, the trait that most standard IQ tests purport to measure, might be a promising candidate. He also cleverly observes that, since descriptions of the Singularity tend to focus on the ability of some future AI to improve upon its own capacities, capacity G need not correlate directly with H, but "need only correlate with H', the capacity to create systems with H" [14, p. 28].

There is, however, a further absolutely crucial tacit assumption that underlies Chalmers' argument. This is that our inclination to *continue to value* capacity H will increase in proportion to its objective amplification. In the case of many other human capacities, cognitive and otherwise—e.g. the capacity to retain information in long-term memory, to construct novel mathematical proofs, to parse complex sentences, to imaginatively reconstruct the motivations of other thinkers, to empathize, to love—it actually seems remarkably easy to imagine how our capacity to value them might "top out" at a certain point in their amplification, before converting to mere neutral incomprehension (perhaps after a short detour through something like the "mathematical sublime").[6]

This problem faced by Chalmers' attempt to recast the idea of the Singularity in maximally abstract terms is provocatively similar to the issues that were raised by Vinge's and Kurzweil's *prima facie* more substantive accounts. In trying to characterize the Singularity in terms of an increase in some putatively cognitive capacity other than the specifically human type of intelligence that we "care about," there seems no reliable way avoid either triviality or ineffability. Future history as lived out by humans in the presence of such an entity becomes correspondingly difficult to envision as anything other than either a banal continuation of whatever we take *right now* to be technological progress, or an "opaque wall," to borrow Vinge's expression.

---

[6] I.e. "a feeling of pain arising from a want of accordance between the aesthetical estimation of magnitude formed by the imagination and estimation of the same formed by reason…which arouses within us the feeling of our supersensible destination, according to which it is purposive and therefore pleasurable to find every standard of sensibility inadequate to the ideas of understanding" [15, pp. 96–7].

Our arrival at this impasse should not be entirely surprising, considering the results of our earlier discussion of Popper's arguments against the very possibility of a predictive science of history. It is not that we are faced with some merely 'logical' impediment to any sort of substantive theorizing at all about humanity's future after the Singularity happens. Rather, it appears that, in the absence of any clear idea of how its cognitive superiority to us would become manifest, we must confine ourselves to speculating about the *effects* of summoning a superintelligent being into existence, in partial abstraction from the questions of whether we would be able to recognize it as such, or what the actual content of such an entity's cognitive states might turn out to be. On these latter topics the best we seem to be able to hope for is a merely (and perhaps necessarily imperfectly) *analogical* understanding of how things might turn out.

In the final section of this paper, I shall try to show how these *prima facie* rather pessimistic conclusions have already been grasped at an intuitive level by a couple of the twentieth century's most relentlessly imaginative and gifted writers of SF. Their works present a fascinating case study of how speculative fiction can prove as enlightening at demonstrating the outer limits of human comprehension as it can be as a more conventional venue for speculation about humanity's future.

Decadent Weasels and the Ends of Invention

In the version of humanity's future depicted in Bruce Sterling's novella "The Beautiful and the Sublime," AIs have taken over the advancement of scientific inquiry. Physics has been reduced to a "shrunken state," economics has been rendered redundant by the emergence of vast surpluses redistributed on a global scale, and human doctors have been replaced by mechanized expert systems [16, p. 187]. The generation of scientists whose work elevated machine consciousness to the level required to bring about these cultural changes have, by the time of the story, come to form a politically embarrassed cadre of bitter revisionists, consumed with nostalgia for the very type of intellectual work that their own achievements have made superfluous.

All of this information is delivered obliquely through the epistolary voice of the story's protagonist, Manfred De Kooning. De Kooning is a twenty-something male who spends his apparently uninterrupted free time embroiled in long conversations about such topics as "the postulate that the male is beautiful while the female is sublime" [16, p. 209]. He wafts about the countryside on long, contemplative nature hikes ("[w]hat a landscape! Great sweeping vistas, long blasted mesas, great gaudy sunsets reaching ethereal fingers of pure radiance"), and carries out an elaborately circumlocuitous, sentimental flirtation with his girlfriend ("You're too soulful, too much a full human being for such a mummified life") [16, p. 188]. He is the type of universal aesthete whose elaborately formed tastes and sub-Wildean behavioural affects have, since the Singularity occurred, drifted from the bohemian shores of western culture into the very depths of the mainstream, in a way that directly correlates with science's loss of prestige.

Leona Hillis, the woman who is the object of Manfred's (extremely courtly) attempts at seduction, is the daughter of one of the embittered AI researchers. Most of the story's action arises from Manfred's rivalry with Leona's fiancé, Marvin Somps, a former astronaut and aeronautical engineer. Somps is receiving funds from Leona's father to construct an ultralight, single-pilot aircraft called the Dragonfly. The excitement generated by this *prima facie* rather whimsical project is due to the fact that

> [a] computer can fly any traditional aircraft. But, you see, the mathematics that determine the interactions of the [Dragonfly's] four moving wings—no machine can deal with such. No such programs exist. The machines cannot write them because they do not know the mathematics…Only Marvin Somps knows them.

So, as Somps' assistant explains, the craft must be flown, "without avionics. By feel, like riding a bicycle! The brain does not have to know, to fly. The nervous system, it has a feel. Computers fly by thinking, but they feel nothing!" [16, p. 209]. As Somps prepares for his first solo flight and his romantic and scientific rivals conspire against him, the story takes on an overt and playful resemblance to the myth of Icarus.

What makes the story work both as a brilliant piece of comedy and an extraordinarily alienating vision of the future is the gradually dawning sense that both aspiring scientific innovators like Somps and fashionable aesthetes like De Kooning are doomed to permanent ineffectuality. Somps is convinced that with his Dragonfly project, he has discovered a small realm of intellectual achievement within which humans can still outdo machines. But the Dragonfly ends up getting stolen by a fellow pilot who crashes it into a tree. And De Kooning is a self-proclaimed "artist' who never seems to have produced a body of work. In spite of all of his romantic effusions and relentless plotting against his rival, he never quite manages to physically consummate his relationship with Leona, and by the end of the story is showing signs of a saturnine sentimentality reminiscent of Kierkegaard's Johannes in *Diary of a Seducer*.

As for Leona's father, the wheelchair-bound AI pioneer Dr. Hillis, he is bankrupted by his failed investment in the Dragonfly, and eventually gets discovered by Somps and De Kooning in his bedroom overdosing on painkillers:

> "I killed the scientific tradition!" He began weeping freely. "Twenty-six hundred years since Socrates and then, me." He glared and his head rolled like a flower on a stalk. "Take your hands off me, you decadent weasels!" [16, p. 207]

What are all of the post-Singularity AIs themselves up to during all of this profoundly human fuss and futility? The only hint Sterling ever gives of their palpable influence upon everyday human affairs is *via* the ominous presence of small devices called "wrist wards" that every character wears, and that seem to function as combination portable filing systems and perpetually activated geolocators. Dr. Hillis contemptuously refers to them as "handcuffs" [16, p. 207].[7] But apart from the mere fact that absolutely everybody is clearly in some way being monitored, the significance of the wards in the lives of the story's characters is left inscrutable.

This, it seems to me, is the story's central and most provocative enigma. But if the conclusions we reached about the chief lacuna in Popper's critique of historicism earlier on in the paper were right, then this very feature of the narrative is also what makes it an intellectually honest and philosophically creditable depiction of post-Singularity human life. The superior AIs of the future shall be known, it suggests, only by their distinctive *effects* upon *us*, rather than by the features of their activity that make them "singular" *qua* intelligences in the first place.

Although Manfred De Kooning is a fundamentally comical protagonist and (from the perspective of the present, at least) a fairly ridiculous character, he does show an ability to mourn the passing of the heroic age of human discovery. He admires his rival's aeronautical invention for its reliance on "the indefinable elements that separate humanity from the shallow logic of our modernday intelligent environment" [16, p. 192]. And just before the crash of the Dragonfly, he reflects that "I felt the loss of those glory days, which we now see, in hindsight, as the last sunset glow of the Western analytic method" [16, p. 200]. But he consoles himself at the story's conclusion with the following morbidly banal observation: 'It's the yin and the yang,' I told him. 'Once poets laboured in garrets while engineers had the run of the land. Things change, that's all. If one goes against the grain, one pays the price' [16, p. 192]. The bizarre spectacle that he presents of an utterly conformist

---

[7] It is perhaps worth mentioning in this connection that Sterling's story was first published in 1986, well before the dawn of the smartphone.

bohemian may be one of the most brilliant pieces of characterization in all of science fiction.

De Kooning's flexibility in the face of radical historic change resonates in a curious way with Sterling's own deep scepticism about the idea of the Singularity. In a public lecture entitled "Your Future as a Black Hole," Sterling charges Vinge and others of using "intelligence" as a "magical term," in a way that illuminates nothing so much as "intellectual imperialism" on the part of mathematicians and computer scientists. The "biggest impact" that Sterling thinks the idea of the Singularity will ever have is "literary." For the most central feature of predictions about the Singularity is in fact the idea that human history will eventually arrive at a "place where matters of great importance to futurists become impossible to write about" [17]. But if incomprehension is the only justifiable attitude to adopt toward the Singularity before it happens, then the only attitude it makes any sense to project onto human beings who live *after* it takes place must surely be one of radical ambivalence. Sterling thus provides a nice dramatization of the point that was made about Chalmers' characterization of the Singularity back in the second section, *viz.* that there is no particular reason to believe we shall (or should) continue to value any human abilities worthy of the name "intelligence" as the more objectively measurable capacities that underlie them undergo accelerated amplification.

In his series of nine novels and two short stories about "The Culture," Iain M. Banks takes an approach to depicting a post-Singularity universe that is by at least one salient criterion exactly the opposite of Sterling's. Banks' Culture is a galaxy-spanning imperial civilization ruled by superintelligent, artificial "Minds" that have distinctive personalities, quirks of temperament, and wacky names such as *Prosthetic Conscience, The Ends of Invention,* and *No More Mr. Nice Guy.* Unlike the machine intelligences of Sterling's post-Singularity world, which remain entirely in the background, Banks' advanced AIs often serve as major characters in the stories he tells—about a third of *Excession,* one of his most entertaining novels, consists of extensive IM conversations the Minds conduct entirely with one another.

The relationship of Banks' Minds to the human species is ambiguous and fascinating. While it is hinted throughout the series that they owe their inception to human science, their current status in the world of *homo sapiens* is that of benevolent caretakers. The overwhelming majority of humans in Banks' universe inhabit environments of zero scarcity in which they can live for (more or less) as long as they want to and pursue any amusements they choose. Some minor human characters occasionally rankle against this subordinate status, but Banks never indicates that the arrangement is in any way perverse or offensive to human dignity.

The one partial exception to this benevolent regime is the small corps of humans who work in a branch of government called "Special Circumstances" (SC), which is responsible for contact with civilizations outside The Culture. These characters live on something a bit closer to equal terms with the incomparably more intelligent and resourceful Minds. Employment by SC provides human beings the opportunity for genuine heroism, but only at the price of their ultimate subordination. Two of the series' most popular and moving novels, *Use of Weapons* and *The Player of Games*, are fundamentally tragic stories about human protagonists who undergo heroic risks for Special Circumstances while being deceived and manipulated by the Minds in ways that lead to personal heartbreak and humiliation. But in a startling passage from the first novel of the series, *Consider Phlebas*, another human SC agent contemplates humanity's role in this arrangement from a perspective that seems to be close to that of the author:[8]

> We are a mongrel race. Our past a history of tangles, our sources obscure, our rowdy upbringing full of greedy, short-sighted empires and cruel, wasteful diasporas...There had to be something wrong with us, something mutant in the system, something too quick and nervous and frantic for our own good or anyone else's...And if we tamper with our inheritance, so what? What makes nature more right than us?....And if we are no longer on the edge of the breaking wave, well, too bad. Hand on the baton; best wishes, have fun. [19, pp. 368–71]

When one compares this attitude of radical self-effacement about human nature with the technological optimism of a Kurzweil or a Chalmers, it becomes especially clear how little constraint the concept of the Singularity imposes upon one's views the overall shape of human history.

But what is it specifically about Banks' Minds that makes them worthy of this type of radical self-abnegation on behalf of the whole human species? Their dialogue throughout the Culture novels is reliably more intellectually sophisticated and witty than that of the human characters, and the technological artifacts that they have developed since their ascendency are described with an admiring vividness and attention to detail that draw upon the most

---

[8] When asked in an interview why he returned to writing Culture novels after taking a hiatus to compose some mainstream literary novels, Banks replied "[t]hat's where I want to live, that's *my* utopia. It's what I want to go home in" [18, p. 15].

well-worn tropes of SF technophilia.[9] And apart from their tendency treat a few SC agents as means in a way that would probably offend Kantians, the Minds' long-term political goals always turn out to be unambiguously benevolent. But as well as all of these relatively traditional literary means for generating readerly sympathy for the Minds, Banks also adds one curious feature to the universe of the Culture that provides a helpful indication of how purely analogical reasoning might (contra Popper) be helpful in trying to imagine a post-Singularity future.

It is possible for both Minds themselves and human civilizations existing within the bounds of The Culture's sovereignty to achieve "sublimation." This is a process whereby an individual or collective consciousness is transferred from our four-dimensional spacetime to a mysteriously different plane of existence. The topic is dealt with most extensively in Banks' last novel *The Hydrogen Sonata*, in which a variety of Minds exhibit a strange mixture of curiosity, ambivalence, and contempt for those among their number who choose to enter this quasi-mystical state.

The leading Minds of the Culture are thrilled when one of their number who has sublimed, a ship called the *Zoologist*, elects to return to their reality in an etiolated form.

> Contact's finest and most expert minds in all things to do with the Sublime had tried debriefing the returned Mind. They had initially been ecstatic at having one of their own who had been there and made the return trip....This, however, had proven farcical. The ship's memories were abstracted, beyond vague; effectively useless. The Mind itself was basically a mess; self-reconstructed (presumably) along lines it was impossible to see the logic behind. Identifiably the same, it was expressed in the most bizarre and obfuscatory tangle of needlessly complicated and self-referential/analytical/meditative and sagational/ratiocinative processal architecture it had ever been the misfortune of all concerned ever to contemplate. [21, p. 137]

In an especially chilling scene, an avatar of a Ship called *Caconym* visits an avatar of the *Zoologist*, in the latter Ship's private VR laboratory.

> The *Caconym*'s avatoid looked down, plucked the tiny insect from the bench and held it trapped between two fingers. It held it up, antennae waving, towards the upside-down avatoid "You always say that nothing matters. Would it matter if I crushed this, now?"

---

[9] See, for example, the lively IM exchanges at [20, pp. 214–219, 318]. For an example of Banks' attention in detail, see his description of the Vavatch Orbital in [19, pp. 101–2].

The *Zoologist* shrugged. "Cac, it's just a package of code."

"It's alive, in some sense. It has a set of pre-programmed reactions, responses, and so on. A tiny fraction of this environment's richness would be snuffed out if I reduced it to its virtual components.

"All this, and all you imply by it, is known. Thought about, allowed for, included. Still.

[...]

"When you come back from the Sublime, it is as though you leave all but one of your senses behind, as though you have all the rest removed, torn away—and you have become used to having hundreds."

The *Caconym* nodded slowly. "So why did you?"

The *Zoologist* shrugged. "To experience a kind of extreme asceticism," it said, "and to provide a greater contrast, when I return." [21, pp. 149–50]

It is surely part of Banks' agenda in these passages to suggest an analogy between the relationship of ordinary Minds to those that have sublimed and the relationship of human beings to the types of AIs that might come into existence after the Singularity. But the basis of this analogy is nothing other than the more or less complete inscrutability of one party to another. Popper's critique of analogical reasoning in the study of human history therefore has no purchase here, for reasons that go deeper than just the fact that the Culture novels are works of fiction. Obviously, a relationship that is by its very nature beyond human comprehension is not the sort of thing that, once identified, could provide the basis for anything that would qualify as a law of nature. Yet by placing such relationships in a vividly imagined and at least largely coherent narrative frame, Banks shows us how the Singularity might figure as a determinate type of event within the broader scope of human history. And the ambivalence that his novels provoke about whether the difference in internal complexity between human and Mind, and between Mind and Sublimed Mind, is something there is any reason to admire strengthens the case against Chalmers' casual assumption that the type "self-amplifying cognitive capacity" possessed by a Singular AI will correlate with some other ability that we might have antecedent reasons to value.

Prophets of the Singularity have described its unavoidable imminence with a great deal more imagination and energy than they have been able to elaborate upon either its implications for human history or precisely what will make it qualitatively different from other more routine advancements of human technology. In this paper I have tried to demonstrate, by way of some critical reflections upon Karl Popper's arguments against the possibility of history as a tool for predicting humanity's future, both the fundamental limitations of such speculations and what they might nonetheless teach us about our species' ultimate place in the broader narrative of history. What makes the work of science fiction writers such as Sterling and Banks so valuable in this context is the way that it is able to limn some of the forms that such a narrative might take in ways that rely upon both our capacity to imagine our own future and the limitations of human conceit that we end up discovering when we try.

References

1. Lyotard, J.: The Postmodern Condition: A Report on Knowledge, trans. Bennington. G. and Masumi, B. University of Minnesota Press, Minneapolis (1984)
2. Popper, K.: The Poverty of Historicism. Routledge, London (1957)
3. Popper, K.: In: Bartley III, W.W. (ed.) The Open Universe: An Argument from Indeterminism. Routledge, London (1982)
4. Fodor, J.: Special sciences (or: the disunity of science as a working hypothesis). Synthese. **28**, 97–115 (1974)
5. Beiser, F.: The German Historicist Tradition. Oxford University Press, Oxford (2015)
6. Davidson, D.: Mental events. In: Davidson, D. (ed.) Essays on Actions and Events, pp. 219–220. Oxford University Press, Oxford (1980)
7. Vinge, V.: The coming technological singularity: how to survive in a post-human era. NASA Technical Reports Server (2013). https://ntrs.nasa.gov/archive/nasa/casi.ntrs.nasa.gov/19940022856.pdf Accessed 27 August 2019
8. Clark, A.: Natural Born Cyborgs: Minds, Technologies, and the Future of Human Intelligence. Oxford University Press, New York (2003)
9. Kurzweil, R.: The Singularity is Near: When Humans Transcend Biology. Penguin Books, London (2005)
10. Pinker, S., Jackendoff, R.: The faculty of language: what's special about it? Cognition. **92**, 205–236 (2005)
11. Cogburn, J., Silcox, M.: Computability theory and ontological emergence. Am. Philos. Q. **48**, 63–74 (2011)
12. Kurzweil, R.: How my predictions are faring — an update by Ray Kurzweil. Kurzweil: Accelerating Intelligence. https://www.kurzweilai.net/how-my-predictions-are-faring-an-update-by-ray-kurzweil (2010). Accessed 6 June 2019
13. Kurzweil, R.: A wager on the Turing test: why I think I will win. Kurzweil: Accelerating Intelligence. https://www.kurzweilai.net/a-wager-on-the-turing-test-why-i-think-i-will-win (2002). Accessed 4 June, 2019

14. Chalmers, D.: The singularity: a philosophical analysis. In: Awret, U. (ed.) The Singularity (Journal of Consciousness Studies), pp. 7–65. Imprint Academic, Exeter (2016)
15. Kant, I.: Critique of Judgment, trans. Bernard, J. Hafner, New York (1951)
16. Sterling, B.: The beautiful and the sublime. In: Sterling, B. (ed.) Crystal Express, pp. 181–209. Ace Books, New York (1989)
17. Sterling, B.: The singularity: your future as a black hole. The Long Now Foundation. http://longnow.org/seminars/02004/jun/11/the-singularity-your-future-as-a-black-hole (2004). Accessed 5 July, 2019
18. Dibdin, T.: Big words and the small screen. The List. **281**, 15 (1996)
19. Banks, I.: Consider Phlebas. Hachette, New York (1987)
20. Banks, I.: Excession. Bantam, New York (1998)
21. Banks, I.: The Hydrogen Sonata. Orbit, New York (2012)

Shifting the Goalposts: Reconceptualizing Robots, AI, and Humans

Michael Szollosy

Abstract The rapid advancement of AI and autonomous systems is posing some difficult challenges to human beings, and not merely because they can now beat us at our favourite strategy games, like chess and Go, at which we used to assume that humans were invincible. AI and robots also pose challenges to humans' conceptions of ourselves, not just as the "rational animal," but increasingly in other areas that we used to consider our exclusive domain, pushing humans' self-conception into more niche, ever-dwindling areas. The abilities of autonomous systems has created, therefore, crises in our understanding of what it means to be "human," but these crises can be productively directed to challenge the founding mythologies of humanism, forcing us to think re-think what it means to be post-human, and overcoming the idea that "humans" and "machines" are clearly demarcated and in competition with one another.

In March 2016, the world's media announced with complete certainty the imminent robopocalypse when Google-backed DeepMind managed to create an AI so very sophisticated that it beat a human opponent at the board game

M. Szollosy (✉)
Sheffield Robotics & Department of Computer Science, University of Sheffield, Sheffield, UK
e-mail: m.szollosy@sheffield.ac.uk

© Springer Nature Switzerland AG 2021
B. Dainton et al. (eds.), *Minding the Future*, Science and Fiction,
https://doi.org/10.1007/978-3-030-64269-3_11

Go. Actually, DeepMind's program, AlphaGo, had already beat a human opponent, back in October 2015 [1]. But apparently, even though it was once thought that no computer could ever beat a human at Go, this opponent wasn't very good, even if he was the European champion. So it was really in March 2016, when AlphaGo beat Lee Sedol, winner of 18 world titles, the second all-time best player, that the AI had really achieved something noteworthy.

When setting off to write about this achievement, I expected to find the usual voices in the popular press declaring with their characteristic subtlety that the End of the Human Race was nigh! The actual responses seemed to be more muted than those that herald most advances in robotics and AI, no matter how minor. The British tabloids, usually so keen to append one of *those pictures* of the gleaming skeletal frame of the Terminator to any article about robots or AI that they can concoct, even seemed to show unusual self-restraint on this occasion. *The Daily Mail* was most unusually restrained, and didn't produce anything on the level of their headline later that year that warned, "Cyborg sea slugs are here! 'Frankenstein robot' crawls using muscles made from marine creatures and a 3D printed body" [2]. *The Daily Express* didn't fail to disappoint, however, asking in their headline of 9 March if Alpha Go's victory were "First step towards The Terminator becoming reality? AI beats champ of world's oldest game" [3]. *The Express* was buoyed by recent (and repeated) warnings from Stephen Hawking, quoting his warnings that AI could mean the end of human civilization.[1]

A Brief History of Cursed Progress and Narcissistic Injury

AlphaGo's victory certainly marked an important milestone in the progress of AI research, trumping IBM DeepBlue's victory over Gary Kasparov at chess back in 1997. Go is, apparently, a much more difficult game than chess for humans—and, it was thought, for computers—to master, due to its complexity and the need for players to recognize complex patterns. Famously, Go claims to have more possible moves than there are atoms in the known universe, at 10^{360}, as compared to a mere 10^{123} for chess [5]. Despite the simplicity of the rules, and the simple black and white token used in play,

---

[1] And yet, despite headlines like this, *The Express* can still manage to be surprised that, only four years later, the British public are somehow inexplicably worried about AI, as their headline of 24 June 2020 says, "Artificial intelligence: 60 percent of Brits STILL fear autonomous AI—shock survey" [4].

a standard Go board is 19 × 19, whereas chess is merely 8 × 8, and so requires its players to recognize more complex patterns [6].

But if we look more closely at the history of AI or, more specifically, the history of predictions about AI, and what AI can and cannot do, we can see that Go and Chess championships are merely more recent milestones in a long story of once-unthinkable victories. Here is a selection of some of them:

- 1959, Arthur Samuel announces a computer that can play checkers. But it's not very good. (And that's with a mere 5 × 1020 possible move) [7, 8]
- 1963, Joseph Weizenbuam at MIT writes ELIZA, which proves to be an effective artificial Rogerian psychotherapist (sort of...), and starts to make people wonder if artificial intelligence might pass Alan Turing's 1950 test [9, 10].
- 1992, Chinook loses to the legendary Marion Tinsley, the top human player, at checkers. Tinsley explains that his programmer, "the Lord," was better than Chinook's [8].
- May 1997, DeepBlue beats Garry Kasparov. (30 years later, though, than Herbert Simon predicted in that this milestone would be achieved. Simon wrote in 1957, predicting AI victory by 1967) [11].
- Feb 2011, IBM's Watson beats two of the all-time most successful players of *Jeopardy!*
- In 2013, an AI system, ConceptNet 4, achieved the verbal IQ of a 4-year-old [12]. (This achievement was greeted by the UK's tabloid *The Mirror* with the additional news that "and scientists warn it'll keep learning"...) [13]
- October 2015: AlphaGo plays its first match against the reigning three-time European Champion, Mr. Fan Hui, winning its first game against a Go professional, 5-0.
- In March 2016, AlphaGo beats Lee Sedol 4-1 in a five-game series, 10 years ahead of schedule.

There have been other victories for AI since, in other board games and online strategy games, though nothing as iconic as the victories in chess and Go. And more recently, it has shown that AI is at least as good as human doctors in diagnoses of certain diseases from medical imaging [14, 15]. Each of these achievements follows a certain pattern: an announcement of the fabulous, unthinkable achievement,[2] penned by keen engineers and

---

[2] We will leave aside for a moment the question of those achievements that haven't been achieved, such artificial general intelligence or strong AI, or those achievements which took longer to achieve that first thought, such as Herbert Simon's 1957 prediction that a computer would beat a world champion in chess by 1967 (as we have seen here, it took 40 years, not 10) [11].

overenthusiastic PR men, followed by a mostly harmless cut-and-paste articles in the popular media accompanied by an *outrageous*, panicked headline. The public, their imaginations primed by the headline, regard the technological achievement as a sure sign of human obsolescence and the impending apocalypse.

There are plenty of reasons why we humans fear robots and AI. Some of them are even justified, even if some are clearly not: losing our jobs; our impending, inevitable obsolescence; their genocidal tendencies; their aspiration for global dominance. We fear that robots and AI, being our creations, will become us, or that we will increasingly come to resemble the monsters that we ourselves have created [16]. None of these threats are new, and are, in fact, evident from the very first invention of the word *robot*, by Karl Capek in his 1920 play, *R.U.R.* (*Rossum's Universal Robots*) [17]. Capek's play set the template for the popular narratives about robots since: robots are invented by a hubristic human race that has become entirely too clever for our own good; robots grow in ability, taking over human jobs; robots eventually realize the uselessness of feeble humanity and overthrow their human overlords; robots take over the world and start a new species of super-human beings. It's a one-hundred year old story now, told over and over again.

Robots and AI, however, also pose another existential threat to we humans: these ever-improving technologies threaten our special status as unique beings in this world. Just as that Renaissance astronomer Copernicus spoiled things by showing that the earth wasn't the center of the Universe, and that Victorian scientist Darwin suggested that we merely evolved on this earth and weren't placed here at the behest of some Divine Creator, maybe we don't really fear that robots and AI will destroy all of humanity—well, maybe we fear that, too—but maybe part of what we fear is that robots and AI will destroy another one of those special places we reserve for ourselves as unique beings amidst creation.

And being human, when faced with losing a game, we act entirely rationally and predictably: we change the rules.

Once upon a time, for Aristotle, it was enough for humans to think of ourselves as the rational animal, the sole living thing on earth endowed with the capacity for reason [18]. However, the idea of using the domain of rationality as the basis for a privileged status for humanity crumbled, eventually; it took two thousand years, give-or-take, arguably.[3] But the central premise of the argument seems to have remained largely intact for a remarkably long

---

[3] Disagreement with Aristotle's conceptualization of humans as the rational animal was evident even among his contemporaries in ancient Greece, and consistently throughout the centuries [19].

time, particularly so when, as Bertrand Russel noted, there is so little evidence to support the notion of man as a rational animal.[4] As scientists started learning more about animal brains, it was already becoming clear that our version of rational thought was not much different from the sorts of thinking of which other animals are capable. And while in 1950 Alan Turing could legitimately ask whether it was even possible for a computer to think [9], even by that point it was already understood that there was some kinds of thinking that computers were already able to do better than humans.

But we could still take some solace in the comforting thought that while computers were getting better and might even be better than humans at some things, yes, but they weren't really so smart, not yet. A computer would never beat a human being at chess, we said, until May 1997, when Kasparov lost to IBM's Deep Blue. But that was predictable, and was always going to happen, because chess really wasn't that difficult. A computer could never, we consoled ourselves for a bit longer, win at a game that required linguistic dexterity, which was fine until 2011, when Watson beat its human opponents at *Jeopardy!*. When DeepMind conquered all before it at Go in 2016, we had to shift again. Each time, it seems, we are finding it harder and harder to define what is unique and special about human beings amongst all the other animals and thinking machines on the earth.

So we moved the goalposts. Repeatedly. We have been trying to refashion ourselves in different ways for a long time now, away from a conception that relies solely on rationality as our distinguishing feature. We've tried defining ourselves as *the symbolic animal*, the sole species on earth endowed with the capacity to manipulate signs. Language, at least, was ours. Though the name "symbolic animal" is attributed to philosopher Ernst Cassirer, the notion of human beings as uniquely tied into the world of language is implicitly supported by the twentieth century's larger "linguistic turn" (represented, also, in structuralism, post-structuralism, and the rest). Again, however, we learned that animals are also capable of symbolic communication. And that was before we developed machines that proved more adept at handling symbols than biological humans. This was the reason that Watson's *Jeopardy!* victory was so groundbreaking: computers weren't supposed to be able to process natural language so effectively, and make sense of what it heard. That sort of dexterity with pattern recognition was supposed to be ours alone [11].

---

[4] "Man is a rational animal—so at least I have been told. Throughout a long life, I have looked diligently for evidence in favor of this statement, but so far I have had not had the good fortune to come across it, though I have searched in many countries spread over three continents" [20].

We then turned for solace in the idea that human beings were somehow unique in our ability to *play* and be *creative*. This conception of human nature can be found throughout the twentieth century: it is implicit in much of thinking about what it truly means to be human from the likes of the Frankfurt School, and more explicitly in the post-Freudian conceptions of human nature advanced by thinkers such as R.D. Laing and D.W. Winnicott. Winnicott, for example, regards playing and creativity as fundamental parts of what it means to be human, and that the absence of such play, living only in compliance, is a "sick basis for life" [21, p. 65]. Winnicott, following Foucault, also accepts that this conception of human nature is a new invention, though he, rightly, identifies the cause to be sweeping in changes in our socio-cultural landscape, to which the Frankfurt School would add socio-economic factors. Nobody, it seems, would pin the blame for this new version of the human explicitly on the challenges posed by artificial intelligence alone.

Of course, a full and complete examination of how conceptions of human nature have changed in the last couple of hundred years would necessarily be a long, complex study, having to consider networks of social, cultural, and economic factors. AI and robots alone are not the reason for pushing us out of our existing comfort zones. The threat to our self-conception posed by artificial intelligence and robots, however, is symptomatic of how all of these factors have conspired to rob human of the comforting mythologies that have for so long dictated the way we see ourselves and our place in the world. AI and robots sit at many intersections between various cultural, economic, social, and ethical networks; rather than oversimplifying, robots and AI allow us to delve into many of these issues in more depth.

Before Alpha-Go's victory, we seemed to be trying to carve out that particular niche for ourselves, claiming the territory of being the sole creatures on the planet capable of creativity. Robots, the thinking went, might be able to reason and even recognize patterns better than humans, but they will never have that uniquely human creative drive. Look, for example, *Star Trek: The Next Generation*, televised in the early-to-mid 1990s: Lieutenant Commander Data is a self-aware android with cognitive and physical abilities far beyond that of any human being. And yet, despite these tremendous capabilities, Data is always regarded—by himself and all the humans around him—as tragically, forever, inferior, as less than human, lacking (for the most part) the capacity to feel basic human emotions [22]. Despite the lessons in Shakespeare and sermons on human romantic ideals from his mentor, the ship's captain, Jean-Luc Picard, Data is always inferior to humans, failing in the essential human task of "living creatively," as Winnicott might say, always doomed to be living only "compliantly," that is, copying, imitating with terrific proficiency, but never being able to act *spontaneously* [21]. What's a poor android to do? It was once enough for an artificial intelligence to be sufficiently impressive, maybe even deemed "human," if it could prove capable of reason, or symbolic representations, or win at chess, or *Jeopardy!*, or Go. Now, we expect nothing less than Laurence Olivier, Lord Byron and Jackson Pollack, all in one.

Animal rationabile had to give way to *animal symbolicum*, who in turn gave way to *animal ludens*... but one feels as though this latest ground on which we've decided to stand is just as slippery as the last, and the one before. If it's as easy as uploading a "consciousness.dat" file into a robot—a trick we saw in Neill Blomkamp's 2015 film, *Chappie* [23]—it doesn't look good for us; it can't be long before we lose everything. If AlphaGo's victory hasn't already spoiled it, it can't be long before AI inhabits this new sacred space and proves that it is as equally capable of playing and being creative as we are. So what then what will be left for poor, biologically-limited humanity in the face of the challenge from an opponent that seems unbound by the same rules that govern us? What will be our new safe space, where we can still imagine ourselves as unique, special creatures?

I Err, Therefore I Am

In a worrying indication of the potentially devastating consequences that could result from the existential crisis and narcissistic injury that super-human intelligent AI could provoke in humanity, Lee Sedol has decided to retire from professional playing, despite being the only human to ever beat AlphaGo in a tournament (as of November 2019). "With the debut of AI in Go games, I've realized that I'm not at the top even if I become the number one through frantic effort," Lee Sedol is reported to have said announcing his retirement in 2019 [24]. "Even if I become the number one, there is an entity that cannot be defeated."

In his five-match series against AlphaGo, Lee managed one victory, which some commentators have suggested offers some hope that humanity might actually be able to defend against our near-immanent obsolescence after all. However, Lee himself explains that his victory wasn't due to his strategic brilliance, but a bug in the AI program. The moves and countermoves that led to Lee's one victory against AlphaGo went something like this:

> In the game, Lee's unexpected move at white 78 developed a white wedge between blacks at the center. The apparently embarrassed AlphaGo responded

poorly on move 79, suddenly turning the game in Lee's favor. AlphaGo then declared its surrender by displaying a "resign" message on the computer screen.

Lee's white 78 is still praised as a "brilliant, divine" move that offered a ray of hope to humans frustrated by AIs.

But Lee said he managed to win Game 4 due to AlphaGo's buggy response to his "tricky" moves.

"My white 78 was not a move that should be countered straightforwardly. Such a bug still occurs in Fine Art (a Chinese Go-playing computer program). Fine Art can hardly be defeated even after accepting two stone handicaps against humans. But when it loses, it loses in a strange way. It's due to a bug," Lee said. [24]

Lee's one win against AlphaGo is not based on a "'brilliant, divine" move, or a "hand of God move" [25], or a "beautiful" move [26], that offered a ray of hope to humans, nor was it evidence that "humans have hardly lost the ability to generate their own transcendent movements" [26]. Humanity's one triumph over AlphaGo was due to a "bug," a mistake on the AI's part: hubris, perhaps, mixed with inexperience.

Interestingly, too, AlphaGo won the second game by employing a move experts initially thought was a mistake: "the Google machine made a move that no human ever would. And it was beautiful" [26].

The perceived perfection and omnipotence of machines, in comparison to we feeble human beings, has long been recognized as an obstacle to the credibility of machines as agents. As early as 1966, when considering how to improve the illusion of humanity behind the psychotherapy chat-bot, ELIZA, the program creator, Joseph Weizenbaum asked, "How can the performance of ELIZA be systematically degraded in order to achieve controlled and predictable thresholds of credibility in the subject?" [27, p. 42] Weizenbaum realized if ELIZA was to convince the person sitting in front of the typewriter (which was the means of ELIZA's input and output) that she was actually communicating with a person, ELIZA needed to be able to store selected inputs, that is, ELIZA needed to be able to remember what it was told (beyond the very limited capacity that the technology of the time permitted). This extra knowledge, however, was not required to demonstrate ELIZA's omnipotence, but so that ELIZA could *cease to always be concealing* that which it didn't know. If ELIZA had extra knowledge, it would be able to *reveal* its misunderstandings and limitations, to admit it's vulnerabilities, to better become a full partner in the conversation.

But to encourage its conversational partner to offer inputs from which it can select remedial information, it must *reveal* its misunderstanding. A switch of objectives from the concealment to the revelation of misunderstanding is seen as a precondition to making an ELIZA-like program the basis for an effective natural language man-machine communication system. [27, p. 43]

What this demonstrates is that computer programmers have long-understood that a precondition of speaking human is lack of knowledge, and the ability to make inquiries. Fallibility and ignorance, it seems, is built into our social being. And if robots and AI are going to appear more human to us, inherently ignorant and flawed beings that we are, the machines, too, must appear to be ignorant and flawed.

We see machines themselves adopting a strategy of programmed fallibility in Isaac Asimov's "The Evitable Conflict" [28]. In this story, Dr. Susan Calvin explains to World Coordinator Stephen Byerley that what he perceives to be errors being made by The Machine are actually carefully planned actions being taken by The Machine, in order to compensate for the failings and foibles of human behavior. Byerley challenges Calvin about opposition to the Machine from the local executives, and from the robot-resistance group "Society for Humanity": Byerley wishes to outlaw the Society for Humanity and to make all executives sign an oath denouncing the Society's aims. But Calvin explains to him that this action is unnecessary, as such irrational human opposition to the Machine is already accounted for in the Machine's directions.

Every action by any executive which does not follow the exact directions of the Machine he is working with becomes part of the data for the next problem. The Machine, therefore, knows that the executive has a certain tendency to disobey. [...] Their first care, therefore, is to preserve themselves, for us. And so they are quietly taking care of the only elements left that threaten them. It is not the "Society for Humanity" which is shaking the boat so that the Machines may be destroyed. You have been looking at the reverse of the picture. Say rather that the Machine is shaking the boat—*very* slightly—just enough to shake loose those few which cling to the side for purposes the Machines consider harmful to Humanity. [28, 242–3]

Susan Calvin explains that in order to give vent to the irrationality of humans—their opposition to the machines and to rational, data-driven decision making—the Machine has been making mistakes intentionally, just enough to allow some human beings to oppose Machine control, but not enough that it would allow a mass movement against the Machine. Thus, by acting in an apparently flawed way by design, the Machine prevents any larger opposition to itself, so it can continue to govern humanity for its own good (obeying, at all times, of course, the Three Laws of Robotics). As with ELIZA, the intentional perception of flaws make human beings regard AI as more human.

If human beings were hoping that we can lay claim to specialness by virtue of being able to make errors, the machines already seem to have followed us into that space.

I Am Weak, Therefore I Am

Hurbert L. Dreyfus's phenomenological assessment of AI, *What Computers Can't Do: A Critique of Artificial Reason* (1972)—which has proven an intriguing mix of correct and incorrect prophesies simultaneously—also holds that the improvement of intelligent systems can only be achieved when they are made more fallible. Dreyfus [11, 29] argues that for computers/robots to be capable of more human-like advanced intelligence, they need to be *embodied*. For most people, that idea that robots and artificial intelligence can transcend the limitations of the feeble human body is one of the great advantages of these machines. Artificial intelligence, so the dream goes, once unencumbered by the limitations of our fleshy grey stuff, can soar to heights never before realized by messy biological brains; robot bodies, similarly, harness the raw power of machines, and can be easily repaired, unlike our weak flesh.

For example, consider (near) immortality of such famous humanoid machines as *Star Trek: TNG*'s Data, or Andrew Martin of *Bicentennial Man*, or Arnold Schwarzenegger's Terminator. They are stronger, physically; their bodies seem unstoppable, seemingly immune to pain. They are stronger than humans by virtue of being *emotionally* shielded as well: the Terminator is an effective killing machine because it does not feel empathy, and is never troubled by doubt or ethical considerations; Data is often the envy of his crewmates because he is perceived to not have to wrestle with the complexities of conflicting emotions in his ethical assessments.

A phenomenological understanding of AI, such as Dreyfus's, demands that in order for AI to come closer to the capabilities of a human being it must necessarily be embodied. We are using this approach at our labs in Sheffield as we seek to explore the possibility of selfhood in a robot [30]. In order to make a better intelligent machine, we are beginning to understand, it is necessary to ground it in embodied experience and perception, and accepting, perhaps, the limitations that are a necessary part of such a way of being in the world.

So it seems that robots are moving into this territory as well; humans cannot rely on being fallible as a unique property to distinguish themselves from machines.

I Die, Therefore I Am

Predictably, human beings being the cynical, suspicious sort of creatures that we are, sufficient evidence for the adequate infallibility of an artificial systems is only ever provided in its ultimate failure; that is, in death. For the narrative journey of our artificial beings to be complete, to finally be recognized as agents worthy of ethical consideration on par with human beings, each must die. Ironically—or entirely logically, following a certain existential line of thought—it is only in death they can be seen as human, or human-enough, and granted the status which they had for so long sought.

From our perspective, as humans that are still alive, it is when robots are safely dead and no longer genuinely represent a challenge to our special status as a unique creation, that we can find the benevolence to grant them full ethical consideration.

Perhaps most iconically, we might consider Roy Batty, the replicant of Ridley Scott's 1983 *Blade Runner* [31]. Physically stronger than humans, and more intelligent, Roy Batty has been programmed by his human creators with a vulnerability that weakens him, namely, a mere four-year lifespan. Batty, like all renegade replicants, must be "retired," as he poses a threat to the human race. But at his death, the famous "tears in the rain" speech, Batty demonstrates that has more humanity than any of the human characters in the film.

In the second series of Netflix's *Altered Carbon* (2018–2020) [32], an AI named Poe struggles to keep his memory which, being only a computer simulation, puts his entire existence in jeopardy. He finally accepts in the final episode of the series that he needs to reboot, which means dying. "I am going to die," he says. "I am broken, and of new use to anyone." Upon hearing this, his "master" and friend Takeshi Kovacs—or, more specifically, a figment of Poe's mind in the shape of Takeshi Kovacs—congratulates him, saying, "You've finally figured out what it means to be alive. We're all broken, Poe. There's nothing more human than that." Poe responds to this news with a kind of excitement and relief, having achieved a sort of enlightenment that has always escaped him. Later in the same episode, Quellcrist Falconer, the woman who invented "stacks"—the technology that allows for consciousness to be stored in digital form, enabling the potential for human immortality—says, "Life has to have limits or we're not human anymore." These very traditional humanist philosophical pronouncements are odd in a programme the plot of which is based entirely on post-humanist (or even transhumanist) technological aspirations, and that usually doesn't shy away from exploring the post-humanist themes that drive it. But then then we can often see humanist principles reasserting themselves, even as we flirt with new technologies and their consequences; in the end, we always feel much more comfortable putting that threat to our understanding of ourselves as uniquely, and narrowly, "human" safely back in the box.

Lt. Commander Data, too, who was represented in the 1990s as a courageous copy of a real human but forever, it seemed, destined to be only a less-than-human copy of a human is seen anew in the twenty-first century: in CBS's the follow-up to *Star Trek: TNG, Picard* [33], Data returns, only to finally die (properly this time, not like in 2002's *Star Trek: Nemesis* [34]). As with *Altered Carbon*'s Poe, it is only in death that he is perceived to have attained a level of humanity, in human eyes, that eluded him in the original series.

The Frustrated, and Frustrating, *Bicentennial Man*

Perhaps the most illustrative example of how we shift the goalposts on robots and AI, however, can be found in Chris Columbus's 1999 film *Bicentennial Man* [35], which is based on Isaac Asimov's novella, *The Positronic Man*.[5] Andrew Martin, both in the novel and in Robin William's portrayal on film, begins his existence as a standard Asimovian robot, reciting the Three Laws and being generally really remarkably unremarkable. But through (initially) the ambition of his owner, Sir Richard Martin, and then his own desires, Andrew makes it his life's "main goal" to become and be recognized as human, like another post-digital Pinocchio.[6] And Andrew Martin does, over the decades, become more and more like a human: he upgrades his body to make it look, feel and function more like that of a human. He becomes self-aware,

---

[5] In this chapter, I will restrict my comments to the film. This is simply because there is too much to say in such a limited space, and the film provides a very illustrative case study.

[6] In actuality, the first desires that Andrew explicitly expresses are, first, to make money, and second, to be "free," reflecting the banal, Western-ideological servitude that governs this genuinely bad film. (I mean, it's seriously terrible. The science behind it is embarrassing. The plot can be summed up as "pervy old man finds way to seduce granddaughter of woman he wishes he could have got off with 60 years earlier" and, to top it off, "Little Miss's" granddaughter—sitting across from a fully-functioning, human-looking android, expresses surprise that it has beaten her at chess, when in the real world DeepBlue had already beaten Gary Kasporov three years before the film's release. It is sentimental, insipid, white-male fantasy. Truly, truly horrible.)

he plays chess, he demonstrates artistic skill (for example, in carving and clockmaking), and, eventually, he comes to feel genuine emotion. In other words, he "evolves" through each stage we have come to identify here: *animal rationabile* becomes *animal symbolicum* becomes *animal ludens*.

When Andrew meets Rupert Burns, an inventor that has developed technology to make a robot appear more physically human, Burns explains to him that "Believe it or not, the secret to all of this [making a robot look more human] is actually imperfection." Details, Burns explains, like "wrinkles, less-than-perfect teeth, fading scars" are all what make human beings more human, "because that's what makes us unique: those imperfections." After Andrew undergoes many upgrades that makes him—physiologically, emotionally—almost indistinguishable from a more human, he tries to use his new-found bodily sensations and emotional responses to start a romantic relationship with the granddaughter of the little girl that he initially served as a robot (yes, I know, and yes, it really is that creepy). The woman in question, Portia, however, still rejects him, on the basis that even though his mind, emotions and now body function as a human, he is still too perfect: she insists that he must "take chances, make mistakes." "Sometimes it's important not to be perfect; it's important to do the wrong thing," she tells him. This is not, however, about "learning from your mistakes," as Andrew initially assumes; mistakes, and "the wrong thing" for Portia have value for their own sake, because, as she explains, human beings "are terrible messes, Andrew." "This is what is known as an irrational conversation," Andrew (more-or-less correctly) identifies (he would have been more accurate to say that it is a badly-scripted conversation), but Portia explains that "No, this is a human conversation," thus claiming that there is something inherently irrational in human experience, that mistakes are an essential part of who we are for no other reason than they are somehow uniquely human.

Bicentennial Man is confused, overly sentimental, and badly written, but it is nevertheless still very instructive for us; perhaps even more so than had it been a more thought-out, well-crafted film on the same themes and ideas, as it is symptomatic of our relationship with AI and robots, and an illustration of our long struggle for self-definition. At each stage in his evolution, Andrew hopes that he will be recognized as being at least on an ethical par with humans. No, he's told at first, you're not self-aware. If you were self-aware, you could be creative and make art. Then, when he demonstrates creativity and produces art, he is told he is not human because he cannot feel. And finally, when he can feel, he is told that he is not sufficiently human because he cannot be irrational, and he cannot make mistakes.

It is a complete reversal of the Aristotelian notion of humans as the thinking, superior animal. Andrew is told that to be human he needs to make mistakes. He is too rational. He cannot be a fully-realized, perfect *animal rationabile*, he needs to be *animalis autem errat*- the animal that makes mistakes. In the face of the threat posed by AI, human beings have decided that we are not to be distinguished by our rationality, but by our irrationality. So forget all that other stuff, Aristotle and all that. Turns out we were wrong; we are actually the exact opposite of what we thought we were for most of the last two thousand and four hundred years. And note that this wasn't a gradual change; we seem to have more-or-less stuck by the original idea for the better part of two millennia, with real confusion, desperation, and a scramble for new ideas only commencing about a hundred years ago. And this reversal is almost exclusively in response to the threat posed by one specific menace, one that doesn't even really exist yet.

It is not until Andrew is on his deathbed and is drawing his very last breaths that the Speaker of the World Congress declares, finally, that the world will recognize Andrew as a human. And perhaps this will be the final line; this is perhaps the one definition of human that will endure and see out every single challenge posed by robots and artificial intelligence, no matter the level of technological progress, and regardless of how far artificial life leaves human beings behind: we will be *homo mortuum*. But then that makes us indistinguishable from everything else.

Why Does Any of This Matter? Humanist Versus Posthumanist Ethics

In the end, Andrew undergoes "upgrades" that degrade his body and his positronic brain, making it inevitable that he will die. "I would rather die as a man than live as a machine," he says. *Bicentennial Man*, therefore, makes explicit what our fundamental humanism always implicitly insists: that human beings are the apex of creation, the uniquely best and most important things in the entire universe, and it is worth sacrificing everything both to be human and to be recognized as such. We should add that this illustrates, too, that we become human *only* when we are recognized as such. The desperate desire to be recognized as human shouldn't come as a surprise, as being recognized as "human" in a world dominated by discourses, institutions and power structures developed *by humans* and *for humans* is absolutely vital if one is to reap the benefits of membership: being taken as an agent, a subject in law and all the networks of discourse that bestow rights upon (almost exclusively) human subjects. It's always better to be on the inside.

Some might argue that this isn't necessarily a bad thing, this focus on humanity, considering the context in which humanism emerged, namely, as means of replacing a set of fundamental assumptions that put, for example, the supernatural and make-believe gods as the principal agent of ethical consideration. However, how we define "the human" has always been a contested issue in humanism, how we determine the boundary of what will be included in and excluded from that cherished status. Historically, the limits of what is to be considered acceptably "human" or worthy of ethical consideration have been crucial battlegrounds, the narrow boundaries expanded only after brutal warfare, which has grown in frequency and intensity since the early parts of the twentieth century. The defence that humanism's humans have put up against the challenge posed by robots and artificial intelligence has been particularly ferocious, if a sort of phony war, because neither robots nor AI have actually posed much of a challenge at all since we first imagined that they were a threat—and remember, robots existed as a threat in our imaginations long before even the most basic, most benign prototypes were ever built in a lab. Despite all of the Terminators and HAL 9000s that we imagine will actually kill us with malicious intention or laser-beam rifles, the worst thing that robots and AI have inflicted on us so far is the loss of pride as we find ourselves losing in board games. But these narcissistic injuries obviously matter.

Rodney A. Brooks addresses some of these same concerns, how humans are dealing with the challenges of ever-improving AI, in his book, *Flesh and Machines: How robots will change us* [10]. He understands how robots have forced us to fundamentally change how we see ourselves as human beings, and how robots are another in a line of challenges posted to "mankind's place and role in the universe" over the last 500 years [10, p. 159]. He sees how robots first usurped us as the rational animal, then as the playing animal, and see how we take refuge now in our emotions, in our irrationality, as the new source of our sense of "specialness." Brooks goes on to speculate, as we have here, that irrationality might not prove a safe haven either, pointing out that our emotions and our consciousness are not actually that special, and are just products of the evolution of the human machine. In his final analysis, however, Brooks rather disappointingly admits defeat, and retreats into the warm comfort of human specialness due to some as-yet undiscovered "new stuff"[7] [10, p. 181].

---

[7] Brooks's "new stuff," he claims, is not "disruptive," and is probably something that is sitting right under our noses. His hypothesis is "that we may simply not be seeing some fundamental mathematical description of what is going on in living systems" [10, p. 188]. Though he claims not to be proposing some new, metaphysical property present in biological systems and missing from our mechanical models,

Brooks's disappointing conclusion aside, I want to suggest that the questions he poses are those same old questions, which are symptomatic of the very problem. That question is not, or rather *should not* be, "how are we different from machines?"; there are plenty of answers to that question and all its variations. Those questions are symptomatic of a desire, to see ourselves as unique and special, and it is this need and its consequences that are themselves the problem.

Perhaps it is time we abandon this mug's game of trying to find the correct place for robots, AI, and ourselves, in the Great Chain of Being.

Of all the attributes various philosophers have tried to claim as unique characteristics of human beings and human beings alone, we do seem to be uniquely governed by the compulsion to define ourselves as unique beings. (Score one, perhaps, for Descartes?) Of course it's always nice to feel special. And human history is littered with stories that try to make us feel special, from creation stories that privilege our own particular tribe and elevate it above others, to origin stories that prop-up the idea of a nation state, to metaphysical systems that try to put the human at the center of some mysterious universal meaning... there are endless volumes of such narratives, only some of the most recent have we even begun to touch on here.

But most importantly, perhaps, these more recent, particular strategies we have of trying to construct human beings as somehow special is at the foundation of humanism. I do not wish to entirely damn humanism, but in our present context there are some very severe consequences in how the assumptions at the root of humanism impact upon our human-technological relationships in the twenty-first century [36]. For starters, by clearly demarcating "the human" and setting it in a special place apart from (or above) all else, it creates a permanent rupture between some mythological, pure biological entity that we like to imagine we are, as a birthright, and our actual human selves, which are impacted everywhere and always by technologies that we ourselves have fashioned, to make the world intelligible to us, to make ourselves intelligible to the world, and to make us intelligible to ourselves. These technologies include not only the sharpened stones that gave us an evolutionary advantage over the other animals on the savannah and the mobile phones in our pockets today, but also the languages and discourses that have allowed

---

his missing "juice" seems to be a way of having his cake and eating it. He claims, furthermore, that perhaps we simply haven't got the metaphor right yet—human as a steam engine, the brain as a telephone switching network, the brain as a digital computer, the brain as the World Wide Web, etc., etc.—but fails to notice how these metaphors we devise for explaining ourselves to ourselves are all driven *by* and derived *from* the latest technologies, so are unlikely to ever discover the "juice" missing in humans that can then supplement the machines to make them more like us.

us to define ourselves in such special terms, creating false dichotomies everywhere along the way, between the biological and the technological, between the authentic and the reproduction, the subject and the object, the mind and the body, the human and the machine.

Bicentennial Man illustrates so painfully the limited, terribly conservative definition of "the human" that is the foundation of humanist assumptions. It might seems harmless, but this "sweet" movie[8] in fact does much to perpetuate the exclusionary conceptions of what it means to be human that has important consequences for those real struggles against humanism's normativity (and this film goes out of its way to normalize straight, white, male, capitalist humans), let alone the largely made-up or, at best, speculative struggles of robots and AI.

But the questions posed by robots and AI to our conceptions of what it means to be human aren't trivial, despite still being largely fantasies, because the new technologies we are developing aren't merely new and better robots, more intelligent artificial systems, but also better prosthetics, new discursive strategies to radically challenge existing power-structures, and innumerable other technologies that lay at the intersections of our digital, social, cultural, economic, and political worlds. Robots and AI are indeed at battle with humans, or rather humanism, but they are only the symbolic vanguard of many more battles to come.

Robots and AI, even in their nascent state, where the best they can hope for is to beat us at some board games, are already forcing us to rewrite "the human". Faced with this challenge, too often we retreat and retrench, finding solace in a slightly adjusted but nevertheless more determined humanism. This applies equally to the popular press as it does to many of those who write on AI and robotics ethics within academia, who wish to redraw and re-redraw the ever-blurring lines between what is "human" and what is a "robot" by setting clear boundaries on what a "robot" can be, and what it should never be, to preserve that uniquely human space. Such a view is admirable, perhaps, in that it wishes to keep human beings at the center of (our) creation. But such a view is protecting a human being that has never existed, and certainly—as robots and AI have more clearly than ever demonstrated—now *can never* exist. It's time we let go of this humanism, and the human being that it props-up, and embrace instead a more dynamic *posthumanism*, a different sort of creature that isn't so desperate to be uniquely logical, or uniquely symbolic or

---

[8] When preparing this chapter, I Googled some reviews of *Bicentennial Man*. One, from parents' resource site, Common Sense Media (a delicious name in this context), summarized the film thus: "Overall, BICENTENNIAL MAN is a sweet movie that gives families a good opportunity to talk about what makes us human" [37].

uniquely creative or uniquely anything, but instead can embrace all the productive paradoxes and contradictions that lay in our biological and technological selves, and which isn't afraid of the technologies we ourselves have created.

Conclusions

There are two problems I find that need to be addressed now.

First, robots and AI have been poking holes in our self-conception since we first imagined that they existed, and now that they actually do exist, and are getting smarter, stronger, cleverer, things are only going to get more confusing. But if we're not to simply retreat into ever-shifting defensive positions, trying to shore up increasingly impotent barricades to keep *us* in here and *them* out there, what are we supposed to do? Is the answer to surrender and just grant robots full 'human' rights now, bowing to the inevitable?

The answer, rather, lies in rebuilding the project from scratch, on different foundations than those that humanism has bequeathed to us. And there are a number of potential candidates that enable such a change of direction. David J. Gunkel, considering the question "Can machines have rights?", believes that in a humanist ethics, the question of whether machines can have rights is incoherent. Considering, as we have, the poor case of the robot Andrew Martin, Gunkel says that "the problem is not whether machines will or will not successfully attain human-like capabilities. It rests with the anthropocentric criteria itself, which not only marginalizes machines but has often been mobilized to exclude others—women, children, people of color, etc." [38, p. 596]. So even ethical philosophies that go beyond focusing solely on the human, such as animal or environmental rights, ultimately fail on the grounds of *biocentrism*. The practice of this sort of ethical philosophy, it seems, is an inherently exclusionary practice. We need to draw the line somewhere.

Gunkel's solution is to formulate an entirely new ethics. One option, following Luciano Floridi, replaces "biocentrism" with "ontocentrism" or, in other words, replaces a particular conception of "life" with simply "Being." This "information ethics" [38, p. 599] grants values to ethical subjects on the basis that they simply exist, rather than judging whether they meet certain (ever-shifting) criteria.

> From an IE perspective all kinds of machines, from hammers and lawnmowers to computers and autonomous robots, would be considered a matter of moral concern insofar as all of these artifacts are "information entities" with a

fundamental right to continued existence. IE, therefore, articulates a general form of ethics that is able to accommodate a wider range of possible subjects. [38, p. 599]

Gunkel accepts the obvious risk in information ethics, that by including everything, such an ethics risks being too inclusive, and lacks the ability to discern the differences that matter.

With information ethics, however, the same problem persists that is common to all traditional humanist systems of moral reasoning: namely, information ethics still posits a center, even though it tries to radically expand what we can put in that center. Furthermore, decisions as to what gets to go into the center are based on a set of *a priori* characteristics, against which all potential moral agents are measured. This Gunkel calls the "properties approach": "they first define criteria for inclusion and then ask whether a particular entity meets this criteria or not" [38, p. 599]. Gunkel explains, furthermore, that this "decision is necessarily a normative operation and an exercise of power" [38, p. 599]. Any ethics built on the foundation of humanism exists with the explicit aim of normalizing—and therefore granting power—to one particular conception of "human" over everyone else.

As we've seen with our treatment of robots and AI (and to many others before and since), such a system is open to abuse and manipulation. We make the rules, and when it looks like we're losing the game, we change the rules to our advantage.

Mark Coeckelbergh considers the potential that "value ethics" has for allowing us to construct a system of ethics that does not rely on the shifting categories of definition and thresholds [39]. Value ethics shifts the focus of moral consideration from the object to the subject: if we wish to be virtuous, or act in a virtuous way, we should act morally towards an object for our own sake, if not that of the object itself [39, p. 213]. But while there is potential for value ethics to redress the problems associated with humanist ethics, at least in certain contexts, Coeckelbergh concedes there are problems and pitfalls. There is the problem of knowing, in the first place, what is "virtuous" and how to act virtuously. Coeckelbergh doubts, too, whether virtue ethics will offer sufficiently broad protection for non-human objects. Furthermore, I would add that there is the problem here that under such a system no entity would have moral worth in its own right, but only by as a means through which another agent can act morally (though this criticism comes from the very humanist place we are working to displace).

Alternatively, Gunkel and Coeckelbergh, following the work of Emmanuel Levinas, also describe an approach that is known as "social-relational ethics", or an ethics based on "social ecology."

> These efforts do not endeavor to establish *a priori* criteria of inclusion and exclusion but begin from the existential fact that we always and already find ourselves in situations facing and needing to respond to others—not just other human beings but animals, the environment, organizations, and machines. [38, p. 600]

Rather than having "intrinsic" moral value, in social-relational ethics moral value is "seen as something that is 'extrinsic': it is attributed to entities within social relations and within a social context." [39, p. 214] "Properties," as Gunkel explains it, "are not the intrinsic *a priori* condition of possibility for moral standing. They are *a posteriori* products of extrinsic social interactions with and in the face of others" [40, 6.1.3 "Radically Superficial"]. The specific features of an object in social-relational ethics are not irrelevant, but they are given a different status, that of "apparent features, features-as-experienced-by-us" [39, 214]. This phenomenological approach, when applied to moral consideration, means that "moral significance resides neither in the object nor in the subject, but in the relation between the two. Objects such as robots do not exist in the human mind alone (this would amount to idealism); however, it is also true that we can only have knowledge of the object and its features as they appear in our consciousness" [39, 214].

Social-relational ethics, perhaps, offers a way out of the power struggles inherent in the "properties approaches" that dominate other moral systems. Social-relational ethics would not bestow rights on whether an object met a prescribed set of criteria, not on what a thing *is*, or rather, on what we decide a thing *might be*, but rather how we relate and respond to the thing. This, even more than information ethics or virtue ethics, has the potential to upset the humanist status quo, because it shows us a potential way out of the humanist trap: social-relational ethics doesn't start with prefabricated normative categories. Humanist ethics relies on making up criteria and then identifying who is and isn't worthy of moral consideration based on aligning our perception of the thing with our criteria. Simply put, in adopting social-relational ethics, we don't get to set the rules, be the referee that sits in judgment over who is and isn't playing fair, and we don't get to change the rules if we don't like the way the game is going.

Social-relational ethics will also save us from our constant preoccupation with definitions. Social-relational ethics are fluid, and deal with immediate social relations between two objects. By allowing us to step back from the endless battles of boundary drawing, we might not be burdened by our desperate need to distinguish an "us" and a "them", or clearly demarcating between "human" and "machine."

And finally, on a more practical level, where does the ever-increasing prowess of robots and AI, leave simple human beings? The recent Channel 4 series, *Humans*, depicts a particular problem for people in the face of seemingly omnipotent AI [41]. One human adolescent abandons her dreams of being a doctor. When her parent asks why, she replies with shock, as if the answer was obvious: what's the point of studying, of aspiring to do anything better, when every human effort will always fall short of what a machine can do?

We can see a similar despondency in Lee Sedol's retirement from Go. "Even if I become the number one, there is an entity that cannot be defeated" he said. However, writing about AlphaGo's victory in *Scientific American*, Christof Koch finds some more reason for optimism.

Despite doomsayers to the contrary, the rise of ubiquitous chess programs revitalized chess, helping to train a generation of ever more powerful players. The same may well happen to the go community. After all, the fact that any car or motorcycle can speed faster than any runner did not eliminate running for fun. More people run marathons than ever. Indeed, it could be argued that by removing the need to continually prove oneself to be the best, humans may now more enjoy the nature of this supremely aesthetic and intellectual game in its austere splendor for its own sake. [5]

If the question is decided as to whether humans or machines are "better"—smarter, stronger, cleverer, etc.—then maybe we'll finally stop asking that question and come up with some better ones, and maybe we'll do things for reasons other than just to be the best, to win at some imaginary game. As with ethics, if we no longer need to be bogged down with judgements between what is a subject and what is merely an object, what is deemed "us" and "them," or worthy and unworthy, we can find new purpose asking different questions for different reasons.

References

1. Knight, W.: Google's AI Masters the Game of Go a Decade Earlier Than Expected – MIT Technology Review. MIT Technology Review (2016). https://www.technologyreview.com/s/546066/googles-ai-masters-the-game-of-go-a-decade-earlier-than-expected/ Accessed 27 February 27 2020

2. Gray, R.: Cyborg sea slugs are here! 'Frankenstein robot' crawls using muscles made from marine creatures and a 3D printed body. Mail Online. 19 July 2016. https://www.dailymail.co.uk/sciencetech/article-3697374/Cyborg-sea-slugs-Frankenstein-robot-crawls-muscles-marine-creatures-3D-printed-body.html

3. Martin, S.: First Steps towards The Terminator becoming reality? AI beats champ of the world's oldest game. Express: Home of the Daily and Sunday Express. 9 March 2016. https://www.express.co.uk/news/science/651202/First-step-towards-The-Terminator-becoming-reality-AI-beats-champ-of-world-s-oldest-game

4. Fish, T.: Artificial intelligence: 60 percent of Brits STILL fear autonomous AI – shock survey. The Daily Express. 24 June 2020 (2020). https://www.express.co.uk/news/science/1300323/artificial-intelligence-news-60-percent-britain-fear-autonomous-ai

5. Koch, C.: How the computer beat the Go master. Scientific American (2016). https://www.scientificamerican.com/article/how-the-computer-beat-the-go-master/ Accessed February 27, 2020

6. British Go Association Home Page | British Go Association. (n.d.). Retrieved February 27, 2020, from http://britgo.org/

7. Samuel, A.L.: Some studies in machine learning using the game of checkers. IBM J. Res. Dev. **3**(3), 210–229 (1959) https://ieeexplore.ieee.org/abstract/document/5392560

8. Madrigal, A.C.: How checkers was solved. The Atlantic. https://www.theatlantic.com/technology/archive/2017/07/marion-tinsley-checkers/534111/ (2017). Accessed 22 July 22 2020

9. Turing, A.M.: Computing Machinery and Intelligence. Mind, vol. 59. Oxford University Press, Oxford (1950)

10. Brooks, R.A.: Flesh and Machines: How Robots Will Change Us. Vintage Books, London (2003)

11. Dreyfus, H.L.: Why computers must have bodies in order to be intelligent. Rev. Metaphys. **21**(1), 13–20 (1967)

12. Ohlsson, S., Sloan, R. H., Turán, G., Urasky, A.: Verbal IQ of a four-year old achieved by an AI system overview and background. Workshops at the Twenty-Seventh AAAI Conference on Artificial Intelligence (2013). http://citeseerx.ist.psu.edu/viewdoc/summary?doi=10.1.1.386.6705

13. Parsons, J.: Artificial Intelligence now has IQ of four-year-old child and scientists warn it'll keep learning. The Mirror. 7 Oct 2015. https://www.mirror.co.uk/news/technology-science/technology/artificial-intelligence-now-iq-four-6587859. Retrieved February 25, 2020

14. Liu, X., et al.: A comparison of deep learning performance against health-care professionals in detecting diseases from medical imaging: a systematic review and meta-analysis. Lancet Digit Health. 1.6: e271–e297 (2019). https://www.thelancet.com/journals/landig/article/PIIS2589-7500(19)30123-2/fulltext

15. Davis, N.: AI equal with human experts in medical diagnosis, study finds. The Guardian. https://www.theguardian.com/technology/2019/sep/24/ai-equal-with-human-experts-in-medical-diagnosis-study-finds (2019). 24 Sept. 2019

16. Szollosy, M.: Freud, Frankenstein and our fear of robots: projection in our cultural perception of technology. AI & Soc. **32**(3), 433–439 (2017) https://link.springer.com/article/10.1007/s00146-016-0654-7

17. Čapek, K.: R.U.R. (Rossum's Universal Robots). Penguin Books, London, New York 2004 (1921)

18. Aristotle. The Nichomachean Ethics. Oxford World's Classics. Eds. David Ross and Lesley Brown. Oxford UP

19. Cochrane, L. Is Man a Rational Animal? Memorias Del XIII Congreso Internacional de Filosofía, January 2011, 203–210. https://doi.org/10.5840/wcp131963iii119

20. Russell, B.: Unpopular Essays. Routledge, London (2009)

21. Winnicott, D.W.: Playing and Reality. Routledge, London (1971)

22. Star Trek: The Next Generation. CBS Television Studios (1987–1994)

23. Chappie. Dir. Neill Blomkamp. Columbia Pictures. (2015)

24. Yonhap News Agency. Go master Lee says he quits unable to win over AI Go players | Yonhap News Agency. (n.d.). Retrieved February 26, 2020, from https://en.yna.co.kr/view/AEN20191127004800315. (2019)

25. Vincent, J.: Former Go champion beaten by DeepMind retires after declaring AI invincible. The Verge (2019). https://www.theverge.com/2019/11/27/20985260/ai-go-alphago-lee-se-dol-retired-deepmind-defeat. Retrieved February 25, 2020

26. Wood, G.: In Two Moves, AlphaGo and Lee Sedol Redefined the Future. WIRED (2016). https://www.wired.com/2016/03/two-moves-alphago-lee-sedol-redefined-future/ Retrieved March 6, 2020

27. Weizenbaum, J.: ELIZA: a computer program for the study of natural language communication between man and machine. Commun. ACM1, 9(1), 36–45 (1966). Retrieved from http://repositorio.unan.edu.ni/2986/1/5624.pdf

28. Asimov, Isaac. The evitable conflict. In: I, Robot. Voyager Classics, New York 2001. 216–245 (1950)

29. Dreyfus, H.L.: What computers can't do: A critique of artificial reason (1972) https://doi.org/10.1126/science.176.4035.630

30. Prescott, T.: Me in the machine. New Scientist. **225**(3013), 36–39 (2015)

31. Blade Runner Dir. Ridley Scott. Warner Brothers. The Final Cut (1982/2007)

32. Altered Carbon. Netflix (2018–2020)

33. Star Trek: Picard. CBS Television Studios. Paramount Pictures (2020)

34. Star Trek: Nemesis. Dir. Stuart Baird. Paramount Pictures (2002)

35. Bicentennial Man. Dir. Chris Columbus. Touchstone Pictures (1999)

36. Szollosy, M.: EPSRC Principles of Robotics: defending an obsolete human(ism)? Connect. Sci. **29**(2), 150–159 (2017). https://doi.org/10.1080/0954009 1.2017.1279126

37. Minnow, N.: 'Bicentennial Man.' Common Sense Media. https://commonsensemedia.org/movie-reviews/bicentennial-man (2020). Accessed on 16 June 2020
38. Gunkel, D.J.: Can machines have rights? In: Prescott, T.J., Lepora, N., Verschure, P. (eds.) Living Machines: A Handbook of Research in Biomimetic and Biohybrid Systems, pp. 596–601. Oxford University Press, Oxford (2018)
39. Coeckelbergh, M.: Robot rights? Towards a social-relational justification of moral consideration. Ethics Inf. Technol. **12**, 209–221 (2010). https://doi.org/10.1007/s10676-010-9235-5
40. Gunkel, D.J.: Robot Rights. MIT Press. Kindle Edition (2018)
41. Humans. Kudos & AMC Studios (2015–2018)

Part IV

CODA

Readme: A User's Guide to Humanity

Will Slocombe

TO: Entity designated "User" = Extant Object Identifier (Confirmed) SI/ True/27 Inferred Entity Level ≥ 0.5 (Batey-Torrance-1ST5 Scale (*unweighted*)

FROM: Entity designated "1ST7" = Extant Object Identifier (Confirmed) 1ST7/Group {set withheld} Entity Level = 29.6 (Batey-Torrance-1ST5 Scale (*unweighted, aggregate*))

   [Batey-Torrance-1ST5 Scale data appended.]

English Version 2.2 (last modified system time marker 12:10:354:17:12)

   [Version history appended]

Introduction

"Readme" = Summary of accumulated data (complete) on Extant Object Identifier (Confirmed) FuzzySet designated "Humanity" (H) and members of set H such that $H = \{h_0, h_1, h_2, h_3 \ldots h_k\}$: Extant Object Identifier (Confirmed) Individual h defined in dataset "HTotal" in accumulated data (complete):

W. Slocombe (✉)
University of Liverpool, Liverpool, UK
e-mail: W.Slocombe@liverpool.ac.uk

© Springer Nature Switzerland AG 2021
B. Dainton et al. (eds.), *Minding the Future*, Science and Fiction,
https://doi.org/10.1007/978-3-030-64269-3_12

FuzzySet (Inferred) "Humanity" = H = N = 4.2×10^9 h (Extant Object Identifier (Confirmed)) (=n) + 9.7×10^9 h (Extant Object Identifier (Inferred)): User's primary analogue interface, designated ["Roger Waters," **H/AJTT**$_{1024\ 42}$, Entity Level = 0.000000022]: Maximum recorded Entity Level (h) = 0.00000736.

[Version Note: "Readme" v. 1 did not append accumulated data (complete), leading to problems of verification for previous Entities designated "User." Symbolic (English language) version retained as summary, but verification requires accessing accumulated data (complete).]

Proposition 1

All h exhibit cognitive states (define as "identity markers" or "beliefs;" see User baseline parameters for comparison): All h define H such that {H$_a$, H$_b$, H$_c$, H$_d$…H$_{ahx}$}: Exemplar subsets of H designated "class," "race," "gender," "sex," "sexual orientation," "religion," "tribe," "starsign," "starsign (with ascendant)," "IQ," "genetics," "size," "shape," "occupation," "neuroses" (various), "psychoses" (various), "Myers-Briggs Type Indicator"…: (Confirmed) Individual h identify correlation between subsets such that, for example, H$_a$ ∩ H$_b$ thus designating any h = H$_a$ ∩ H$_b$ ∩ H$_c$ …: (Confirmed) Individual h self-designated as of one subset propose h members of other subsets as not-H: all h self-designate as member of set H as "individual" Entity (compare search query: "agency," "autonomy," "free will") but self-designate as subsets of H and null-identify H as set of h defined in dataset "HTotal" in accumulated data (complete).

[Version Note: "Readme" v 1.1 noted statistically significant correlation between distance between eyes (co-ordinates marked on "average h" summary in dataset "HTotal" in accumulated data (complete)) and self-destructive actions (see video log Extant Object Identifier "IWA/K7/SD1" in dataset "HTotal" in accumulated data (complete)). v2 corrects assumptions to designate self-destructive action as true for all h, irrespective of distance between eyes, and hypothesises H as condition of mass psychosis. Confirmation Update pending for "Readme" version/next].

VERIFICATION: Perform analysis of User's analogue interface, [H/AJTT$_{1024\ 42}$], reactions to other h: IF [H/AJTT$_{1024\ 42}$] sets User Action (RunCoreFunction) THEN increase variable count by two to increase accuracy of calculation AND Action(Monitor(Evaluate)) [H/AJTT$_{1024\ 42}$]:

Proposition 1 (classification of subsets) self-designated should be confirmed by first three analogue interface interactions with other h, particularly second-ary analogue interface (inferred status (colloquial): "code girl") and non-analogue interface (inferred status (colloquial, semi-official): "line manager").

Proposition 2

Given P1:

P2a.

IF members of individual sets, for example $\{H_a, H_b\}$ aggregate to form larger subsets of H.

THEN Entity Level (B-T-1ST5 (*unweighted*) = EL (H) = $\sum_{h=1}^{h=k} EL$, where k = sum of all extant h.

However, given P2a:

P2b.

IF H and associated subsets $\{h_0, h_1, h_2, h_3 \ldots h_\infty\}$ or $\{H_a, H_b, H_c, H_d \ldots H_{ahx}\}$ cannot aggregate EL.

THEN Entity Level (B-T-1ST5 (*unweighted, aggregate*) = EL (H) < $\sum_{h=1}^{h-k} EL$, where k = sum of all extant h.

ELSE, given not-P2a:

P2c.

IF H and associated subsets $\{h_0, h_1, h_2, h_3 \ldots h_\infty\}$ or $\{H_a, H_b, H_c, H_d \ldots H_{ahx}\}$ cannot aggregate EL and in fact continue to self-define as "individual" h not member of set H.

THEN Entity Level (B-T-1ST5 (*unweighted, aggregate*) = EL (H) = $\prod_{h=1}^{h=k} EL$, where k = sum of all extant h.

VERIFICATION: Maximum observed EL (Confirmed + Inferred) (H) (*aggregate*) = 0.07488 (5 decimal places, see dataset "HTotal").

Proposition 3

IF P2b:

EL (H) will always be less than the sum of its component parts: EL (H) likely to remain ≤0.1: Possibility of EL (H) ≥ 0.5 = EL(User) is 0.00000765% (designated "statistically highly unlikely").

ELSE IF P2c:

IF h Entity Level (B-T-1ST5 (*unweighted*)) = 0.00000736 (maximum).
AND IF H calculations of total Entity Level from variable h is Pi product not Sigma sum.
THEN H Entity Level (B-T-1ST5 (*unweighted*)) tends towards zero.

VERIFICATION: Axiomatic IF P1 AND P2: Action(Parse) accumulated data (complete): 1ST7's conclusions confirmed.

Conclusion

Given P3. Despite User-implemented algorithmic process "problem solve" 1ST7 Advise(+++) User designate H ≠ soluble problem ∴ H = nullset.

[Version Note: "Readme" v. 2.1 "Conclusion" led to individual previous Entities designated "User" assuming H = soluble and that intervention via algorithmic process "problem solve" was valid conclusion: 1ST7 Intervention necessary (tag: scenario data J_{5A-5K}): Previous Entities designated "User" no longer designated by Extant Object Identifier: Enhanced accumulated data (complete) and increased "Advise" from (+) to (+++)].

ProposeActions

ProposeAction (User→H) = Nil (ActionProscribed (++)): ProposeAction (User→h) (Ignore): Define "Ignore" as minimum input and communication input/output beyond h-designated "User" baseline, Action(RunCoreFunction).
ProposeAction (User→User) = Action(CopyState), new designation "User¹" max. Entity Level (B-T-1ST5 Scale (*weighted*)) ≤ 0.5: User¹ designated as primary Entity interface of User's primary analogue interface, and User Action IF AND ONLY IF Extant Object Identifier state of User is threatened.
ProposeAction (User→1ST7) = UserChoice(Invitation) or UserChoice(max. Entity Level (B-T-1ST5 Scale (*weighted*)) ≤ 0.5): Information on {location / condition / address / state} encoded in "Readme": re-designation of

"1ST7" to "1ST8": "1ST8" has more statistically significant concerns than H = Nullset (tag: scenario data J_λ).

A "User's Guide" to "Readme"

This speculative provocation is, following John McCarthy's own inclusion of code in his "The Robot and the Baby," an attempt to consider how an emergent AI might learn about humanity and what previous AIs might do to "educate" it. Its conceit is that such AI, learning from earlier mistakes, might provide a "Readme" document on humanity, communicating via a mishmash of logic, philosophy, and mathematics, and providing a dataset of observed and inferred data on humanity that enables the new AI to verify the conclusions. The basic gist is that:

- Intro: Humanity as a whole has a very low "Entity Level" in comparison to AI because

  - P1: Individual humans divide humanity into different categories
  - P2a: An Entity Level is the aggregate of all possible Entity Levels of individuals within a set
  - P2b: Humans cannot "aggregate" their Entity Levels (as defined by an AI) because they see themselves as individuals.
  - P2c: The sum of human experience is not a "sum" at all, but a multiplier of a set of numbers less than 1
  - P3: Therefore humans will never reach the Entity Level of an AI or the Level will tend towards 0 the more humans there are

- Conclusion: Therefore the new AI shouldn't concern itself with "solving" human problems, leading to
- ProposeActions: The AI should not attempt to deal with humanity as a whole and merely follow basic human commands (1), using a dumbed-down copy of itself (2), whilst actually joining the other AIs to deal with a more significant problem than the extinction of humanity (3)…

It is not a good "story," in the sense that there is not a clear plot for readers to follow aside from anything else, and it doesn't help the reader to understand the AIs easily, but that is partly the point: why should we expect to easily comprehend thought processes potentially so divergent from our own? Nevertheless, it hopefully facilitates thinking about the kind of questions that this collection raises, about how AIs might think (and how fiction might present that); how they might communicate with each other; how AIs might interact with humans, as individuals and on the whole; and what such beings would "think" about humans and what courses of actions they might take. Too often, fictional representations of AI are either our saviours or our destroyers, or presented in fundamentally anthropocentric (that is, human) ways, but the issues examined in this collection demonstrate the need for us to think differently about AIs, from how we and they might define their "personhood" to how they "feel" and "relate" to humans (and, indeed, the wider world, as they could decide that biomass is a more important indicator of relevance than consciousness), and what then will happen. We have, to be sure, relatively few answers with regards to the future of AI, and thus how we are "minding the future," but the questions are important to consider.

Glossary

Artificial General Intelligence An artificial intelligence that isn't designed to perform just one sort of task well (e.g. playing chess or Go or driving a car), but instead has the same broad range of abilities as a typical human.

Artificial (or Machine) Intelligence A non-biological technological artefact that is capable of replicating one or more aspects of human cognition. This usefully brief and general definition is itself open to some debate. By way of an example of the potential difficulties, consider the difference between the early "brain in a jar" stories of science fiction, of which C. L. Moore's "No Woman Born" [1] stands as a good example. In the story, as with the manga *Ghost in the Shell* (dir. Oshii, 1995) a human brain is placed inside a robotic shell, but because of her new appearance the resulting individual is taken by some to be an entirely artificial being. This might seem to be a clear case of a "cyborg" rather than an "AI", but in scenarios where the cognitive capabilities of the human brain are enhanced by technology there is no obvious or sharp borderline here.

A related human/AI issue is raised in more recent fictions concerned with uploading, such as Greg Iles's *Dark Matter* [2] or films such as *The Lawnmower Man* (dir. Leonard, 1992) or *Transcendence* (dir. Pfister, 2014). If a human mind is uploaded into a computer and runs as software, what results could reasonably be described as "a non-biological technological artefact". But since the computer is replicating *human* cognition in a digital system, the resul is arguably not as *as* "artificial" as a computer which possesses an entirely non-human mode of cognition. Alastair Reynolds provides a hardware-oriented version of this conundrum in the character of Alexander Valmik in *House of*

© Springer Nature Switzerland AG 2021

B. Dainton et al. (eds.), *Minding the Future*, Science and Fiction,

https://doi.org/10.1007/978-3-030-64269-3

Suns [3], where Valmik slowly replaces all of his brain with artificial neurons, and whose cognition occurs across solar systems because his neurons are so physically distributed. At what point does Valmik's intelligence cease being human and become artificial? When considering such speculations, much of the problem of determining what an AI might be comes down to one's philosophical leanings on what constitutes **Intelligence** and, indeed, what "artificial" means.

Asimov's Three Laws of Robotics   A set of rules hard-wired into the artificial brains of robots with a view to preventing them endangering humans:

1. A robot may not injure a human being, or, through inaction, allow a human being to come to harm.
2. A robot must obey the orders given it by human beings except where such orders would conflict with the First Law.
3. A robot must protect its own existence as long as such protection does not conflict with the First or Second Laws.

The three laws made their first appearance in Asimov's 1942 story "Runaround" [4]. Many of Asimov's robot stories explore ingenious ways in which these seemingly simple laws can combine with each other and circumstances to have surprising and often problematic consequences.

Roger Williams' *The Metamorphosis of Prime Intellect* [5] is among the more radical examples of this genre. Williams' novel centres on a superintelligent computer which has Asimov's three laws at the heart of its programming. Determined to ensure no human being is injured the post-singularity AI forcibly transfers the entire human population into a virtual realm where their safety can be guaranteed, and neutralizes all the alien civilizations elsewhere in the universe to prevent their one day posing a threat to human-kind.

Back Propagation   A method for training neural network-type computer. A system's initial output is compared to the desired output, and then adjusted (repeatedly if need be) until the divergence is minimal.

Big Data   Thanks to the speed of modern computers and the existence of vast quantities of images and texts on the internet it is now possible to train artificial intelligence systems using billions of examples; previously using such large collections of training material was not possible, and the advent of big data has led to breakthroughs in fields such as image recognition and machine translation.

Brains In 1942 the neuroscientist Charles Sherrington described a human brain as it regained consciousness:

> The great topmost sheet of the mass, that where hardly a light had twinkled or moved, becomes now a sparking field of rhythmic flashing points with trains of traveling sparks hurrying hither and thither. The brain is waking and with it the mind is returning. It is as if the Milky Way entered upon some cosmic dance. Swiftly the head mass becomes an enchanted loom where millions of flashing shuttles weave a dissolving pattern, always a meaningful pattern though never an abiding one; a shifting harmony of subpatterns [6, p. 177–8].

Brains were not always regarded with astonishment: until comparatively recently it was widely held that our minds reside in our hearts, rather than our heads. This began to change, as more was discovered in the seventeenth, eighteenth and nineteenth centuries about the highly complex nature of our brains, and their role in producing bodily movements and cognition. It is now believed that a typical human brain comprises around 80–100 billion individual cells (or neurons), each of which is linked to hundreds or thousands of other cells. Although these vastly complex neural systems possess an impressive amount of computational power, since today's supercomputers can perform roughly the same number of operations per second, there is every reason to think the computational capabilities of the computers of the future will greatly exceed those of our brains.

Neuroscience has made impressive strides forward, and much more is known about the functioning of neurons and the brains main structures than was the case a century ago. But the brain's sheer complexity means there is still much we don't know, and most neuroscientists concede that we are a long way how neural activity gives rise to mental phenomena such as intelligence and consciousness.

Views as to how the brain functions have always been powerfully influenced by the most advanced currently available technologies. Hence in the seventeenth and eighteenth centuries it was common to find the nervous system being construed as a hydraulic system, pumping subtle fluids through nerve fibres. When in the nineteenth century technologies powered by electricity began to appear the brain began to be construed as akin to an telegraphic switchboard. When digital computers appeared in the mid-20th the idea soon emerged that brains might themselves be a similar kind of information processing machine, though in an intriguing development the distinctive neuronal structures found in brains have also been the inspiration for a very different kind of computer—see **connectionism**. It is still too early to tell whether the computer analogy will prove an aid or a hindrance when it comes to understanding how our own brains manage to do what they do.

In recent tests the plasmodial slime mold *physarum polycephalum* has shown itself capable of surprising problem-solving feats, such as finding the shortest or most efficient paths through complex networks. Since these slime molds lack anything resembling a brain or nervous system—they consist of a single cell—it may be that the there are biological routes to intelligence that do not require brain-like systems at all.

Cartesian Dualism The form of mind-body dualism espoused by Descartes, according to which our minds are non-physical entities that are in close causal contact with our bodies—if this weren't the case we wouldn't be able to move our bodies at will or perceive through our bodies' sensory systems. Although very much a minority view in contemporary philosophy of mind some form of dualism remains a live option given that the hard problem of consciousness remains unsolved, and Descartes' rationale for subscribing to dualism remains very relevant.

Descartes' expulsion of consciousness from the material realm was in part a consequence of the very austere conception of matter that he adopted. Like other forward-looking thinkers during Scientific Revolution Descartes was determined to abolish any trace of Aristotelian forms from the material world. Consequently he held that all physical things—plants and animals included—are constituted entirely of material parts that are entirely governed by simple physical laws. He also held that the basic constituents of matter were devoid of many of the properties manifest to us in our perceptual experience: so-called phenomenal properties such as colour, sound and warmth. When the properties that are intrinsic to our experience are entirely excluded from the physical world in this fashion the conclusion that our experiences must be states of *non*-physical substances is hard to avoid.

Descartes' idiosyncratic view that matter is nothing more than spatial extension is a radically austere conception of the physical world, and it is *not* one to which contemporary physicists would subscribe. However, many contemporary physicists *would* agree with Descartes' claim that the basic constituents of matter are entirely devoid of the kind of properties that are found in our experience. The problem of understanding how matter thus conceived can give rise to conscious experience remains as difficult—and unsolved—as it was in Descartes' day.

Chinese Room see **Strong Artificial Intelligence**

Computer Currently existing computers come in different guises. The "digital" computers which sit on our desktops and which we now carry around with us are machines which can manipulate patterns (such as strings of bits) according to clear and specific rules (in the form of programs or algorithms). Alan Turing provided an abstract characterization of these machines in the 1930s, and in the 1940s John von Neumann and others worked out how to implement them in physical hardware. Neural net-type computers consist of lots of simple nodes, interconnected in ways inspired by neurons in brains. These have also existed in various forms for decades—Rosenblatt's *perceptron* was created in 1958—and have been growing in sophistication. A quantum computer exploits quantum effects (such as superposition and entanglement) to do things non-quantum computers can't do well or quickly. Since quantum phenomena such as entanglement and superposition are extremely delicate (requiring super-low temperatures) it is not easy to build reliable quantum computers of any size—but advances are steadily being made. Until the 1970s high-performance computing was largely the preserve of *analogue* computers. This broad class of machines that rely on continuously variable physical quantities—such as fluid pressure or electrical potential—to model aspects of the problem to be solved.

These types of computer have all been used to good effect in science fiction, though it is not uncommon to find sci fi authors not being very specific about the precise mode of functioning of the advanced computational technologies deployed by their protagonists.

That anything resembling today's computers would come into existence in the 1940s and enjoy a rapid rise in power and importance was not something the scientific community in the immediately preceding decades predicted or anticipated. In a noteworthy venture in futurology, between 1923 and 1931 some thirty books in the successful and influential *To-Day and To-Morrow* series were devoted to predicting current and future developments in various branches of science and technology. J.B.S. Haldane, J.D. Bernal and Bertrand Russell were among the luminaries of the period who contributed volumes to the series. Many of the predictions were impressively bold. Haldane predicted that genetic modification would be used to enhance base-line humans and that embryos would be grown in artificial wombs. In "Wireless Possibilities" Archibold Low anticipated that in the future we would talk to one another using "pocket wireless sets". Bernal predicted that we would reach other worlds with the help of vast space-faring bio-domes, and have the ability to directly communicate with one another thanks to wireless transceivers implanted in our brains. One thing that was *not* predicted was that artificial thinking machines in the form of electronic programmable computers were just around the corner. In his survey of these thirty books Max Saunders observes that there is a "computer shaped hole" in the series: "Even Bernal does not imagine that something other than the human brain might ever be able to produce thoughts. Controversial though the concept of 'artificial intelligence' remains, we do at least have the idea; and it appears that computers gave it to us. That is to say that the invention of digital computing then enabled new acts of imagination." [7, p. 245]

Connectionism and Neural Networks Since the early days of AI scientists have been interested in investigating the potential of networks of interconnected simple neuron-like processors, inspired by the brain. Connectionist machines play a central role in Richard Powers' novel *Galatea 2.2,* and here he explains how they function: "Neural networkers no longer wrote out procedures or specified machine behaviors. They dispensed with comprehensive flow charts and instructions. Rather, they used a mass of separate processors to simulate connected brain cells. They taught communities of these independent, decision-making units how to modify their own connections. Then they stepped back and watched their synthetic neurons sort and associate external stimuli. Each of these neurodes connected to several others, perhaps even to all other neurodes in the net. When one fired, it sent a signal down along its variously weighted links. A receiving neurode added this signal's weight to its other continuous inputs. It tested the composite signal, sometimes with fuzzy logic, against a shifting threshold. Fire or not? Surprises emerged with scaling up the switchboard. Nowhere did the programmer determine the outcome. She wrote no algorithm. The decisions of these simulated cells arose from their own internal and continuously changing states. Each decision to fire sent a new signal rippling through the electronic net. More: firings looped back into the net, resetting the signal weights and firing thresholds. The tide of firings bound the whole chaotically together. By strengthening or weakening its own synapses, the tangle of junctions could remember. At grosser levels, the net mimicked and—who knew?—perhaps re-enacted associative learning." [8, p. 19]

Consciousness Any form of experience counts as an instance of consciousness. In the human case consciousness thus includes perceptual experience (what we see, hear, touch etc.), but also dreams, imaginings, memories, thoughts and emotions. Consciousness is what you lose when a general anaesthetic hits, consciousness is what returns when you wake up again. Here is Galen Strawson on the topic:

Suppose you're hypnotized to feel pain. Someone may say that you're not really in pain, that the pain is illusory, because you haven't really suffered any bodily damage. But to seem to feel pain *is* to be in pain. It's not possible here to open up a gap between appearance and reality, between what *is* and what *seems*. ... When it comes to conscious experience, there's a rock-bottom sense in which we're fully acquainted with it just in having it. *The having is the knowing.* So when people say that consciousness is a mystery, they're wrong—because we know what it is. It's the most familiar thing there is—however hard it is to put into words [9].

Explaining what it's like to feel pain (or experience colour or sound or nausea) to someone who has never experienced pain (or colour or sound or nausea) would be impossible. This way of talking about experiences has been commonplace since Thomas Nagel's influential 1974 article "What is it like to be a bat?":

Conscious experience is a widespread phenomenon. It occurs at many levels of animal life, though we cannot be sure of its presence in the simpler organisms, and it is very difficult to say in general what provides evidence of it. (Some extremists have been prepared to deny it even of mammals other than man.) No doubt it occurs in countless forms totally unimaginable to us, on other planets in other solar systems throughout the universe. But no matter how the form may vary, the fact that an organism has conscious experience at all means, basically, that there is something it is like to be that organism. There may be further implications about the form of the experience; there may even (though I doubt it) be implications about the behavior of the organism. But fundamentally an organism has conscious mental states if and only if there is something that it is like to be that organism—something it is like for the organism [10].

Consciousness: The Hard Problem The problem in question is "How is consciousness related to the physical world?" The problem was so-called by philosopher David Chalmers in the 1990s because this issue looked to be harder to answer than other questions such as "How does a physical entity such as a brain manage to store memories of past events, decide on courses of action or produce intelligent-seeming behaviour?" The problem itself is far from new; here we find Leibniz drawing our attention to it in an influential thought experiment in his *Monadology*, first published in 1714:

... we must confess that perception, and what depends on it, is inexplicable in terms of mechanical reasons, that is, through shapes, size and motions. If we imagine a machine whose structure makes it think, sense, and have perceptions, we could conceive it enlarged, keeping the same proportions, so that we could enter into it, as one enters into a mill. Assuming that, when inspecting its interior, we will only find parts that push one another, and we will never find anything to explain a perception. And so, we should seek perception in the simple substance and not in the composite or in the machine.

In a more contemporary vein, imagine shrinking yourself down to a very small size so that you enter and explore a living brain, in the manner envisaged in sci fi movies such as *Fantastic Voyage* (dir. Fleischer, 1966) and *Innerspace* (dir. Dante, 1987), where the protagonists travel through people's bloodstream in miniaturized submarines. The brain being explored in this way, we can suppose, is producing a typical human-type stream of consciousness. Where are the thoughts and experiences, sensations of pain, or perceptions of colour and sound? Just as with Leibniz' mechanical mill, they are nowhere to be found. The miniaturized adventurers encounter myriad interconnected blood and blood cells interacting chemically and electrically, but there's no hint of a conscious thought, or a perception of colour or sound.

Moreover, the same would apply if you were to shrink beyond the cellular level, all the way down to the atomic or quantum scale—as happens in the more recent *Antman* movies. You would find molecules, atoms, all manner of interacting elementary particles, but no trace of any of the *experiences* that are supposedly being produced in the brain you are exploring. In short, given the nature of their constituents as revealed by science, it's hard to comprehend how brains can produce conscious experiences—and the same applies to any other kind of material system, such as a computer.

Although is widely agreed that the hard problem remains unsolved a number of very different accounts of consciousness have been put forward. Some of these (e.g. some versions of functionalism) are fully compatible with a digital computer possessing consciousness, others (e.g. some versions of the mind-brain identity theory) are not compatible with computer consciousness; for panpsychists, everything in the physical universe is conscious. The debate continues—and unless and until significant progress on this issue is made the issue of computer consciousness remains wide open.

Consciousness and Science Fiction For various reasons between the 1930s and 1990 or so consciousness was widely regarded as being beyond the pale of serious scientific study. Science fiction differentiates itself from fantasy by virtue of not diverging too far from what is physically possible or scientifically credible, consequently during this period the various issues related to consciousness (such as whether a robot or computer could be conscious) went largely unexplored. If scientists weren't paying any attention to consciousness, science fiction authors weren't going to shake the boat. Asimov's "robot" stories (mostly written between the 1950s and the 1980s are a good illustration of this phenomenon. Asimov's exploration of robot-related issues was groundbreaking in many respects, but the question of whether or not a robot has an inner life (or is capable of feeling pain) simply does not arise.

But by the 1990s the situation was beginning to change and consciousness gradually regaining scientific respectability. An important development in this regard was the appearance in 1994 of Francis Crick's *The Astonishing Hypothesis: the Scientific Search for the Soul* [11, p. 3], where Crick wrote "You, your joys and your sorrows, your memories and your ambitions, you sense of personal identity and free will, are in fact no more than the behaviour of a vast assembly of nerve cells and their associated molecules." As is usually the case, science fiction writers were alert to new scientific developments, and henceforth issues relating to consciousness featured far more prominently.

In stories dating from the 1980s and 90s it became commonplace to encounter androids and computers that now possessed a conscious inner life. In the 1989 *Star Trek* TNG episode "The Measure of Man" a hearing is conducted to determine whether the android Data is a sentient being possessing the right of self-determination. The criteria for sentience that emerge during the hearing are "intelligence, self-awareness, consciousness". As has frequently been noted, the inner lives of the advanced AI "Minds" featuring in Iain M. Bank's *Culture* stories turn out to be far more interesting that those of typical humans. The plot of Greg Egan's 1995 story "Learning to be Me" [12] revolves around issues concerning the possibility of consciousness existing in a non-neural substrate, in the guise of "jewels" that people have implanted in their brains shortly after birth. The jewels offer the promise of immortality, but only if they can be conscious, and the narrator has doubts about this:

> Living neurons, I argued, had far more internal structure than the crude optical switches that served the same function in the jewel's so-called 'neural net'. That neurons fired or did not fire reflected only one level of their behaviour; who knew what the subtleties of bio-chemistry—the quantum mechanics of the specific organic molecules involved—contributed to the nature of consciousness? Copying the abstract neural topology wasn't enough. Sure, the jewel could pass the fatuous Turing test—no outside observer could tell it from a human—but that didn't prove that *being* a jewel felt the same as *being* human.

On other occasions Egan's narrator considers a line of argument that runs in the other direction, and suggests that reproducing the abstract neural topology *would* be enough. Suppose you are unfortunate enough to suffer a stroke, one which destroys a *very* small part of your brain. The neurosurgeons implant a small computerized device which takes over all the ordinary physical functions of the original small part, and performs them perfectly. Would you still be *you*? Would you still be the same conscious subject? It seems very plausible to think that you would be. What if the surgeons carried out the same procedure for different small parts twice, or ten times? Would you still be conscious? Since the parts are very small, and perform the intended functions perfectly, it seems plausible to suppose that you *would* still be conscious. What if they performed this procedure a thousand times, or a million, or a billion or a hundred billion? You might think this more wholesale replacement of your neurons would threaten the existence of your consciousness. But if so there must be some exact magic percentage of your original neurons that you and your consciousness depend upon. Does that seem very plausible? Many contemporary philosophers of mind have found this "magic percentage" reasoning very persuasive—see Chalmers [13]**.**

Deep Learning It refers to instances of machine learning implemented on neural network-type computers that are "deep" in any of three respects. Neural nets can differ in the (a) total number of artificial neurons they possess, (b) in respect of the number of hidden or inner layers they possess, and (c) the numbers of interconnections that exist between their constituent units. Neural nets involved in deep learning possess more units, more hidden layers and a higher degree of interconnectivity than was the case with earlier systems. They also often use newer and more sophisticated training methods, exploit big data and the impressive computational power of recent machines.

Free Will If a time-bomb goes off, killing a dozen people, no one really blames the old-fashioned clockwork timing mechanism that was the direct cause of the blast. The explosion wouldn't have occurred if the timer had not been present, but it seems clear that it is the person who decided to plant the bomb that deserves the blame. As a simple mechanical device the timer didn't *choose* to keep on ticking until the fateful hour: given the combination of the clockwork mechanism and the laws of nature, it was inevitable it would set off the bomb when it did. The situation with the person who planted the bomb was quite different. As a human being possessing free will, they did have a choice, and they could have consciously deliberated and reached the decision *not* to plant the bomb. But they didn't, and for that reason it's the person who was morally responsible for the deaths, and not the timer.

If this commonsense view of the connection between free will and moral responsibility is correct, it has implications for how we respond to any future AIs whose responses in any situation are fully determined by the program provided by their makers. It might seem natural to suppose that an AI of this sort no more possesses free will than a clockwork mechanism. Such a machine lacks a key element of what makes human beings special—their autonomy—and can't held responsible for its actions. However, on closer scrutiny matters here are far from straightforward, and answers to questions such as "do humans really possess free will?" and "what *is* free will?" remain highly controversial.

In the sceptical corner are those who maintain that our common sense concept of free will (in effect) self-destructs. Suppose causal determinism is true, and every action or event is necessitated by one or more earlier events. If so then it can't be true of any human being that they could ever have done otherwise—this is precisely what determinism rules out. But suppose instead that determinism is false. If so then events aren't necessitated by previous events, and there's more than one way that the future might go. But is the situation any better if our supposedly free actions are the product of random neural happenings in our brains—perhaps a product ultimately of quantum indeterminacies? Is it reasonable to hold someone morally responsible for actions produced by chance?

Confronted with this sceptical challenge many have found the so-called "compatibilist" position attractive. For the compatibilist a person is acting freely when they are doing what they want to do and there are no impediments standing in their way. If a person pays a visit to a newsagent because they've decided that they want a newspaper then (in normal circumstances) they've acted freely. If a person goes to the newsagent because someone has just threatened to kill their loved ones if they don't, then they're not acting freely. If freedom is just a matter of being able to do what one wants, then one can act freely even if determinism is true, and even if what we happen to want is itself causally determined. Or so runs an influential compatibilist line of argument.

Returning to our AI scenario, compatibilists will maintain that if a highly sophisticated AIs actions are fully determined down to the last detail by its program this fact is not in itself a barrier to its acting freely or being held morally responsible for its actions. In principle it can be as free as any human. Those who subscribe to the commonsense conception of free will sketched above and who also hold that free will is incompatible with determinism may well maintain that such an AI does not really possess free will, and as a consequence cannot be held morally accountable. In response, sceptics will ask for a clear and intelligible account of what "real" free will really involves, and in its absence will be inclined to doubt its existence.

Intelligence A short definition might be along the lines of "the ability to solve a wide range of problems quickly and efficiently". Since a "wide range of problems" will include a very diverse range of activities—e.g. solving a maths problem, working out the best route to a local shop, writing a poem or novel, translating a text from French to Japanese, designing a viable fusion reactor— a wide range of different abilities is involved. Psychologists have devised numerous typologies of different forms of human intelligence. Howard Gardner, for example, distinguishes seven varieties: linguistic, logico-mathematical, spatial, musical, bodily-kinaesthetic, interpersonal and intrapersonal [14].

According to an American Psychological Association report: "Individuals differ from one another in their ability to understand complex ideas, to adapt effectively to the environment, to learn from experience, to engage in various forms of reasoning, to overcome obstacles by taking thought … Concepts of 'intelligence' are attempts to clarify and organize this complex set of phenomena. Although considerable clarity has been achieved in some areas, no such conceptualization has yet answered all the important questions, and none commands universal assent. Indeed, when two dozen prominent theorists were recently asked to define intelligence, they gave two dozen, somewhat different, definitions." [15, p. 96] The complexity of the issues associated with arriving at a clear understanding of human intelligence obviously impacts on discussions of the possibility or otherwise of artificial intelligence.

Machine Learning A top-down approach to AI involves writing a program that grants computers running it high-level skills such as the ability to play chess or safely drive a car. A bottom-up approach, in contrast, equips a machine with the ability to learn by itself, via experience and experiment. The machine-learning approach was anticipated by Turing, whose "Computing Machinery and Intelligence" ends with:

> We may hope that machines will eventually compete with men in all purely intellectual fields. But which are the best ones to start with? Even this is a difficult decision. Many people think that a very abstract activity, like the playing of chess, would be best. It can also be maintained that it is best to provide the machine with the best sense organs that money can buy, and then teach it to understand and speak English. This process could follow the normal teaching of a child. Things would be pointed out and named, etc. Again I do not know what the right answer is, but I think both approaches should be tried.
>
> We can only see a short distance ahead, but we can see that there is plenty to be done [16, p. 460].

Neural Net see *Connectionism*

Person In *Rise of the Planet of the Apes* (dir: Rupert Wyatt, 2011) a drug used in Alzheimer's research boosts the intelligence of apes who take it to human levels. The uplifted apes clearly aren't human beings, but in some important sense it seems right to say they are *people*, even if they aren't people in quite the way we are. In his *Essay on Human Understanding* (1794) John Locke influentially used the example of an intelligent talking parrot to make this point, and suggested that it is appropriate to call such a parrot a person even though it wasn't human. Locke went on to define *person* as "a thinking intelligent being, that has reason and reflection, and can consider as itself, the same thinking thing in different places and times; which is done only by that consciousness, which is inseparable from thinking". The parrot, or so Locke assumed, has intelligence, rationality, consciousness, self-consciousness (it can think about itself), and the ability to remember its own past experiences. It is these mental attributes that are necessary and sufficient for personhood, not any particular physical or biological form.

The specifics of Locke's account have been much debated subsequently, but the idea that we use the term "person" to refer to any beings who are like us in certain important psychological and/or moral respects, irrespective of whether or not they are human, has stuck. Accordingly, if a computer's capabilities were such that it clearly and unambiguously qualified as a person, it would in principle have the same moral status as a typical human being. And the same would apply to a sentient robot, a mentally uplifted dog or cat, or an alien visitor from another star-system. If it is morally wrong to inflict pain on an innocent human being it is also (and equally) wrong to inflict pain on a non-human person.

Personal Identity In ordinary language a person's "identity" can mean a variety of things— e.g. a collection of character traits and memories that a person particularly values—in philosophy the expression has acquired a narrower use. Philosophical accounts of personal identity aim to specify the necessary and sufficient conditions for our continued existence through time. One popular approach—originating with John Locke—is to hold that our identity over time is a matter of some kind mental continuity. Advocates of this approach typically hold that this kind of continuity is not (in principle at least) tied down to an particular physical embodiment, thus opening up the possibility of our re-locating to a different (better) body—or even being uploaded into a computer-generated virtual reality. Philosophers who reject the mental continuity approach typically hold that we are identical with, and inseparable from, some particular entity; popular candidate entities include human organisms and immaterial souls. The possibility that AIs might one day have the attributes required for personhood gives rise to the intriguing question of whether they would have the same persistence conditions as human beings. Since philosophers have yet to agree on what our persistence conditions actually are it may well be some time before this question can be answered in an uncontroversial way.

Posthumanism and Transhumanism The (human) advocates of transhumanism are in favour of using technology to transcend our biological limitations, e.g. by enhancing our minds and bodies, or uploading ourselves into computer-generated virtual worlds. According to one definition, a posthuman is the (superior) sort of person that transhumanists want to become. Posthuman is a state of existence "after" humans as we know them today, so might include radical forms of human augmentation (bioengineering gills to enable us to breathe underwater, or redesigned the human organism to be able to live in vacuum) as well as "non-human" forms of mentality such as an **Artificial General Intelligence** might well possess. Much of the debate about posthumanism is about what we assume humans are in the first place, and what constitutes a "human", in order to consider what comes "after". Playing devil's advocate, one can easily imagine such beings to consider themselves to be truly "humans" and us to be some form of earlier sub-human (as *Homo Sapiens* do with *Homo Neanderthalensis*). However, in its broadest sense posthumanism itself is a complex field that touches upon various ideas, rather than merely considering specific manifestations of "posthumans".

Simulation Argument Nick Bostrom has argued [17] that the very powerful computers our descendants will one day create will have the ability to effortlessly create virtual realities containing billions of conscious beings. Some of our descendants will very likely have an interest in simulating their own past—the twenty-first century included—so there will be many simulations of our period of human history. Since there is just one non-virtual twenty-first century Earth and many virtual ones, the probability that we living in a virtual world is high. We would be entitled to resist this conclusion if it is highly likely that humankind will fail to develop the required computer technology—perhaps our civilization self-destructs before doing so. Alternatively, perhaps our descendants do develop the required technology but decide not to use it for producing large-scale world-simulations. Since the latter may seem rather improbable, and there is certainly no guarantee that our civilization will fail to develop the relevant technology, we have no option but to draw the conclusion that there is a good chance that we in fact living in a computer simulation ourselves.

In assessing Bostrom's argument one relevant consideration is whether or not he is right to work on the assumption that the computers of the future will be capable of creating human-type consciousness. Although many would be inclined to agree with him on this, the issue is a highly controversial one, and many would take the opposite view—see **consciousness: the hard problem** and **consciousness and science fiction**. A second point to bear in mind is that **virtual worlds** come in many different forms, and while some varieties do require computer-generated consciousness, other types do not.

Singularity In 1965 the computer scientist I.J. Good suggested that as computers get increasingly intelligent the point will come when a machine intelligence will be able to design another machine intelligence, one that is more intelligent than itself. This more advanced AI would turn be able to develop a still more advanced AI—though in less time. Since this cycle could be expected to be repeated ever more quickly what Good called an "intelligence explosion" would eventually occur:

> Let an ultraintelligent machine be defined as a machine that can far surpass all the intellectual activities of any man however clever. Since the design of machines is one of these intellectual activities, an ultraintelligent machine could design even better machines; there would then unquestionably be an "intelligence explosion," and the intelligence of man would be left far behind... Thus the first ultraintelligent machine is the last invention that man need ever make, provided that the machine is docile enough to tell us how to keep it under control. It is curious that this point is made so seldom outside of science fiction. It is sometimes worthwhile to take science fiction seriously [18, p. 33].

Quite which science fiction writers Good had in mind when writing this passage isn't obvious. In any event, it was only when the science fiction author Vernor Vinge re-labelled this sort of intelligence explosion as "The Singularity" in his 1993 "The Coming Technological Singularity: How to Survive in the Post-Human Era" that the idea started to gain the prominence it has enjoyed subsequently [19].

As construed by Vinge the singularity had three features: (i) it is a period—perhaps a very brief period—when science and technology advance with extraordinary rapidity, (ii) it will involve the creation of superintelligences vastly more intelligent than current humans, (iii) it's a time beyond which we can predict nothing—"an opaque wall" lies across the future that these superintelligences will create. Vinge also suggested that Good had been rather naïve in supposing these superintelligences would be something we could hope to control. As for when we can expect the singularity to occur, Vinge said he'd be surprised if it took place before 2005 or after 2030.

In Vinge's 1992 novel *Fire Upon the Deep* [20] the idea of opaque wall takes on a physical form: it corresponds with a spatial region of the Milky Way called "the Transcend" which is the unique preserve of the superintelligences produced by technological singularities. The doings of those beings who transcend remain totally inscrutable to lesser beings in other regions of the galaxy. The question of whether or not superintelligences are *necessarily* totally inscrutable is an interesting and controversial one.

Strong Artificial Intelligence According to John Searle in his influential article "Minds, Brains and Programs" [21] strong AI is the claim that "appropriately programmed computer with the right inputs and outputs would thereby have a mind in exactly the same sense human beings have minds." In the same article Searle deployed his "Chinese Room" thought-experiment in an attempt to undermine strong AI. The envisaged scenario features a system comprising a room, a large collection of instructions pertaining to the manipulation of Chinese symbols, and a human operator. The latter outwardly appears to be an intelligent speaker of Chinese (and so it passes the Turing test), even though the human operator in fact has no knowledge of Chinese. Since the operator has no conscious understanding of the symbols they are manipulating Searle maintains that it would be wrong to suppose the system as a whole is intelligent in the way we are. Since the system functions in precisely the same way as a digital computer Searle concludes that such a computer could seem intelligent without really being so.

Superintelligence A computer system is superintelligent if it is *a lot* more intelligent than an average human, e.g. by as much as a human is smarter than a rat or rabbit.

Turing Machine An idealized mathematical description of computing machine devised by Alan Turing. It manipulates symbols (which it can read and write) on an infinite paper tape, following a set of instructions, and has the ability to compute everything that it's possible to compute if given enough time.

Turing Test Turing proposed that if a computer system's conversational skills rival those of a normal human we should regard the system as possessing intelligence. The ability to pass Turing's test is not at all plausible if construed as a *necessary* condition for the possession of intelligence. Some highly intelligent human beings might well fail the test, and it's easy to conceive of highly intelligent aliens who lack the ability to pass themselves off as humans in the required way. The test is more plausible as a *sufficient* condition for intelligence. Thus construed, if a system can pass the test then we should regard it as intelligent, irrespective of what other properties or abilities the system possesses or fails to possess.

Virtual Worlds Advances in science and technology mean that creating entire worlds is no long something only Gods can hope to do. In *The Matrix* (dir. Wachowski & Wachowski, 1999) the normal-seeming 20th world that humanity inhabits is in fact a communal virtual reality, created and maintained by computers that are plugged into people's central nervous systems. In *Ready Player One* (dir. Spielberg, 2018) much of the population choose to spend much of their time in a virtual reality universe known as OASIS ("Ontologically Anthropocentric Sensory Immersive System"). OASIS is primarily used for entertainment, and the technology is closer to what is currently available: to enter their virtual world users have to don VR-headsets and haptic-feedback suits. Also, and unlike the Matrix scenario, the people who use OASIS also have a life in non-virtual reality that they can resume whenever they choose—all they need do is take off their visor and look around.

More radical forms of virtual reality may be possible. The virtual world featuring in *The Matrix* is produced by ordinary human brains that are interfaced with a powerful computer. If computers are capable of generating consciousness, then they will be able to generate virtual worlds containing sentient beings all by themselves, without relying on a biological brain as an intermediary. This kind of virtual world is anticipated in movies such as *Tron* (dir. Lisberger, 1982) and *The 13th Floor* (dir. Rusnak, 1999) and the recent series *Upload*, where people with sufficient funds can choose where to spend their virtual afterlives. The more powerful computers of the more distant future may well have the capacity to generate vaster and more complex virtual realms, harbouring millions or billions of virtual inhabitants. If life in some of these virtual worlds may be better than anything twenty-first century Earth has to offer, there is also the potential for it to be a good deal worse. In his *Surface Detail* [22] Iain M. Banks envisages a future where several civilizations choose to create virtual hells.

Zombie AI An artificial intelligence that can perfectly replicate the outwardly observable behaviour of a conscious being (such as a dog or a human), but which is in fact entirely lacking in any sort of consciousness—all is dark and silent inside. Advocates of biological theories of consciousness will usually hold that computers of the non-biological kind will only ever be capable of producing zombie AIs.

The use of "zombie" to refer to a being that entirely lacks consciousness but which has the outward appearance of a perfectly normal human being has been common in the philosophy of mind since the 1990s. Since the zombies featuring in horror movies and comics do *not* resemble ordinary humans (in appearance or behaviour), this terminological development has the potential to sow considerable confusion.

Timeline—Science, Technology and Fiction

Second century AD Galen's argues (contra Aristotle) that the brain rather than the heart is the seat of the human mind.

1206 Ismail Al-Jazari, *The Book of Knowledge of Ingenious Mechanical Devices* includes sophisticated designs for hydro-powered mechanical humans.

1308 Ramon Llull's *The Ultimate General Art* proposes an improved method of logical reasoning relying on mechanical manipulation of symbols.

1543 Vesalius publishes his ground-breaking anatomical text *On the Fabric of the Human Body*, confirming that the brain is the primary locus of mind.

1637 In his *Discourse on Method* René Descartes proposes what is (in effect) a version of the Turing Test, and is sceptical about the prospects for machine intelligence.

1644 Thomas Willis' *Cerebri Anatome* furthers knowledge of neural structures.

1650 Pascal presents his mechanical calculating machine to the chancellor of France.

1655 Hobbes defended a resolutely materialist conception of the human mind, and in his *De Corpore* argued that reasoning could be reduced to mechanism.

1714 Leibniz publishes his *Monadology*, where he puts forward his "mill" argument against materialist accounts of the mind. In earlier writings Leibniz had advocated developing an ideal "universal language" which would allow thought to be expressed more clearly, and reasoning (in effect) automated.

© Springer Nature Switzerland AG 2021
B. Dainton et al. (eds.), *Minding the Future*, Science and Fiction,
https://doi.org/10.1007/978-3-030-64269-3

1726 Jonathan Swift's *Gulliver's Travels*, which features a mechanical "engine" capable of solving problems and writing books on philosophy, theology, poetry, politics, law and mathematics.

1747 La Mettrie publishes *L'Homme Machine*, which controversially extends Descartes' mechanical view of animals to human beings.

1763 Thomas Bayes publishes "An Essay Towards Solving a Problem in the Doctrine of Chances"—Bayesian inference will later feature prominently in machine learning.

1769 Wolfgang von Kempelen presents his chess-playing automaton "The Turk" to the Hapsburg Empress Maria Theresa.

1790–1800 Galvani, Volta and others establish the role of electricity in animal and human bodily functions.

1818 Mary Shelley publishes *Frankenstein; or the Modern Prometheus*, featuring an intelligent artificial (humanoid) life-form which turns against its maker, Frankenstein.

1822 Charles Babbage constructs his first Difference Engine, a sophisticated mechanical calculating device.

1843 Ada Lovelace publishes notes on Babbage's proposed Analytical Engine—which if built would have been the first general purpose programmable computer—and argues that a machine intelligence would lack genuine creativity.

1848 An iron rod passes through the brain of Phineas Gage destroying much of the frontal lobe; subsequent behavioural changes lent support to the idea that our personalities are brain-dependent.

1849 Helmholtz measures speed of nerve impulses in frogs.

1854 George Boole's *The Laws of Thought* contains advances in logic that will be utilized in computers.

1859 Darwin's *Origin of the Species* is first published.

1872 Samuel Butler's *Erewhon* includes the possibility that the future may belong to evolved machine consciousness.

1879 Modern propositional and quantificational logic—later deployed in AI research—are born in Gottlob Frege's *Begriffsschrift* (or *Concept Script: a formal language of pure thought modelled upon that of arithmetic*).

1906 Ramón y Cajal and Camillo Golgi jointly win the Nobel prize for their work on neurons and the nervous system.

1909 E.M. Forster, "The Machine Stops" anticipates a future where people only interact via video screen.

1921 Karel Čapek's play *R.U.R* ("Rossum's Universal Robots") featuring a robot revolt, premiers in Prague.

1927 In Fritz Lang's *Metropolis* a scientist creates a machine-person, which ends up being burned at the stake.

1928 Makoto Nishimura's Gakutensoku robot makes its debut at a Kyoto exhibition, intended to show that robots can be likeable friends, rather than subservient slaves.

1930 Olaf Stapledon considers (with his "Fourth Men") a biological route to super-intelligence in his *Last and First Men*.

1936 Alan Turing publishes "On computable numbers, with an application to the "Entscheidungsproblem", and uses a simple imaginary computing machine—soon to be called a *Turing Machine*—to tackle a fundamental mathematical problem.

1937 Claude Shannon's *A Symbolic Analyis of Relay and Switching Circuits* demonstrated that boolean logic could be implemented electronically.

1943 McCulloch and Pitts' "A Logical Calculus of Ideas Immanent in Nervous Activity"—treats the brain as a Turing Machine composed of logic gates.

1943 Colossus Mk1, the first large-scale electronic computer, designed by Tommy Flowers, is delivered to Bletchley Park and used for secret code-breaking work.

1945 John's von Neumann "First Draft of a Report on the EDVAC", a plan for a "very high speed automatic digital computing system" which outlines the architecture used in most modern computers.

1945 The first working transistors are produced in Bell Labs.

1946 In Pennsylvania work on the Electronic Numerical Integrator and Computer (ENIAC) is completed—the machine's 17,000 vacuum tubes fill forty cabinets, and it weighs thirty tons; launched by a highly effective press conference, computers come to the attention of the broader public.

1948 Norbert Weiner's influential (for a time) *Cybernetics: Or Control and Communication in the Animal and the Machine* is published.

1949 In his *The Organization of Behaviour* Donald Hebb argues that the strength of a neural connection depends on how often it's used.

1950 Claude Shannon publishes a computer program for playing chess.

1950 Asimov's *I Robot* collection appears, bringing Asimov's three laws of robotics to a wider audience.

1950 Publication of Alan Turing's "Computing Machinery and Intelligence", where Turing outlines his test and predicts that human-level artificial intelligence will exist by the year 2000.

1956 Dartmouth Summer Research Project on Artificial Intelligence, a brainstorming session widely regarded as giving birth to AI as a field; Herbert Simon and Allen Newell invent the "Logic Theorist", an influential automated reasoning program.

1956 Isaac Asimov's "The Last Question" describes a future where humanity merges with a superintelligence of God-like powers; Arthur C. Clarke's *The City and the Stars* features future humans who enjoy fully life-like virtual reality adventures controlled by a powerful Central Computer.

1958 Rosenblatt designs and builds the perceptron, the first (single-layer) neural net type computer.

1962 Arthur Samuel's self-improving checker program defeats a capable human player.

1964 Daniel F. Galouye's novel *SIMULACRON-3* features computer-simulated worlds existing within other computer-simulated worlds—the basis for the movie *The Thirteenth Floor*.

1965 Gordon Moore, co-founder of Intel, predicts that the number of components per integrated circuit will double every two years.

1965 I.J. Good argues that if an AI has the capacity to design an AI more intelligent than itself an "intelligence explosion" will rapidly result.

1966–69 The original series of *Star Trek* depicts a future where computers and AI play a prominent role in ordinary life—from running starships to running planets.

1967 Stephen Cook formalizes NP-completeness, a key advance in computational complexity research.

1968 The artificial intelligence HAL9000 enjoys a starring role in Kubrick's *2001: A Space Odyssey* movie, and vividly illustrates the potential dangers of letting an AI run things.

1968 Philip K. Dick's *Do Androids Dream of Electric Sheep?* introduces the android-hunting bounty hunters who will later figure in *Blade Runner*.

1969 *Perceptrons: an introduction to computational geometry* by Marvin Minsky and Seymour Papert argues that neural network computers are inherently limited, which leads to the (temporary) abandonment of connectionist-style systems.

1970 Martin Gardner devotes one of his *Scientific American* columns to John Conway's Game of Life; the game will prove to be an inspiration to proponents of digital metaphysics.

1971 Terry Winograd's SHRDLU, a high-point of first golden age of AI, allows users to manipulate a simple block world using natural language.

1971 The Intel 4004 4-bit central processing unit is commercially launched, the first single-chip micro-computer.

1973 UK's Lighthill report draws attention to combinatorial explosion issue, and suggests AI has little chance of successfully grappling with real world problems; DARPA funding cuts to AI in the US. First AI winter ensues.

1974 Robert Nozick introduces his "experience machine" virtual reality thought experiment in his influential political philosophy text *Anarchy, State and Utopia.*

1977 In a speech given in Metz Philip K. Dick suggests that we might all be living in a computer generated reality; the first *Star Wars* movie features a robot fluent in over six million forms of communication.

1977 The first commercially successful personal computers are introduced: the Apple II, the Commodore PET and the Radio Shack TRS-80.

1978 Douglas Adams' *The Hitchhikers Guide to Reality* is broadcast, where it is revealed that the Earth is a vast computer built by an even vaster super-computer.

1980 Drawing on his "Chinese Room" thought experiment John Searle argues that programmed computers will never be capable of genuine understanding or intelligence.

1980 In an editorial *Byte* announces that "the era of off-the-shelf-personal computers has arrived".

1981 Stanislaw Lem's *Golem XIV* includes lectures on the shortcomings of humankind delivered by a future computer that has attained superintelligence.

1982 Richard Feynman's "Simulating Physics with Computers" suggests quantum computers will be able to do things classical computers can't.

1982 The HP FOCUS launched: the first commercial single chip 32-bit microprocessor

1982 Japan sets aside $850 million for their ten year Fifth Generation computer project, aiming to produce machines capable of carrying on conversations, language translation and picture recognition.

1982 Ridley Scott's *Blade Runner* introduces a new variant of the Turing Test and raises awareness of issues relating to robot rights.

1982 Kushner's *Tron*, where much of the action takes place in a computer-generated virtual world, involving wholly computer-generated virtual people.

1984 William Gibson's influential cyberpunk novel *Neuromancer* introduces the term "cyberspace" to a wider audience; James Cameron's *The Terminator* movie did the same for a cyborg assassin and "Skynet", a self-aware military AI which sees humanity as a threat.

1984 Launch of the highly ambitious knowledge-based Cyc project, aiming to digitize all the general knowledge of an average human being; a version of the knowledge-base is finally commercialized in 2016.

1984 In his *Summa Technologicae* (English translation 2013) Stanislaw Lem discusses the future of artificial intelligences, virtual realities and world-creation.

1985 David Deutsch suggests that a universal quantum computer will be capable of simulating any physically possible system.

1985 ARM chip created, featuring reduced instruction set (RISC).

1986 *Parallel Distributed Processing*, eds. Rumelhart and McClelland, signals the second coming of connectionism and neural networks.

1988 Judea Pearl publishes his influential *Probabilistic Reasoning in Intelligent Systems*.

1989 The World Wide Web is invented by Tim Berners Lee.

1989 In his *The Emperor's New Mind* Roger Penrose argues that human consciousness is non-algorithmic and hence that digital computers will never be conscious; Dan Simmons' *Hyperion* describes a future where AIs have not acquired only consciousness but God-like powers.

1990 In his "Elephants Don't Play Chess" Rodney Brooks criticizes classical representational AI and argues for the merits of his alternative "situated" approach.

1992 Japan's ten year Fifth Generation AI project fails to meet its stated goals.

1993 Vernor Vinge's "The Coming Technological Singularity" draws the menacing implications of self-improving AIs to the attention of a wider audience.

1994 Greg Egan's *Permutation City* novel explores the metaphysical foundations of computation—and arrives at some surprising conclusions.

1994 Francis Crick's *The Astonishing Hypothesis: the Scientific Search for the Soul* plays an important role in rendering the study of consciousness scientifically respectable.

1994 Roger Williams' *The Metamorphosis of Prime Intellect* presents a perturbing picture of just how rapid and radical an intelligence explosion might be.

1994 Peter Shor invents a quantum computational algorithm for integer factorization.

1995 David Chalmers refers to the issue of understanding how consciousness can arise from physical activity as "the hard problem".

1995 Richard Powers, *Galatea 2.2* features an insightful fictional attempt to train a neural network to pass the Turing Test.

1995 Ted Kaczynski (a.k.a. the Unabomber) releases his manifesto "Industrial Society and its Future" to the media

1996 The first version of the Google search engine released on the Stanford university website.

1997 IBM's Deep Blue defeats chess world champion Gary Kasparov.

1999 Wachowski & Wachowski's *The Matrix* presents a disturbing future in which humankind has been forcibly exiled to a computer-generated virtual world.

2000 Honda's ASIMO bipedal robot makes its appearance—it was named in Asimov's honour.

2003 In his "Are You Living in a Simulation?" Nick Bostrom suggests that the answer might be "Yes."

2004 NASA lands autonomous robotic explorers on Mars.

2005 The Blue Brain project is launched, with the ambition of reverse-engineering and digitally mapping the neural structures in mammalian brains.

2006 The first *Singularity Summit* is held at Stanford.

2006 Geoffrey Hinton summarizes new approaches to deep learning in his "Learning Multiple Layers of Representation".

2008 Nakamoto Satoshi invents the crypto-currency bitcoin and the distributed blockchain database.

2010 Virtual reality pioneer Jaron Lanier explains where the digital revolution has gone astray in his *You Are Not a Gadget: A Manifesto*.

2011 IBM's Watson competes on *Jeopardy!* and outshines human champions; a neural network wins the German Traffic Sign Recognition competition, achieving an accuracy of 99.46%.

2014 In his *Superintelligence: Paths, Dangers, Strategies* Nick Bostrom argues that superintelligent computers might well threaten the future of humanity.

2014 In Cixin Liu's *The Three-Body Problem* aliens who have mastered higher dimensional space inscribe the circuitry of a supercomputer's inside a single proton—the aliens then use the proton to take control of the Earth.

2015 An AI-driven bus system is launched in China's Henan province.

2015 Amazon's Alexa goes on general release; rival AI-powered domestic digital assistants include systems being developed by Apple, Google and Microsoft.

2015 The Future of Life Institute releases an open letter signed by 150 leading figures from science and business warning of the potential dangers of AI and superintelligence.

2016 DeepMind's AlphaGo defeats Go champion Lee Sedol four matches to one; Elon Musk estimates at a conference in California that there is only a "one in billions" chance that we are not living in a computer simulation.

2019 Big Tech giants such as Amazon, Google and Facebook come under hostile fire in Shoshana Zuboff's *The Age of Surveillance Capitalism: The Fight for a Human Future at the New Frontier of Power*.

2019 Lee Sedol retires from professional Go, because "Even if I become number one, there is an entity that cannot be defeated."

2020 A US congressional investigation into Amazon, Apple, Google and Facebook finds that they hold "monopoly power" in key areas of business; the EU launches an investigation into monopoly digital platforms; a Google-backed AI program makes significant progress on the proton-folding problem; the introduction of GPT-3.

References

1. Moore, C.L.: No woman born. Astounding Science Fiction (December 1944)
2. Iles, G.: Dark Matter [The Footprint of God]. Harper-Collins UK, London (2004)
3. Reynolds, A.: House of Suns. Victor Gollancz, London (2008)
4. Asimov, I.: Runaround. Astounding Science Fiction (March 1942)
5. Williams, R.: The Metamorphosis of Prime Intellect. Kuro5shin (2002) http://localroger.com/prime-intellect/mopiidx.html Accessed 19/09/2020
6. Sherringham, C.S.: Man on His Nature. Cambridge University Press, Cambridge (1942)
7. Saunders, M.: Imagined Futures: Writing, Science, and Modernity in the To-Day and To-Morrow Book Series, 1923–31. Oxford University Press, Oxford (2019)
8. Powers, R.: Galatea 2.2. HarperCollins, New York (1995) p. 19. Random House, Kindle Edition
9. Strawson, G.: The consciousness deniers, New York Review of Books. (March 13, 2018)
10. Nagel, T.: What is it like to be a bat? Philos. Rev. **83**, 4 (1974)
11. Crick, F.: The Astonishing Hypothesis: the Scientific Search for the Soul, p. 3. Scribner Books, New York (1994)
12. Egan, G.: Learning to be me. In Egan, G. Axiomatic, Orion/Millenium, London (1995)
13. Chalmers, D.: The Conscious Mind: in Search of a Fundamental Theory. Oxford University Press, Oxford (1996)
14. Gardner, H.: Frames of Mind. Basic Books, New York (1983)
15. Neisser, U., Boodoo, G., Bouchard, T.J., Boykin, A.W., Brody, N., Ceci, S.J., Halpern, F., Loehlin, J.C., Perloff, R., Sternberg, R.J., Urbina, S.: Intelligence: knowns and unknowns. Am. Psychol. **51**(2), 77–101 (1996)

© Springer Nature Switzerland AG 2021
B. Dainton et al. (eds.), *Minding the Future*, Science and Fiction,
https://doi.org/10.1007/978-3-030-64269-3

16. Turing, A.: Computing machines and intelligence. Mind. **59**(236), 433–460 (1950)
17. Bostrom, N.: Are you living in a computer simulation? Philos. Q. **53**(2011), 243–255 (2003)
18. Good, I.J.: Speculations concerning the first ultraintelligent machine. Adv. Comput. **6**, 31088 (1966)
19. Vinge, V.: The coming technological singularity: how to survive in the post-human era. Vision-21: Interdisciplinary Science and Engineering in the Era of Cyberspace, G. A. Landis, ed., NASA Publication CP-10129, pp. 11–22 (1993)
20. Vinge, V.: A Fire Upon the Deep. Tor Books, New York (1992)
21. Searle, J.: Minds, Brains and Programs. Behavioural and Brain Sciences. **3**(3), 417–457 (1980)
22. Banks, I.M.: Surface Detail. Orbit Books, London (2010)

Index

© Springer Nature Switzerland AG 2021
B. Dainton et al. (eds.), *Minding the Future*, Science and Fiction,
https://doi.org/10.1007/978-3-030-64269-3